Hard Travellin' Man Blues

A LIFETIME OF STORIES BY DENIS HAYES

Denis Hayes

PARTRIDGE

A Penguin Random House Company

ISBN: Hardcover   978-1-4828-9039-6
             Softcover   978-1-4828-9040-2
             Ebook   978-1-4828-9041-9

To order additional copies of this book, contact
Toll Free 800 101 2657 (Singapore)
Toll Free 1 800 81 7340 (Malaysia)
orders.singapore@partridgepublishing.com

www.partridgepublishing.com/singapore

Other books by the same author.

Silly animal stories for Kids
Silly Fishy Stories for Kids
Silly Ghost Stories for Kids

Silly Alien Space Stories for Bigger Kids
Silly Alien Space War stories for Bigger Kids
Silly Alien Space Time Travel Stories for even Bigger Kids
Out of this World Stories
All the above available on www.sillystorycentre.com.

Adult Books. Joint website to be decided.
The Misadventures of Wunderwear Woman
The Misadventures of Wunderwear Woman in America
Bye Bye Baby Boy Big Boy Blues

Author's note

All the characters portrayed in this book actually lived and all the events really happened. Any views and opinions expressed are those of the author's.

Names have been changed where necessary to protect the privacy of innocent and guilty alike. Any readers who claim to recognise themselves do so at their own risk!

For convenience some events have been combined, several different experiences have been grouped together, not necessarily in strict chronological order and frequently several characters have been made into one.

Hard Travellin' Man Blues

(words and music by Denis Hayes. Medium tempo standard 12 bar blues in E major).

I got those hard travellin' hard travellin' blues,
I got those hard travellin' hard travelling'Blues,
Gotta wear those hard, hard, hard travellin' man shoes.

Live out a suitcase, sleep just where you can,
Live out a suitcase, sleep just where you can,
That's the life of a hard, hard travellin' man.

Don't fall in love, but take it where you can,
Don't fall in love but take it where you can,
That's the way of that hard, hard travellin' man.

So it's goodbye baby, good bye baby good bye,
So it's goodbye baby, goodbye baby good bye,
When I done gone you can hang your head and cry.

You can talk bad about me honey, 'cos really I don't care,
You can talk bad about me honey, 'cos really I don't care,
By the time you finish talking I could be anywhere.

I've done some hard travellin' got hard travellin' man blues,
I've done some hard travellin' got hard travellin' man blues,
I done wore out those hard travellin' man shoes.

PART ONE

Hard Travellin'

The Cross Country Spectacular

Louise was a lovely young lady. Good looking with a strong firm body. I liked her because she always made herself available whenever I came by.

She had two drawbacks. She had a fiancee and she lived in lodgings with a landlady who didn't believe that young women should get involved with young men. There was certainly no nooky allowed on her premises.

So we had to make do with hotel rooms in the winter and nature in the summer.

As it was one of those rare beautiful early summers we saw a lot of nature.

We were so healthy and horny that we never fancied driving or walking too far. We would rather spend the time and energy on screwing the daylights out of each other. So we found local secluded spots, banged away and hoped for the best.

Once or twice I asked her about her fiancee and how she felt about all this. She was quite comfortable with the situation. Her boyfriend was serious and steady. I was not. He was great future husband material. I was not.

I was a terrific fuck. He was not.

So there you had it.

She even suggested taking me on their honeymoon but although flattered I declined.

We were driving around looking for new likely places when we spotted an orchard with a wide open gate. Nothing else could be seen for miles around.

Yeah.

We drove in and ran well down between rows of trees loaded with fruit. A few more weeks would make them ripe and ready.

I had a girl with me who was ripe and ready right now.

I turned the engine off. Wound the windows down to get a closer feel for the countryside and dived onto the back seats.

We were kissing, missing, panting and grabbing at everything in sight and feeling for a lot that was hidden. Fumbling was paramount.

Not for long. Buttons were undone, straps loosened, pants and panties came off and abandoned out of the window and exciting bare flesh was eagerly grasped by fingers and lips.

The car was a hive of feverish activity.

We explored everything and everywhere before that gorgeous moment when a rampant dick gets placed in an open, welcoming pussy.

I went deep and we both got lost in pushing, pulling, thrusting, mounting, demounting, changing places as we worked our way towards our first big climax.

Just as it arrived I threw my head up and Louise threw her head back.

Our eyes met several others.

We were looking out and they were looking in.

Outside the car, running on the spot, were a group of cross country runners, breaking their necks to get a closer look at the love fest.

They had numbers on their chests but the significance of that took a while to sink in.

I arched my back and lifted my head higher while Louise sank down but not before the crowd had a bird's eye view of a pretty face and a couple of wonderfully shaped firm breasts with nipples that stood out like strawberries.

I looked at the runners. The runners eventually looked at me. Louise was hard to look away from.

The reactions were mixed. Some were openly appreciative, some were nondescript and a few were definitely disapproving.

They moved on. Slowly. The disapproving ones the slowest of all.

A noise behind me made me look over my shoulder.

There was another group at the other window.

They had a view right up a delicious pair of long female legs with the top blocked off by a bare backside which was actually still pumping away in between.

Louise had gasped out, "for goodness sake don't stop now."

I didn't.

So we finished off as the two groups went on their way.

We recovered and then started again. Slower but more persuasive than before.

We were really into it when a pair of pants dropped on my head and a voice said, "are these yours mate?"

I took my head out from between Louise's legs only to see a different group looking through the windows.

Louise couldn't easily be seen as were were having a go at soixante neuf with me on top.

I checked both sides of the car. Yep, we were surrounded again.

We decided that it was far too late for modesty so we just sat demurely side by side and waited for them to go.

They were in no hurry.

Eventually they moved on but something to do with the numbers on them made me call one back.

"You've got numbers on. You're number 52 right?"

"Yeah so?"

"Well how many of you are there then?" I asked fervently.

"Well it's a county run mate and there's about three hundred of us so if I was you I'd either move on or start selling tickets. There's a lot more to come."

Louise and I looked at each other, shrugged our shoulders, wound up the windows, steamed them up and carried on for another couple of hours.

Zany in Zurich

The Zurich Hilton was on a hillside on the outer edges of the town. We were staying there with others attending the Swiss Industries Fair in Basle.

We commuted between the two cities everyday.

First stop on returning each day was the bar. It was usually quiet there at first but livened up a lot later on.

This particular evening it was absolutely roaring from the start.

Holding centre court was a large Belgian we knew well. We normally stayed clear of him. He was dangerous in a non violent way. He was inclined to get tanked up and then rope you in for a ride out to the airport at over two hundred kilometres an hour in his rented Ferrari. He would find car parks or lay byes on the way and perform wheelies or hand brake turns screaming out "oh yeah" or "oh fuck this baby" at the top of his voice. If you survived that he would put together a flight plan and take you for a spin in his Cessna through the mountains. At night??!!

That was hairy enough but he took great delight in telling you he was so pissed that he could hardly see and was certainly not in control. What made it worse was that you just had to believe it.

We saw him and swerved back towards the door just too late. He spotted us and waved us over.

We were swept up in huge Huggy Bear hugs, dumped in places of honour beside him, handed glasses of champagne and heard him announce in a voice loud enough to wake up William Tell, "now we really get going. See these two here? They are real party animals, take note boys and girls, take note." He swept his arms around in a grand gesture.

We shook our heads sheepishly in disagreement but our reputation had already been established.

However we did manage to get an agreement with the bartender that he would pass us over on refills unless we nodded our heads.

Undoubtedly this saved our lives and our livers without destroying our credibility.

The bar was ours for the night and a buffet was installed.

Inevitably the call went out, "bring on the girls."

This was totally unnecessary as there is nothing more attractive to women than flamboyance, laughter, free food and booze and of course money, money, money. It was all there and so were the women.

Most were attractive but some were not. This made no difference in the end because with dimmed lights, jaded senses and buckets full of liquor everyone was looking beautiful before very long.

We stayed close to Belgian Cave Man but there were three Australian girls who stayed closer. They were gorgeous but far too upfront to be real.

No subtlety with these three. If it had been possible to stick their pussies on their heads they would have done.

Belgian loved it. He wasn't one of those who professed to like the chase. He wanted the sure thing right away.

He did have patience though once he knew he was onto a sure thing. He wasn't going to spoil the party by leaving early. He wanted the lot. Drinking games and contests were going on all over the place, most with sexual overtones. Party games were organised also with sexual overtones. Twister was the favourite with far more positions being discovered than were ever envisaged by the originators.

I kept my reputation by not actually joining in but either betting on the outcome or offering helpful remarks for those who were stuck in the more bizarre situations. In this way it was possible to see things that probably would have been better hidden, at the same time as performing hilarious tricks on the actual performers.

Around about one in the morning the management called time.

Everyone was drifting off in a good mood when Belgian caught hold of us and said we would have a nightcap in his room with the girls.

The three Australian girls of course.

Room service was already in attendance and a few of us kept the party going until about two am.

Belgian suddenly roared out, "okay, fuck off everyone. Sleep for you, fucking for me. The neighbours have complained so clear off now."

We thanked him but his mind was elsewhere. It was obviously in his dick because he was fondling the Aussie girls.

We went, they stayed.

We slept like logs until eight o'clock. Showered and went down to breakfast.

Bloody hell the three girls were there looking fresh as daisies.

They called us over. We joined them as breakfast and everything else was on the Belgian.

We asked how he was. They giggled and said they had fucked him to a standstill. He was still out cold, done in but highly satisfied.

We asked them how they had managed that as the Belgian had a huge appetite.

"Easy man, easy," they laughed, "we play according to Aussie rules. Go flat out right from the start, none stop through to the end. Team work!"

"I've seen you here for a few days," I said, "are you here on business or what?"

"Or what," came the answer, "we're tourists who like to fuck. So we fuck our way all round the world. If we stay in the posh places there are always gentlemen who will take care of us. We never stay in backpacker's hostels. They're full of guys who think we'll do it for love. No hope losers too full of themselves. We travel in style."

"Yeah," said another girl, "you two got room for us tonight as I reckon Belgian's had enough for a day or two?"

"Don't be so sure," I said, "he'll come roaring back."

"No, not a good idea, management and security have their eyes on us. We may have to move on," she said, "we could go out with you though and come back later."

"Woah, not so fast," I chuckled, "I come cheap, you come expensive. No deal girls, no deal."

Suddenly my colleague smarmily chirped in with a silly smirk that he obviously thought was making him seem a man of the world, "don't be so hasty, maybe we could help these young ladies out. You know three in a bed and all that."

"Are you nuts?" I exclaimed, "you heard them. You are not even in the backpackers class let alone the Belgian's. You want it you pay but you're on your own."

He looked hurt. I didn't care.

"Sorry girls, but tell me, how do you get away with it?"

"If we worked alone it wouldn't work," they said, "it would look like a pro job. But with three of us it seems like enthusiastic amateur innocence, a holiday spree, not a set up, so the guys love it. We tell them they were the best ever and they were usually so pissed they can't remember and go along with our made up stories of how great they were. What sucker can resist that. They not only pay our bills but give us a tip. Sometimes we get a good fuck out of it as well but not often. How about you? You look likely. Fancy a go?"

"Me? No way, try my mate here. Mind you I might change my mind if you paid the bill."

They shook their heads and grinned, "bye bye poms, bye bye."

So we went.

Hypermarket Hysteria

Supermarkets were out—old hat. Hypermarkets were in if you could get planning permission. In England that was a problem. In France it was the way to go.

So we went.

All of our senior executive level on a fact finding mission. We had been the pioneers of Supermarkets so we felt we needed to be in the advance guard of the Hypermarket development.

We went across the Channel by ferry and were picked up by coach on the other side. We had a local French driver and a guide.

We covered two projects before lunch firmly believing that we had remained inconspicuous. How thirty-five prim English business men sticking their noses in everywhere asking questions in pidgin French could pass unnoticed by the French Hypermarket staff and management didn't occur to us. We were undercover and that was that. The French weren't too bright, were they?

It did occur to me and a colleague called John that if we were so much smarter why were we in France on a spying mission in order to copy them?

Never mind, our mythical low profile was about to disappear.

It was lunch time. Due to traffic hold ups we were running a bit behind time so we decided on a working lunch at our next port of call.

John and I were accompanied by a colleague called Paul. Paul was a relatively young and inexperienced University graduate who had become one of a quota. Companies decided that in order to appear with it and fashionable then they needed to be able to boast of more university graduates at executive level. So Paul was shoed into a senior position and needed to prove himself.

He was nice enough but practically useless. Theory great but practice poor.

So Paul, being a University smartass, had developed a strategy.

He would attach himself to the more experienced senior personnel, follow them around, listen in, ask questions and then present the answers as his own before anyone else got a word in.

He attached himself to John and I. He tried his usual gambits along the lines off, "it's good and well done but I don't think some things are quite right are they?—There could be some improvements don't you think?—What are your impressions then?—I know what mine are, what about yours?"

Originally we had fallen for it and had opened up only to find that Paul had put a report in first and stolen the glory. His star had been on the rise.

We adjusted. We deliberately fed him misinformation. We had done this for some time and he wasn't doing so well. We felt a bit treacherous and had a little guilt but not too much. He had no compunction about shitting on everyone else.

Anyway John and I detached ourselves leaving a puzzled Paul to wonder how he had missed so much of what we had just told him.

John and I decided to go French for lunch. We bought a crusty French loaf, a bottle of Perrier, a hunk of cheese, an onion and a plastic bottle of red wine filled cheaply from a cask with a tap on it. We sat on a curb in the car park beside the coach and dined like the fine fellows we thought we were.

It was not long before we attracted the attention of colleagues who had been at a loss how to get a bite to eat and drink on the move.

They fell in with the idea wholeheartedly and we were soon joined by small groups entering into the spirit of the thing. Unfortunately the spirit took over and the wine dominated more than the bread and cheese. By the time we got back on the coach things were starting to go out of control.

Several members of our party were jubilantly holding up bottles of wine that they had kept in reserve for the journey and to fortify themselves for the business ahead. They were free with the fortification, passing it around, and starting a singsong.

The pop songs were soon replaced by bawdy rugby songs and our CEO decided that enough was enough as there were ladies in the party. This remark brought forth hearty laughter and risque comments that so upset one woman she started to batter her male neighbour with very unladylike forthright abuse.

A few were so far gone that they were prepared to risk their futures. They carried on carrying on, in fact staggering down the aisles exhorting us all to sing and dance. The more senior members, although not happy, decided in the end to go with the flow and our deputy chairman, who had a fine Welsh tenor voice, let loose with a fantastic rendition of "We'll keep a welcome in the Hillsides" which so impressed even the most far gone that it actually quietened things down.

Unfortunately it was a little too late. No one was in any condition to sensibly carry on so we didn't. We headed for the nearest hotel which didn't have enough vacant rooms so as punishment for our somewhat naughty boy behaviour we had to double up and in our case to treble up.

John and I were to share with another colleague called James.

We had a room with a single and double bed. Adequate enough.

John and I were in the doghouse being viewed as the subversives who had started the whole thing. No amount of protests could change the impression so we just enjoyed the dubious notoriety hoping that memories would soon fade. Paul was making sure that the powers to be could see that he was being such a good boy and was preparing a mental dossier on everyone else.

We had an early dinner and it was recommended that we should put the day behind us, get an early night and start afresh in the morning.

Most tried and co-operated. Some didn't.

One guy, David, decided that the party wasn't over. We retired to the bar.

Of course this soon became rowdy and the wiser amongst our group retreated and went to bed.

John, James and I decided to stay. We weren't among the wiser ones.

The bar was situated in a garden type aviary. Almost a jungle of plants.

The bar was eventually closed in a hurry as the barman realised if he kept open then it could be an all night session.

This was not good news to David.

He somehow convinced the barman to leave it open. He did so and washed his hands off the whole thing. David promised to list everything that we drunk assuring him it would be paid the next day.

David looked around at those few of us left with a triumphant look on his face and a glass of white wine flourished high in his hand. This put him off balance and we watched as he slowly staggered backwards falling into the trees, disappearing with a loud crash.

We all rushed forwards in mock horror expecting to find a casualty needing hospital attention.

Instead before we got there the bushes were parted and a shining face appeared with the most dozy, sloppy look on it. It was David holding up his glass with not a drop spilt out of it.

We decided that that was a good place to stop and go to bed.

We all did.

The three of us drew straws as to who would get the single bed and I won. John and James would share the double. It was all a bit surreal as none of us were very stable and sober. Even so we managed to get into bed, turn out the lights and settle down.

James then went into the bathroom.

Suddenly the lights blazed on and James was screaming and pointing to his tongue.

We tried to ignore him but he wouldn't shut up.

We were forced to examine his tongue which wasn't pleasant as his breath was vile.

His tongue was a worry. It was very swollen and coloured purple, nearly black.

We finally calmed him down, convinced him to wait for the morning when we would ensure he received treatment. John and I slept well for the few hours left in the night but James sat on the end of the bed examining his tongue every few minutes.

Fortunately when daylight arrived his tongue was almost normal.

Nothing else was normal as most were very hungover and hangdog and the rest of the trip was very serious and subdued. We eventually successfully built and ran a number of Hypermarkets.

Girl's Time Out

I t was a girl's night out heading for the usual gossip, giggling, flirting and hang overs.

The normal boring, forgetful stuff was breathlessly trotted out with no indication that this chatter would turn out to be any different to any other night. However although they didn't know it everything was going to change with just a few sentences.

The company encouraged bonding and girls from varying branches and at different levels got together from time to time to have a bit of fun.

Well that's what they called it.

They were grouped in a corner of a wine bar, all talking at once, across different groups, excitedly joining and leaving conversations when they felt like it. That was except for Miss Miserable.

Judy sat a little aside, on her own, being ignored, looking as though the end of the world had come.

She had said nothing of interest all evening and didn't appear to be listening.

One girl was going on and on about her oh so handsome new boyfriend who they would just all die for and who simply adored her. She could do no wrong and their sex life was incredible.

"Huh! That's nothing. I give the best blow job in the whole bloody world and if you don't believe me ask Gary Grendle."

Suddenly there was dead silence. Slowly all heads swung round towards Judy who had just gone from zero to hero in a matter of seconds.

Gary Grendle, who although not nearly as good as he thought he was, happened to be a very senior executive in the company.

This was real news.

They held their breath in case Judy clammed up but she didn't. She opened up.

She revealed that she and Gary had been having a torrid, secret love affair for months. He had gone on holiday the week before with his wife and she was about to go on holiday with her husband. Gary and Judy would be apart for more than three weeks and it was unbearable.

The morning Gary had been leaving he managed to slip away for a quick phone call to Judy. Could she meet him for a quickie before he went. Judy was up for it but she was also up somewhere else. Or actually her husband was. At the time of the call Judy was mounted astride her husband bouncing away like mad when she reached over to take the phone by the bedside. She shouted "okay, I'm coming, I'm coming," and both Gary and her husband thought she was talking only to them. They were both right.

Judy was now the centre of attention. All the girls were focussed on her alone.

Two of them went up to the barman and asked him to turn the music down.

"Why?" he asked, "it's not loud and everyone likes it."

"Well we don't. If we wanted to listen to fucking music we would have gone to a disco or a concert. Turn it down."

He did.

The girls returned to the group with triumphant, satisfied expressions on their faces.

All the girls were hoping for more.

Judy didn't disappoint.

"I got away okay," she said, "hubby always turns straight over and goes off to sleep. Says it's a compliment. I satisfy him so much. Gary and I got together, had a quickie behind the toilets in the park, gave each other moah moah air kisses and we left each other in tears. It's not as though we've not had blow jobs before. Of course we have. Gary says his wife's not bad at it and my husband likes it but with Gary it's so different. He fingers me while I'm blowing him so that we both come at the same time. He reckons that when I gasp sucking his cock I give him the thrill of a lifetime."

All eyes and ears were wide open. Could there be more?

Apparently not. Judy sank back into her previous melancholy.

Two days later she went on holiday remembering little of the conversation totally unaware of the stir she had caused.

The whole company knew the story because all the girls had told at least one other friend in complete secrecy.

The week's wait for Gary to return seemed like a lifetime.

He came back to work tanned, revived and full of himself as usual.

He seemed puzzled at the attention he was receiving especially at people passing his desk making sucking noises and giving moah moah air kisses into vacant space.

When he looked at them with an unspoken question on his face they glanced back and said, "all right Gary mate? Feeling fit are we?" and moved on giving a thumbs up sign.

As I was one of the few who didn't join in any of this it was inevitable that he came to me saying, "right then, what the hell is going on? What's the big joke."

"Sorry pal," I replied, "not sure really, just gossip as far as I'm concerned. Reckon you'll have to ask Judy when she comes back."

Silence.

"What's it to do with Judy?" he asked feigning puzzlement.

"Good try but not good enough." I thought.

"Like I said, I dunno really. You'll have to ask Judy," I smiled encouragingly at him, "she's back soon isn't she?"

"How should I know," he replied, "where is she anyway?"

Brave effort Gary but if you only knew??

No one let on so Gary was on tenterhooks and so were we until the following Monday.

It was obvious the pair of them had been in contact over the weekend. We were greatly disappointed in them because they deliberately stayed miles apart. Not at all what we wanted.

We wanted drama.

We were not to be denied for long.

Judy suddenly appeared on the floor looking distraught.

She was also looking for Gary.

Gary pretended she wasn't.

We were all looking at both of them.

Judy, tired of trying to attract Gary's attention quietly, ran over and literally dragged him outside.

Everyone rushed to the windows.

We couldn't actually hear what was being said but whatever it was made them both gesticulate frantically.

They were in a state of panic.

Gary made off.

Judy returned to the office trying to appear unconcerned only to be told that her husband wanted to see her in the lobby.

She said she didn't want to see him. But we did!

The poor guy had a continuous stream of people flowing past him telling him that Judy would be out shortly.

She wasn't so he asked to see Gary. He was told Gary had hopped it.

"Lucky Gary," he said, gave up and left.

Judy came out of hiding and demanded to know who had told her husband about Gary.

Everyone tried to play the innocent but failed. It could have been anyone as it was common knowledge.

Gary and Judy were the only two who seemed unaware of how bad and extensive the damage had been.

Judy then got a call from Gary's wife. A furious row erupted. She had been informed of the situation by an over helpful friend who only wanted to assist of course. Gary's wife was the one who had phoned Judy's husband.

The cat was now really out of the bag.

Gary returned to tell Judy that his wife had dumped all his things in the front garden only to be told that Judy's husband had put their washing machine in the middle of the road to make it easier for Judy to wash their dirty linen in public.

Eventually it all got sorted and a divorced Gary and Judy married each other and settled into a turbulent but happy marriage.

How to Survive the
Great Earthquake

The news came through to company HQ in the UK. San Francisco had been hit by a devastating earthquake and suffered further damage from heavy aftershocks. So turn on the TV and get updates from CNN. We did.

We had major commercial operations in the airport and downtown around Union Square. Our offices and warehouse were situated halfway between the city and the airport.

I was due to leave later that month on an inspection trip to our shipping interests in Florida, mainly in Miami and Fort Lauderdale. I was told to bring it forward immediately but first divert to California.

Reservations were changed and I went. The earliest we could get was to New York, on to Chicago and connect to San Francisco. Anything more direct was booked out for some time due to the Earthquake.

The brief was that on top of my normal business I was to check and report on the situation, not just in San Francisco, but to see if there were any knock on effects in LAX and downtown Los Angeles. The report was to be a bullet point overview from an outsider as the insider reports from our staff on the spot were facts but quite naturally mixed with emotion.

I arrived late evening at O'Hare Airport, Chicago from New York, with a one night stay. I had an early morning onward flight.

I checked my luggage into my room and didn't bother to shower or change. I was making a beeline for Buddy Guy's Blues Club and I didn't want to waste a minute. You have to make time for the blues.

I had no idea where it was but reckoned that a cab driver would. The first two or three didn't. The blues was not their style—from the sounds of their radio Ummel Kelsum was favourite. The door man found a driver who said he would take me right to the door. He explained he thought it was a bad area so I needed to go straight in and when leaving come straight out. Call a cab first.

He looked a bit bewildered when I said, "Yeah! that's why they call it the blues."

There was a huge black guy on the door, built like a tank, who looked down on this more lightly built white guy.

"Yes sir, can I help you?" he said politely but insinuating he really meant, "Can I help you on your way?"

"Yes, I've come to hear some Blues."

"You've come here on purpose to hear the Blues?"

"Yeah, a long way, from England. I've heard that there is some good stuff here, that right?"

He turned to a buddy standing further back and said, "this gentleman here has come from England to hear the Blues, what do think of that?"

His friend replied, "I think we should darn well get him inside, sit him down and get him a drink. That's what I think."

They did. I was home.

I only managed two hours sleep as I was invited to join a small group going on to a late night jam session in another club.

We finished up at four in the morning. We had moved on from electric blues, to old style acoustic and bottleneck blues, to blues rock and then to flat out mainstream and modern jazz jam sessions. The tenor sax player, a young tex mex, who had invited me, played an incredible twenty minute Coleman Hawkins style solo on Lady Be Good.

What a night. Just unbelievable.

I made up some sleep on the flight.

The African-American had originated four of the major influential art forms of the 20th century, Jazz, Blues, Gospel and Rock and Roll and I was not going to miss a chance to hear any of it live. They had changed so much in music, dance and the world.

It was amazing to me that out of sadness, repression, humiliation and slavery came beautiful music played in a way no one had before and others could only copy. World music and the dance was revolutionised and enriched along with style and colour.

They have a different life in the 21st century but opportunity doesn't seem to have produced the creativity that repression did. Ironical isn't it?

Out of ugly repression came some beauty, out of beautiful freedom came some ugliness.

Not just in the USA!!!??

I arrived at San Fran. airport around midday, picked up my hire car, skipped lunch, and went straight to the warehouse. A quick survey confirmed that my report would be simple. No casualties, no losses, little damage but there were now two warehouses instead of one. The earthquake ran straight across the middle of the building and left a neat open air corridor about two feet wide between the two sections.

Simple report but no simple solution.

The area manager needed to get up to the airport urgently so I told him to take my car and bring it down to my hotel later. We could meet up, survey downtown and then go out and eat. I would take a cab.

I was picked up half an hour later by a cabbie who had come from the city, dropped off a fare locally and was pleased to have a passenger on the return trip.

Consequently he was full of chat and friendship.

After the usual, "where you from?" and "oh gees," I thought I'd ask him about the earthquake and if it had affected him.

"Not too much man, I had a long distance fare well out of town, gone for hours.

Had problems getting back, pretty damn bad, freeways and bridges down, fires and floods in some places, buildings in dangerous condition and accidents everywhere. Casualties all over the place. Not good.

Me I was worried about my girlfriend. We live in an apartment in a badly hit part of town. It's not in too good a shape, a bit like my girlfriend.

She ain't great, a bit like the building, but she's all I got. We ain't got much, but we got each other, we're company, you know? She's real big. I'm big but she is sure one big hunk.

When I made it home I found all the neighbours out in the street.

Fire fighters, police and medics were around all looking up at a crane lifting workers in a big sling. They were swinging around a window on the fifth floor. I tell ya, the window had been taken out and the pieces of it were down in the street.

When I went to go in, the police prevented me, telling me the building had been declared unsafe.

I told 'em, huh, what's new, you come late fellas! I need to check on my girlfriend, I left her on her day off work, she was sleeping.

The cops looked at each other, told me the whole building had been evacuated and all had been accounted for.

So, where's my girlfriend?

They asked me my room and floor number. I told 'em.

Right, they said, your girlfriends okay, but she's still up there. We're trying to get her out now.

I thought, "What! Oh my god, what's going on? but all I could get out was, "how?"

So they told me she was very big, yeah I knew that for sure. They told me that the room was not much bigger than the bed. Yeah I knew that too, so what?

Well the earthquake had thrown her out of bed and she had slipped a bit between the bed and the wall. The aftershocks had dropped her even further down and she was stuck, stuck fast.

Rescue workers and neighbours had heard her crying out for help but couldn't get in 'cos when she fell the bed moved over to wedge the door. Man, she was stuck, the bed was stuck and the door was stuck. They smashed down the door, beat up the bed but still couldn't lift her out.

They were taking a sling up there to hook underneath her and use crane power to lift her up and out the window. They had already widened the space.

I backed up in time to see my girlfriend swinging out of the window. She was crying, laughing and shouting and so was I.

They dropped her slowly down but when she landed she couldn't get up. If she's down and wants to get up she needs help bigtime.

We got it, helped her to the ambulance and except for a few bruises and grazes she checked out okay.

We got a new apartment now, the old one is done for."

He finished and looked at me.

What could I say?

I just said, "wow!"

Most of the cities in the USA lack character, and have become increasingly more alike over the years. Perhaps because so many are surrounded by stunning countryside the Americans don't bother about their towns. Not San Francisco.

It is easily my favourite city in the states.

I've never been across to Alcatraz, my timing has always been wrong but I have flown under the Golden Gate Bridge in a seaplane so I've been under it, across it and over it. Triple whammy.

Free evenings were always spent down on Fisherman's wharf. The seals and sea lions were always a treat to watch but the real draw was the Blues again.

A lady with character ran a bar on the first floor above a fish restaurant, She was no longer young but she was once. The evidence was a huge portrait of her along a side wall, young and naked. She was posing a la Maya.

She was open 24hrs and featured blues and jazz bands at any time they wanted to come along and play. Evenings and late nights were packed. Beers flowed faster than the waters outside. She was totally ruthless with slow payers and even slower drinkers—they were swiftly evicted. Drink and you were in, hang around and you were out. Great gal, great days and even greater nights.

I picked up a smart sweat shirt that had graphics and a slogan that said, "I survived the great San Francisco earthquake." I wore it with pride.

When asked by wide eyed out of towners how I survived I told them that it was easy—I wasn't there!

Boy I can lose an admiring audience quicker than anyone.

There was little that I could add to the efforts of our staff. San Francisco is one of those places where people pick themselves up, dust themselves down and get on. Once the initial shock wore off recovery began and rebuilding started up. Business moved on, affected areas were replanned and sorted.

Extra-ordinary energy.

I flew to L.A.

A different city entirely where most of the citizens seemed wrapped up in themselves. It was one large smog ridden urban sprawl that appeared to have grown without any overview. Of course it had its attractions but they were virtually all orientated to the spectacular and visual entertainment.

It had some wonderful views backing up into the mountains but the tours were not directed towards nature, only to celebrity housing and wealth. In the midst of incredible natural and human creativity was a cultural desert.

Yes Disneyland and International Studios were there but you had to go to Florida for Epcot and the NASA experience.

We had recently rebuilt the commercial facilities at LAX and they and the downtown enterprises were doing well. No damage had been recorded in the area but there was nervousness around.

LA was built on the San Andreas fault and both official and public opinion was that a quake was overdue. The San Francisco disaster had not calmed down any anxiety but of course life went on as usual. Good for them.

I caught the red eye to Miami.

This flight enables you to do a full days work on the west coast and then fly overnight to the east coast arriving in time to do a full days work there. Because of flight times and the coast to coast time difference it didn't work the other way round.

We were in the process of moving our Miami office to Fort Lauderdale just up the coast.

Because of the nature of our business we worked very odd hours. We were a world wide organisation on which the sun never set. Always as one office shut another was opening up and didn't want to be told it had to wait for its work to be dealt with. It was frequently difficult to get away.

Some of our staff had been having trouble when going to pick up their cars from the car park in the early hours and in spite of additional security the harassment continued. We decided to move.

Fort Lauderdale was safer but I had to do Miami first.

I stayed in a hotel on Biscayne Bay, at the mouth of the Miami River. There was no chance of sleeping in.

At six every morning, just around sun up the Customs boat exited the river, engines throttled back to a harsh roar. As soon as they hit the bay the customs guys, in exact unison, reversed their baseball caps, strapped themselves in, settled down and opened up the engines. Such power.

The boat lifted up out of the water into the plane position and shot forward like a rocket. The customs officials' heads shot back, then forwards, then sank lower to avoid the spray. The noise was incredible. It was enough to wake the dead on the moon let alone around Miami.

They had to have that sort of power and facility to be able to compete with the smugglers boats that could be seen in inlets all over the intra coastal.

While there I saw one or two drug busts in the bay.

The entrance to the sanctuary of the Miami River was covered by a lift up road bridge.

The bridge was automatically controlled and allowed road passage for a set period then changed to allow the boats to enter. Countdown was shown in big digital lights.

Consequently there was often a build up of boats in the bay waiting to go up the river and also many waiting to come down and out. They were mainly sailboats, the power boats generally used other jetties further up the coast.

Frequently when the build up was at its height the Customs boats would roar in and call a halt while instigating searches.

They put sniffer dogs on board. These hounds were unbelievable.

They seemed to know where to go almost immediately. If there was no scent then there was no activity, and they just sat down patiently waiting for the humans to do their thing. If they caught any sort of scent then the reaction was very different. They jumped up at their handler who knew to let them loose.

They went straight as an arrow to whatever it was that attracted them. One day a dog went directly to the curled foresail, barked, sat down and pointed to the sail.

The boat owner was directed to lift the sail and sure enough a load of packages fell to the deck. Blue flashing lights went up, sirens sounded and two other customs boats closed in. It was a bust and onlookers cheered, rather cynically it seemed. I asked why and was told that while the customs were arresting this one about five others got through. The smugglers ran the numbers game. Lose one, gain five. The viewers all knew it and played a bit of a guessing game as to which of the other boats were runners or not. They probably guessed better than the customs!

The Merchandise Manager for our Cruise Ship contracts in Florida was Melvin. Mel was a great character, previously a food and beverage man, so he liked his little tipple. Sometimes not so little.

Some months earlier we had met up with suppliers in New York and were taken to dinner at Smith and Wolenskys. During the first course we noticed a cockroach climbing up the wall besides our table. The management supplied free glasses of wine with apologies. During the main course there was a slightly smaller cockroach running down the wall. The management this time supplied two free bottles of wine with profuse apologies. Unbelievably during dessert yet another cockroach ran along the wall. The management supplied a bottle of champagne with red faced apologies and moved us to another table. We nearly fell over it.

Mel and I needed the toilet. We were staggering and definitely did not want to see any more cockroaches. When we got to the toilet we had to hold on to anything in sight but did manage to keep away from each other. I think we managed to pee on target and tidy ourselves up only to find our hosts staggering along the corridor.

They were holding on to the walls, with inane grins on their faces. Thank god no one was driving that night. But cockroaches in Smith and Wolenskys???

Mel had asked me to vet this supplier in Miami who had some fabulous, gems, jewellery and antiques and see what I thought. Apparently his product was great but the guy himself made everyone nervous.

He was shown into Mel's office carrying two large bags. He was big, not huge but he was as hard as nails. There was not an ounce of spare flesh on him. However he did not flash it around like many show offs with cut off vests and shaven heads. He didn't need to, he was hard.

He was around thirty years of age, wearing an expensive suit, neat haircut and what passed for a smile. When this man smiled it was not reassuring. His lips crinkled but his eyes remained cold.

We shook hands, sat down, exchanged a few pleasantries and got down to business. He loved what he had and it was soon covering the desk.

Loose gems, minerals, fine jewellery and Spanish treasure. It was all mixed up. I couldn't make head nor tale of it, there was so much. I asked him if he was worried about carrying all this value around Florida and just for a second his left eye twitched before he said slowly no, nobody bothered him.

I believed it.

I thought we should get it all a bit organised and sorted so I suggested that we group the merchandise into categories and relax. He agreed we should relax. He put his hand in the waistband of his trousers and pulled out a Colt 45 automatic and placed it on the top of some computer printouts on the desk. Before we could attempt to relax he then pulled out another weapon from a shoulder holster and put it alongside the Colt. Mel and I were looking down the barrels of both of them so we relaxed by sliding down in our chairs, moving slightly sideways, so that we could just about see over the desk but were definitely below the firing line.

We managed to get a satisfactory deal even from the discomfort of our low position and a few weeks later the product was aboard on a free trial. I had a feeling that we should leave ourselves a quick way out because It seemed to me he didn't worry too much about the business end of it possibly due to money laundering. Later events proved this right when there was an investigation fortunately long after we had terminated our business with him. We also found out that he was an organised crime enforcer. Thank goodness no one had upset him!!??

I had met up with a number of my UK colleagues one evening who were determined to make whoopee. Basically a night of wine, women and song.

I was never intentionally a party pooper but bowed out of this one.

I had just turned out my light when there was a gentle but insistent tapping on the door.

I ignored it.

It carried on.

I switched on the light, slipped on a pair of shorts and peered out through the spy hole.

No one.

I had just turned round swearing to myself when the knocking came again.

All right what silly bastard was playing games after midnight?

I swung open the door and before I could prevent it an absolutely stunning, gorgeous blond had slipped past me into the room. Obviously well practiced.

"Oi, you," I called out from the doorway, "come back here."

She walked towards me doing that American style hip swinging walk that they think makes them look sexy and attractive. The Americans are just too bloody obvious. The problem is so many copy them.

I grinned.

"What are you doing here?" I asked, "I didn't order any room service. You've got the wrong room."

"I haven't," she purred, "you're Denis and I'm in the right room. You're friends ordered the service. I and my girl friends met them in a bar, great fun guys. I loved 'em!"

"Yeah, I bet," I laughed, "one at a time or all at once?"

"Huh?"

"Never mind," I said, "look you're wasting your good time and money, so be my guest keep your pay and let me sleep, okay?"

"Heck I haven't been paid," she complained, "they said you'd pay."

"No way, sorry," I said, "anyway out of interest just what do you charge?"

"Two hundred and fifty dollars US," came the brisk reply.

"Bloody hell," I exclaimed, "what do you do for two fifty for goodness sake?"

Five minutes later she still hadn't finished. Boy this girl gave value for money!

"Woah, woah, hold it there," I interrupted, "I can't do all that. That's a lot more than I can manage even on a good day with the wind behind me."

She looked puzzled and wriggled about which was quite pleasant as she was facing me across the narrow entrance pinning me to the wall with her size 42Z cups.

"I mean, see, give me a break. What do you do for fifty dollars," I asked hopefully.

"You're funning me" she moaned, "for fifty dollars I don't fuck, I fuck off."

And she went, wriggling her arse all the way down the corridor as I watched.

I watched her all the way.

We had a number of cruise ships coming into Miami and Fort Lauderdale over the next few days and so had to get the logistics correct. The ships docked early but it took time for the passengers to disembark, clear immigration and customs and then for the officers to stock check and seal up all facilities while in port. They would then allow us and new product to go on board after it had been checked and cleared. Old product and waste would be landed. Everything under strict control.

The ship sailed again at six in the evening, fully loaded with a new passenger list. We only had a short time frame to get everything done and cleared for the outward journey.

Our trucks were all lined up, cleared by officials, allowed through the gates and onto the dock. We also had a few new staff and crew members to join the ships. They were either fresh members or recycled ones, not necessarily new to cruising but new to these particular vessels.

Miami and Fort Lauderdale were ports where the majority of ships could come alongside the dock.

Some ports could not handle the big stuff and so ships had to be serviced by tenders and lighters while at sea. This was a huge challenge and ship owners showed us no mercy if we failed to shape up and deliver.

I had a lot of new inventory, staff training, systems and marketing to cover. Getting a lift to the decks we needed was no easy task. The ship was being loaded at all levels and grabbing a lift was a fight.

We got one, already occupied by an unshaven guy in stained light blue chinos, sweaty white shirt, bald head at the front and a pigtail behind. He had a wide smile and asked us where we were headed. Feeling important we told him we were going up to see the captain. OK, he said, so was he. We thought, "Oh yeah."

We got out on the appropriate deck and we all walked along to the Captains quarters. When we got inside the guy turned round and said, "Okay people, welcome, what can I do for you?"

He was the captain.

Well that was Carnival Cruises. It would never have happened on Holland America!

Carnival Cruise line offered people non stop fun and adventure. You did not go on Carnival to relax.

Most frightening were the women. They came in all shapes, sizes and ages. As soon as they got on board they formed packs and went hunting. They were not hunting to hold hands or share a joke. They wanted a man and they wanted him right away. If they shared a cabin they shared the man. We were hunted many times and the offerings and propositions were quite startling and inventive. We smilingly rejected the eager beavers and told them we had to leave the ship as we weren't sailing, we were mere working executives. Some didn't care, they were into quickies anyway. We explained we weren't.

Happy sailing guys!??

During these visits it was essential to maintain good relationships with the crew. Most important for us was the Cruise Director. His job relied on keeping the passengers happy. If we supplied all the basics and frills to help him then he was happy. If we slipped up then he was upset and that was not good. Bad reports were bad news and were to be avoided.

This Director was happy, we were okay.

He told us the story about a trick our General Manager had played on a new staff member. The Captain was mystified to see a person in the foremost bow of the ship, a prohibited area at sea, peering at the horizon with a pair of binoculars.

What the hell was going on?

He was told it was a member of our staff.

The phone call came down to our General Manager—the Captain wanted to know why that person was where he was.

The answer went back.

"Sorry for not informing you sir, but he's a new staff member of the watch shop and we put him on pocket watch. He's been told he will shortly be relieved."

"Fine," said the captain, "commend him for his diligence, just keep me informed."

The captain spread the news to the whole crew who were roaring with laughter. Poor guy.

I managed to cover everything I needed to get done but as always it was a close run thing.

We prepared ourselves for the next ship which was due next day. It belonged to the Chandris line, a Greek company.

I had little business to deal with them this time but I had been asked to look into a difficult matter that needed to be kept low key and discreet.

In order to enact good practice we moved staff around from ship to ship periodically. Life on board a large or small tin can was quite incestuous so relationships could get intense. In order to relieve this we moved staff around.

I was frequently asked to take messages from ship to ship and port to port so that friends could meet up sometime or relationships could be continued or terminated. No problem. Messages were okay, parcels or packages were definitely not.

On this occasion the Captain had objected to a member of the Spa being transferred. He didn't like or want the new masseuse and had notified us that he would land her in Fort Lauderdale. If we didn't give him back his previous masseuse then he would sail without any and close down the Spa. Although this was an arbitrary decision and contrary to all our contracts we didn't want to make a big issue. So solve it please.

I interviewed the tearful reject as soon as she landed. She told me that the captain was a horrible, dirty old man. He had come down for his evening massage and she had asked him what was his pleasure and how could she help him. What could she work on. He had opened his dressing gown, looked down at his erection and told her to work on that. This girl was a skilled physio and she had screamed and run out.

The captain reacted, accused her of goodness knows what and told her to leave the ship.

Oh boy, I could see a biggie here. Captains were mainly at sea and were difficult to prosecute under any law. We had to rely on the Company to co-operate and discipline its own officers and I knew we were going to get nowhere with this one. Two girls would have their reputations compromised and the captain could come out a hero. Ranks would close. Bad news.

I calmed the girl, told her she would soon be re-united with friends. I told human resources to put the original girl back on the ship. She had been upset at being moved and was delighted to return.

It was against strict company policy but what the hell. Give the captain and girl what they wanted and get a decent girl out of harm's way. In the long term we could figure out a way to sort out the captain.

We didn't have to. He was an alcoholic who had fantasies of greatness when drunk and depression when sober. A little later he got out of control, caused damage due to neglect and although escaping direct punishment he was retired without an official stain on his character but with his reputation in ruins.

They shoot badly damaged out of control dumb animals don't they? I feel that there are occasions where some humans also come into this category.

Dictators beware!!

I had the Noordam in at the same time. This was a Holland America ship and to our British minds was run how a ship should be run.

Discipline, cleanliness and detail were everywhere without spoiling the fun and relaxation of cruising.

It could be done and they did it well.

We had a refit in one of our onboard areas which could not be finished in one day.

The renovators had to sail with the ship, work at night and early morning as quietly as possible, and do any noisy stuff during the day without disrupting the passengers enjoyment. Not easy.

The captain wanted the job done swiftly and the workmen off his ship earliest.

We made arrangements for them to be put ashore in Jamaica and then flown home. I was sailing with the ship for a few days until Porto Rico, doing systems and staff training. I would then switch ships to go to St. Thomas in the Virgin Islands.

On reaching St. Thomas I met up with a colleague who had just flown in and we checked into the hotel together.

Great view but when I wanted to check the news on CNN I found a gap on the study table. In the gap was a note.

"Dear honoured guest, this card is left in the space where the TV should be. The TV was ordered sometime ago and will eventually turn up. The delay is usual and is part of the charm of the islands. We apologise and hope that the beautiful sun, sea, sand, and sin will make your stay enjoyable."

Well we were working so the sun, sea and sand were out but where was the sin?

The two of us were sitting in a jetty bar relaxing with cold beers. We thought we looked a bit scruffy and dilapidated after a day scrambling on and off of ships making sure everything went well and was okay.

However.

Two attractive girls came in, looked around for a few seconds, and made straight for us. Us?

They were a little chubby, obviously American, too loud and too confident, and asked if we wanted a drink.

Why not?

While we were drinking one of the girls said, "when we finish our drinks can we go on your boat? Can we sit on your boat awhile and maybe—you know?"

Ah, so that was it.

"Well that would be nice but there's a problem," I said. "That would be difficult."

"Why? There's no problem, let's go, have fun."

"You don't want to hear my problem?? I think you should."

"What's a matter with you? We all got problems. I won't bother you with mine, you don't bother me with yours."

"I think you'd better hear my problem."

"You weird? We just want you and your boat, no problems. We have sex and sail, OK?"

"I am a bit weird I think, but you must hear my problem."

"What is it with you fucking Brits? Okay, for god's sake tell us your problem."

"We haven't got a boat. That's the problem. We haven't got a boat, OK? Do you get it now?"

They got it all right. They glanced at each other, nodded, stood up and left without saying a word.

They also left us with the cheque.

We heard a great hoot of laughter behind us, turned round to the bar and saw the two barmen grinning and pointing fingers at us.

"Smart move, buddy," one of them said, "those chicks are hunters. They go on your boat, they don't come off easy and when they do, you find some one is looking for you with their hotel bill. What the hell did ya say to 'em?"

"I told them we had no boat."

"Jesuz, that's genius, do you mind if we spread the word?"

"Nope, be my guest."

"You're in St. Thomas, and they believed you had no boat? Man, you guys are something."

We decided to quit while we were still heroes.

As we left he was still shaking his head saying, "jeez all mighty, they said they had no boat."

The next day the weather turned rough. No cruise ships were allowed in, they were all diverted except for one. I worked on it all day and left just before it sailed at six in the evening. I hadn't realised things had got so bad. You couldn't see more than a hand in front of you. I was stuck way down on the dock with little shelter so I thought, "What the hell," and ran for it.

After a quarter of a mile I had second thoughts but I was too far gone to go back. I was drenched. I saw a few buildings ahead and ran for the only one that had lights on. I burst through the door, panting and soaked.

The small crowd inside looked at me, laughed and said, "you look as though you need a towel and a drink."

I did, and got both, gratefully.

I couldn't believe that anyone would still be out there on the docks at that time with nothing moving. What were they doing?

They were not smugglers or drug runners as I first thought. They were setting up a submarine tour centre and were opening soon to the public. They were still doing test runs and were trying to pluck up enough courage to go out with their supply boat to two submarines that were out in the open sea waiting to be refuelled and victualed. Usually the subs would be tied up alongside the supply ship at night and worked on for the morning sessions.

That was impossible in this type of severe tropical storm as the supply ship could not safely stay out at sea. It would have to be a hit and run affair but nobody wanted to do the hit and run bit. The subs, once supplied could stay submerged for hours, about one hundred feet down and ride out the storm raging above them. Time was running out.

Only the supply ship's captain and one other was eager to go but they were alone and not quite enough.

Suddenly a voice said, "are you taking volunteers?" It was mine.

I was jumped on.

I tried to back out by saying, "ah, I mean I would go but I don't know what to do."

"That'll be no problem, we can brief you on the equipment on the way out, it's simple and straight forward. That's the refuelling, the rest is just chucking things over and making sure it all lands on the sub. OK, you in?"

"Oh, what the hell, yes!"

Within minutes I had on wet weather gear, boots, sou'wester and life jacket.

The supply ship was all ready and was much smaller than I expected. Never mind, too late now.

We cast off and almost immediately ran into a heavy swell and we hadn't even cleared the harbour.

I was shown a clasp on my life jacket. This I was to clip on to rails running round the vessel if and when I left the shelter of the cabin.

We could not see a thing except for flashes of lightning straight ahead. When we hit the open sea we really rocked and rolled. We climbed up, stopped dead, then shot down. As we started to pull up again the ship was covered in dense spray. It was a roller coaster ride in the pitch dark.

This was crazy. The wind was howling, the rain was lashing almost horizontally, the ship was tipping dangerously sideways and we were hanging on unable to communicate because of the noise. What was I doing?

How the captain knew where we were or where we were going was a mystery. He appeared to navigate purely by instinct.

After about forty minutes he throttled back and said, "look out down on the port side. We are almost over one submarine and we don't want it coming up directly underneath us. An exact pin point rendezvous is impossible under these conditions."

It seemed more than good enough to me. "Does the sub know we are here?"

"Of course, that's why he's coming up. The other one will stay down until summoned." He was talking away all the time on the radio.

Then we saw it, just below the surface, a few yards away. Incredible. It was a yellow submarine.

After surfacing, the hatch opened, two guys in uniform climbed out, fastened themselves to a safety line and pulled themselves into our side.

After some fumbling and cursing by my co worker I started to get everything right and finally became a help and not a liability. Well I needed some practice.

The sub was refuelled at the same time as we were passing over other packages. There was no criticism from the submariners, they were amazed and delighted to see us.

I couldn't believe they were so casual about spending a night underwater in the storm.

The sub cast off amid jokes and insults and the captain called up sub number two.

It came alongside just as we were hit by a succession of larger than normal storm waves. It was thrown against us with a bang and scraping noise before it could be properly secured.

Our captain had a red face as he said that although the damage was not serious the company would not be happy.

I asked him if they would surely take into consideration the weather conditions.

"You gotta be kidding," he said.

The pilot on the sub shouted something across which the wind blew away and I didn't hear.

The captain said to me, "go on then."

"Go on what?"

"Go on the sub and take a trip."

"What, is that okay?"

"Yes, your reward man."

They manhandled me over the side onto the sub. The weather was too bad to use the passenger hatch so I had to enter through the small conning tower.

Once I dropped down inside it was like entering a luxury bus.

The driver was called the pilot and he sat in a luxury chair surrounded by controls very much like an aircraft. His area up front was enclosed within a large transparent bubble so that he could see all around him.

Behind me, in the stern were the passenger stairs. I walked along a central gangway. On either side was a step down to a swivel seat and large viewing porthole. There were three crew members including the pilot. I had a free choice of seats and chose one immediately behind him. He explained that the submarine could go up and down, forwards and reverse, turn left, turn right and slip sideways. Some of them at the same time. He could make it dive while turning left but also slip sideways. The cabin was pressurised and air conditioned. The air was continuously recycled. We had taken on fresh batteries which were recharged by the engines but which needed renewing after a certain period of time. He said we were okay for more than twelve hours.

Oh, oh, that didn't mean me I hoped.

We went down to 150 feet and leveled off.

There was no turbulence at all and the sea creatures carried on about their business undisturbed.

We saw a couple of sharks, a marlin and a large group of tuna. The tuna got the crew excited and they radioed base. If the weather improved then there would be fishing boats out on the hunt as soon as it was daylight.

They took me close to the reef, still very much alive and haunted by myriads of multi-coloured, multi-varied fish.

After about thirty minutes we circled, slowly rising, contacting and searching for the supply ship above. We also had to be aware of the locality of the sister sub. We surfaced although it was not apparent below as the portholes were below the water line. I clambered out, spilling onto the heaving deck, nearly missed the helping hands, slipped sideways, but managed to grab the ladder to the ship which was in non stop bobbing motion.

My climb was not very graceful as I was dragged bodily to safety.

Never mind, the job was done and we started on the return journey. This was more hairy as the big waves were coming from behind us, not from the front.

The ship seemed stalled as they first loomed high over the stern apparently going to topple over and swamp us.

Then we would agonisingly slowly lift until we appeared to be facing straight down to the bottom. After what seemed an age the wave would pass below us and we would sink back down into the trough only to start the process over and over again.

Fortunately I don't get seasick, airsick or carsick.

My companions thought that this was a good sign.

We could actually see through the weather now. The wind, rain and cross currents were not so strong. I still couldn't understand how the captain could find his way around in a huge storm safely in the pitch dark and meet up with his objective without landmarks and tracking systems. Yes he had charts, radio and radar but it was still one hell of a feat.

The captain was in a good mood. This would count as a success under extreme conditions and would look good on his record. We'd had a slight bang but finished the job.

We returned to the dock, secured the ship and went into the office. Only the security were there. The rest had gone home. I was given a lift to my hotel where I showered and changed. I was amazed to see that it was only eleven o'clock at night. The rain stopped.

Right time to celebrate.

Up the hill to Jimmiz'.

I joined a crowd who loved my story and were eager to celebrate my nautical success. This crowd always wanted to celebrate any success even if it was a failure.

We closed Jimmiz' that night.

Seven of us piled into a jeep on the way down. One guy was really making out with a girl completely oblivious to the crowd. Then the girl's boyfriend said to the guy, "look man if you want to make it with my girlfriend then get out of the car." They did. They rolled around panting, gasping, moaning and groaning in the grass beside the track until they finished—unfortunately not at the same time, much to our disappointment. We had watched the whole thing offering advice or putdowns at precisely the wrong moments of course.

The pair then got up, brushed themselves down, tidied up and climbed back in the jeep. The boyfriend put his arm round the girl as though nothing had happened and we drove on.

Well it takes all sorts.

The next day, or more correctly, the same day, I flew back to Miami.

Anyone who has experienced the St Thomas take off is never likely to forget it. The aircraft cannot take off facing out to sea due to adverse currents so the plane taxies out to the sea end of the runway. It turns and faces the mountains at the other end. As the engines start to rev up and roar the Captain comes over the intercom and says, "Hi good people, many of you are wondering why we are facing the wrong way. Unfortunately we are not.

In order to get a good run at them there mountains we have to push the engines nearly to maximum with the brakes full on. When we feel that the kite is about to fall apart we let go and race like hell down the runway hoping to get enough height to clear the big fella there right in front of us. The more perceptive among you will realise that we can't make it so we have to swing hard to the right and then swing back hard to the left so as to avoid the other big fella out there. Now if my co-pilot gets it just right we shoot out between the two over the sea on the other side of the island. He is going to do it. I won't as frankly the whole thing scares me to death! Welcome folks to the St. Thomas take off."

This was a ritual and I bet they are still doing it.

I had to meet up with Paul our West Coast Manager in the evening and then fly to L.A. with him the next morning. We had a ship on a World Cruise docking in San Pedro that appeared to be short of some essentials. I wondered if they had run out of coffins because the average age of World Cruisers was at the extreme edge of Biblical Forecasts. Every cruise took a number of coffins on board at the start and most had been used by the end. Great way to go.

Paul was notorious for being outrageously gay and pathologically late. I warned him several times that I expected to see him at breakfast no later than 6.30. He must be showered, packed, paid up and ready to go in the lobby by 7.30. Our flight was from Miami, not Fort Lauderdale, so we needed added travel time. Talking to Paul was like talking to a wet sponge. Most dripped out, little went in.

Breakfast at 6.30—no Paul.

Lobby at 7.30 no Paul.

Six phone calls later to his room finally got an answer. Paul sounding irritated said that he was ready and on his way down.

He wasn't.

He eventually appeared at 8.00, wet, disheveled and sort of packed. He had luggage okay but also had about a dozen pink, tightly stretched plastic bags that closely resembled used condoms. He flounced into the lobby, hot and bothered and demanded to know why I had been harassing him while he was trying to get ready. I had slowed him down.

"Bollocks, Paul, you didn't get up until my calls woke you up and got you moving. You're still not dry and your make up has run. So get a grip."

"Oh, all right," he pouted petulantly and looked about a bit lost.

I shouted at him to get moving. The taxi had been waiting for 30 minutes and we were going to be very tight for time.

He picked up his two cases and told me to pick up his plastic bags.

"Do what? Paul I am not going to be seen with them attached to me in any way, they look disgusting. What's in them for god's sake?"

"Just things, things for friends," he said coyly.

"Right then, give me a case, you carry the plastic." I said.

"Oh, all right then, let's go." And he pranced off.

Apparently the Cruise Directors loved him and I suppose his mother did once but frankly I could have killed him.

Everywhere we had to stop Paul got in a state with his pink bags. At check in they told him he would have to carry them onto the flight or buy another case to put them in. He argued until I pulled him away. At security he tried to pretend some were mine and I didn't like the looks the security personnel gave me. I denied it of course but they still looked at me suspiciously especially as Paul put on a theatrical hurt face.

We were so late that we had been personally called three times. We charged down the gangway, screamed through the door of the plane, plastic bags flying around to be greeted by angry faces, stony silence and accusing looks, and that was the staff. The faces of the passengers were positively hostile. Even the door slamming behind us sounded aggressive.

Paul paused for breath, stood still, looked around him slowly, gave everyone a beautiful smile and said, "Well then, here we are, where's my gin and tonic?"

The guy may have had no balls but he sure had style.

Asian Values in the Gulf War

The Gulf War was at its height. Air travel was considered dangerous so few were flying.

Even film stars renowned for their carefully constructed macho images were grounded.

I was called into a meeting.

I was presented with a request.

Certain parts of our Asian contracts were needing attention. They needed a few problems fixing. Would I go?

"Yep, no problem."

Sighs of relief, smiles and affirmation that they had picked the right man.

I was chuffed that I had been their first choice.

I hadn't been. Three others had turned it down!

Never mind, they got to me in the end.

First stop would be Thailand, then Hong Kong, Seoul and Tokyo. At least a four week trip.

Appointments were arranged. Flights and hotels booked.

I was the man.

I arrived at Heathrow and was waiting for my flight when the news circled about that a BA flight had just landed from Scandinavia with only seven passengers on board. Passenger numbers had been falling sharply for days but this was a new low.

We hardened travellers all scoffed and felt very superior. Long distance hard men would show those short haul cowards how it was done??!!

We boarded our BA Jumbo only to find it wasn't much better occupied. We could nearly all fit into first and business classes. So we all did.

Oh boy it was one big party all the way. One or two were party poopers who either preferred to sleep or watch a movie. One even wanted to work! Everyone else was up for it.

No specific details will be given here to protect reputations.

As we landed in Bangkok the pilot came over the public address system with some unusual comments.

Basically they were as follows :-

"Those of you on the left hand side of the aircraft will have the first view of an imposing array of military might. That will be our escort. Other lines are forming up on the right hand side, our front and rear are already covered. I am told that this is solely for our protection and that we are in no immediate danger. I asked for clarification as to why we needed protection if there was no danger and received no sensible reply. We will shortly arrive at our gate and will disembark. Please remain seated until the seat belt sign is removed. British Airways thank you for flying BA and wish you a pleasant stay and a safe journey."

I looked out of the window and saw a tank, two armoured cars and two jeeps with light machine guns mounted on overhead crash bars. That was just on my side.

What the hell was going on?

We disembarked between rows of steel helmeted troops all armed with modern weapons looking very serious and on the watch for potential troublemakers.

That wasn't us.

Most of us were jet lagged and had the mother and father of all hangovers.

We were hoping that the party poopers would stand out strongly from our small crowd and be picked on but much to our disappointment we were all totally ignored. The soldiers just gazed vacantly at some remote space over our heads. Other military personnel ushered us along to immigration. The usual immigration and customs officers had been replaced by servicemen and women all of whom sported rows and rows of campaign ribbons and paratrooper wings.

What had they done to earn them? What countries had Thailand been at war with? I didn't know that there were that many countries anyway. No disrespect but Asian countries seemed to dish out medals like smarties, particularly to the high rankers.

I'm sure they were tough cookies but it did look a bit overdone.

I made it out to the taxi rank and was relieved to find that they were normal taxis and not military vehicles. I told the driver my destination, "Royal Orchid Sheraton," and we were off.

Three roadblocks later we arrived.

I had never had this before and was even more puzzled when my taxi driver was too nervous to discuss it.

At the first roadblock we were just waived through but at the second we were stopped, pulled over and a white helmeted trooper motioned me to wind down the window. He then promptly stuck the barrel of his rifle on the end of my nose and said, "passport."

I hesitated, a bit pissed at such treatment, started to protest, when he shouted a command and immediately half a dozen men surrounded the taxi pointing their weapons, mainly at me. The taxi driver nervously urged me to comply. I did so slowly hoping to impress but it didn't. I got poked in the neck with the barrel.

I got out my passport, handed it over, telling him that I had better get it back but he ignored me and gave it to an officer standing behind him.

After careful scrutiny he looked up and asked, "Ingrish, Farang?"

I said, "yes sir," very politely.

He gave me back my passport, snarled something at the taxi driver who rammed the cab into gear and shot off.

I wound up the window and said, "OK, what's all this? I've never had this in all the years I've been coming here. What's going on?"

Before we could answer we came up to another road block. We were now almost into the city.

I groaned, "not again."

But I needn't have worried, we slowed, the troops waved us through banging hard on the roof telling us to go, go go.

The driver needed no second telling. He went.

We arrived at the hotel and after paying off the cab and organising my luggage with the doorman I got a chance to look around.

Oh no! Sandbags and soldiers in the lobby and after checking in I found them on every floor by the lifts with a sentry on the stairs.

The bellboy who delivered the luggage told me that the government had taken measures to protect foreigners during the Gulf War and I would be safe while staying in the country.

I had served in the army, been in wars and combat and this didn't look like protection to me.

The military were everywhere. Bus depots, railway stations, post offices, embassies, radio and TV stations, government buildings and royal palaces were sandbagged and guarded by tanks and armed units.

I never did understand why at one road block they let us through, at another they banged hard on the car and at another they stuck a weapon in my face. Maybe it was the location or maybe it was my face.

After several days and numerous meetings I managed to sort out that the business misunderstandings arose because of the Thai inability to say no. They would always be polite and say yes. But there was "yes, we understand and agree." Then there was, "yes, we understand, like it, but probably won't do it unless there are some changes." And finally, "yes, we understand but don't like it and won't do it."

I had to sort out which yes was which. I found out later that I was successful with about 70% and had to go back later to clear up the remaining 30%.

I met up with a French expat at the bar on the last night.

I decided to go fishing for info.

I told him that although no one would go into details, all were impressed with the protection that was made for foreigners, and didn't mind the inconvenience.

He roared out laughing, looked at me as though I was a greenhorn, and explained it all in a couple of short sentences.

"Protection my arse, we are in the middle of a military coup. Thailand is in the process of being oppressed by a military dictatorship who have got fed up with the government's incompetent corruption and are establishing a better organised corruption that favours them of course."

I just said, "Oh, so thats it," and ordered a few more beers.

Time to leave. The early morning journey in the Hotel's highly recommended limo was uneventful.

I went to the Thai Airways check in counter.

Before I got near the clerk was anxiously waving me away. I wondered if he had gone mad. He hadn't but he was getting there.

He was shouting, "you no check here, no fright for you, fright full awleady."

I took no notice, walked up and said, "here's my business class ticket to Hong Kong, my passport, check in please."

"No, no, you go, no go."

"Are you all right?" I said, completely and utterly baffled but determined to get a result, "listen, I have appointments in Hong Kong this afternoon, very important, just check me in and get me there."

"Cannot, you go other airrine, not Thai, fright fu'."

"Well," I said angrily, "what other airline, find me one and I might, just might co-operate."

"OK, ret me see, Quantas full, Thai full, Blitish Airways full, Galuda full, China Airrines OK, Cathay Pacific Airrines full, Rufthansa full, blah blah blah //////////"

"Wait a minute, you said China Airlines OK, didn't you? What time, can you do, is it direct, is it available?"

"Yes."

"Then let's do it, do it please, no more mucking about, I've got to go."

"I can't do it."

"What, no way, just do it."

"Cannot."

"WHY NOT?" I shouted in exasperation.

"Must go to Thai information desk, endorse ticket and check in China Airrines.

He looked at me a bit slyly, "you reary, reary wan' go China Airrines, reary?"

"If that's what I've got to do to go from here to there, then yes, what's wrong?"

"Nothing, nothing, but you go now, go now prease."

This was too much, "I'll go but you must take me and explain, ok?"

"Cannot."

"Can and will."

"Cannot, prease sir, go now."

"Why," I asked.

He nodded over my shoulder.

I turned round and saw lining up behind me five white helmeted fully armed soldiers with an officer in a peaked cap.

The soldiers made a circle round me facing outwards while the officer checked with the clerk and then explained what should have been told to me thirty minutes ago.

There was a Middle Eastern Islamic Delegation finished at an economic convention and about to check in for the flight to Hong Kong where they would connect with another airline taking them to Kashmir for an Islamic conference. There were nearly a hundred of them, all fervent believers, and it was thought better for me to take a different flight.

I agreed. Where was the China Airlines desk?

"We will be your escort, protection, as the Delegation has already arrived in departures. This way sir."

We set off on a roundabout route to avoid confrontation, with the soldiers grouped around me as if I was a President whose life had been threatened.

This swiftly became claustrophobic as only the officer was sure of the direction, but often changed his mind, so we others had to frequently adjust.

We were continually stopping and starting. The point was they were all little guys and I was a six footer who could see way over their heads. I felt like their early warning system.

Then I had enough. Several times when we stopped abruptly, rifles that were slung over short shoulders, had nearly poked up my nose and this time one actually did.

I rocked my head backwards only for it to bounce off a helmet behind me. The guy immediately swung about, rifle at the ready, looking for trouble. That was it. I was familiar with weapons but objected to having them poked at me and in me. I pushed his weapon aside and explained to the officer that frankly I felt safer on my own or even with the Islamic party.

We argued a little but I was adamant. We went our separate ways.

I breathed a sigh of relief and saw the Thai Info desk a few yards away.

They asked me if I was sure I wanted to go by China Airlines.

Yes.

They did the necessary and one of the attendants escorted me to the China Airlines check in.

I was met with smiles and the question that was being constantly repeated.

"Did I really want to travel with China Airlines?"

What was it with this airline?

Shortly after check in I was to find out.

Not good.

A fellow passenger, attempting to be helpful told me that it had a poor maintenance and safety record and that passengers and crew were not usually well behaved. Flights were frequently cancelled or were delayed.

Now they tell me.

However our flight was called only fifteen minutes late.

We boarded and it soon became clear that the fifteen minutes were going to become forty five or more.

The attendants in an attempt to get an over active passenger list seated, belted and pacified had issued food trays and drinks.

The passengers obviously found the food to be unsuitable as they started to throw bread rolls at each other, hooting with laughter, diving, ducking and throwing bread all over the place. One venturesome girl chucked her drink at a friend who got the cup full in the face. Fortunately it was clear plastic. The Airline had presumably experienced such scenes before and so the food offered was cold and the cups half empty.

After thirty minutes the food and passengers were exhausted and things settled down.

Just when we actually start moving, two very old ladies ignored the seat belt signs and staggered down the aisle. Attendants rushed to take them back to their seats but they insisted that they had to go to the toilet. Why now and why two of them?

It appeared that they were somewhat incontinent and incapacitated and had to go together to help each other on and off the toilet.

This was explained to me by a business man sitting on the other side of the aisle, who was splitting his sides with laughter at the whole show. I would have joined in but time was ticking away and the plane was stopped again to allow the old girls to proceed without danger.

Suddenly there was a commotion towards the back. I glanced over my shoulder and saw a couple opening the overhead baggage compartment and getting out two small wooden crates. They lifted the lid on one and feathers flew.

There was a clucking and feverish fluttering with the couple desperately trying to contain a fight between chickens stuffed in the crate. The chickens turned on the humans adding to the confusion. The attendants rushed to help completely forgetting two old ladies exiting the toilet and groping their way forwards to their seats.

The ladies stopped in their tracks completely bemused but then laughed happily as they grabbed at the feathers drifting slowly around in the aircon. They showed them to one another and eagerly stuffed them into their handbags. You would think that it made the whole trip worthwhile for them.

The flight was full. Apparently the Gulf War didn't worry them. Probably didn't even know where it was or what it was about.

We did eventually arrive in Hong Kong but nearly two hours late.

The guy who met me was not happy, we were pushed for time and had to go straight to our first appointment. He wanted to know why the hell I had taken a ticket on China Airlines.

I told him that he really, really, didn't want to know.

A little over ten years later China Airlines had been transformed into a modern airline and bore no relation to its earlier days. A pity in some ways.

We managed to catch up and sort out our appointments and bring the problem solving up to date.

The next day I caught the MTR out to an industrial district in the New Territories. This was not a residential or office area so consequently was a frantic hive of activity. The buildings were strictly functional not fancy and trying to get into the lift lobby was a work of grim determination. Finding a place in a lift was a work of art and sheer luck. You had to be in just the right place at the right time to jump over the trolleys being pushed out and leaping in front of the overloaded trolleys being shoved in. Getting out at your floor was a race before the doors closed and the lift moved on.

Today the problem was different.

I found the address, entered the lift during a break time, not very busy, and pressed my floor button. There were a half a dozen women office workers in with me. I was fifteen minutes early.

Unlike the countries in South East Asia, being on time here was business like and professional and time was money.

Between the third and fourth floors the lift shuddered, creaked and groaned and stopped.

The women showed the whites of their eyes and were close to panic. Whereas I could see myself being stuck up in the air they could obviously see themselves hurtling to the bottom!

I suggested pushing the emergency button. This was done.

We could hear bells clanging in the distance.

A voice came on the intercom shouting in Cantonese. All the women shouted back something different at the same time.

The voice repeated itself. So did the women. This was going nowhere.

I thought I had better intervene.

I asked the voice if it spoke English. It did. Right what did it say?

It said, "what was the problem?"

Oh god, what did it think it was? "We're stuck."

"Where?"

"In the lift you berk, where do you think?"

"What lift?"

"The lift that's stuck, dumbo."

"Every lift has a lobby and code number, what is it? We can get to you easier and more quickly if we have it."

"Okay, where is the number?"

"It's on the ground floor, besides the maintenance card in the lobby."

"Listen, we are stuck in the lift between the third and fourth floors, how the bloody hell can I get down and read the numbers. If I could do that then there wouldn't be an emergency would there?"

"Why are you shouting at me, I am trying to help you?"

"Well then why don't you get off your backside and go looking for us? We're stuck, we shouldn't be too hard to find should we?"

"Right, stay where you are, don't move too much, we'll send an engineer."

I exploded, "we can't fucking well move can we and"—but he had gone.

The women had congregated on the other side of the lift looking at me as though they had been confined with a lunatic. I smiled at them reassuringly but it didn't work. They moved even further away.

We settled down for a long wait. I was now twenty minutes late.

Thirty minutes later there was activity. Doors were prized open above us and a voice shouted down that they would try to winch us up and get us out.

Great.

Minutes later we started to move very slowly up and the women started to relax and chatter.

We came up until our eyes were on a level with the floor and then we stopped. The gates were forced open.

An elderly man's face appeared, peering in, flattened sideways against the concrete. He smiled best he could with a flattened face and said that they couldn't get us up any further with the hand winch so they had sent for a team that had machinery that would do the job. Did we mind waiting? He was very sorry.

I gritted my teeth and said, "no, we didn't mind waiting, in fact we were thrilled."

"Good stuff," he replied and disappeared.

A little after this there was a commotion above and a shrill woman's voice rang out, "Mr. Hayes, Mr. Denis Hayes. Is there a Mr. Hayes in there?"

"Yes I'm here, I want out, can you do something?"

"Mr. Hayes, you are very late. Mr. Foo has been waiting for two hours and cancelling his appointments. We are experiencing problems because of you. Mr. Foo is an important, influential man you know?" She said in a high pitched sharp voice.

"What is with this woman?" I thought.

What I said was, "Well if he's so bloody important and influential, and you can shut up yelling at me, perhaps you could get him to get this bleeding lift working so I can go to the toilet and have a very, very long piss. Do you understand?"

Silence.

Then a cultured man's voice came through, "Mr. Hayes, I am terribly sorry and embarrassed that this has happened to you in my building. I own this and several other properties and this is the first time such a thing has happened.

I have requisitioned an emergency team and they will be here shortly. I apologise again."

"Mr. Foo?"

"Yes, don't worry my friend, we will have our meeting a little later than planned and then go for a dinner at my very special, favourite restaurant afterwards. I am sure we can settle everything."

We did.

Later that night I decided I would indulge my curiosity. Before leaving the UK, John, one of our directors had called me over and made a request. A few years before, he said, he had found a bar in Kowloon, near the Hong Kong Hotel, just off Nathan Road, that had become his favourite. He wanted me to see if it was still there and recommended a visit. He told me it was very upper class so I should dress accordingly and behave well. He said the name would be up in lights and entry was through a narrow passage. He told me to enjoy it.

Sure enough on the other side of the road I saw the name well lit up. I stopped to look before crossing. Almost immediately I became aware of frantic activity on the other side. A gaggle of shabby old ladies were dancing up and down waving to me. I looked around, surely not me, but it was.

Halfway over the road several of them rushed at me, seized me by my arms and literally hurled me down the alley.

I was swept into a dilapidated, run down bar. Surely this was not it— but it was. I had been beautifully set up.

They plonked me down in a chair, running their hands all over my body, massaging my arms, legs, shoulders and neck. It was quite pleasant and not intrusive.

"You wan dlink?" I looked up through the cigarette fog and focussed on a gorilla in an oversize grubby twin set and a voluminous tweed skirt.

"I guess so, okay."

"We got beer, you have beer, yes?"

"Yes."

The gorilla ambled away.

She returned shortly with two mitts full of green looking liquid in tiny glasses.

"These for girls, okay?"

Girls!!!??? "Okay."

My beer arrived as an afterthought. In fact after a second round for the girls.

The massage was great and I had only just relaxed and said so when three or four hands dived down my trousers each trying to beat the other grappling very dangerously around in the dark.

I said, "Woah, massage good, this not good." I removed the hands ashamed that I was responding to them.

"You not like?" they said more or less in unison.

"Oh yes," I lied, "No disrespects but you're all a bit old for this aren't you?"

"No, we good, but we get girls for you. Velly, velly good girls, young, all virgins, all legal age, still at big girls school, college. Help pay way through. They do good job, experienced, rike old men."

I was mortified. Experienced young virgins liking old men? Oh my god.

Anyway—"Where and how," I asked tentatively.

"You hotel. You go we bling, we know night men at hotel, okay?"

This made me roar with laughter. I could just picture this bundle of old ladies ushering a load of college girls through the streets and into the hotel at midnight. No way.

I graciously declined and made my excuses with the gorilla and women hanging on to me until almost at the lobby of my hotel even though I'd paid a fortune to escape. They only gave up as I went through the automatic doors into the lobby.

Great, what an experience. Thanks a lot John.

I sorted out more business and moved on to Seoul in Korea.

We always called the country Korea, not South Korea. At that time North Korea was just a poverty stricken non entity and everyone overlooked it but at the same time kept an eye open in case it decided to be silly and threatening.

It occasionally did but then backed away when confronted. Nowadays, North Korea like a number of other countries, still has dire poverty, but has formidable weapons. The leaders of these countries seem to think that threatening neighbours and world peace is better than steady economic progress for their people. No wonder they are backwards and barbaric.

The problem I was facing was a local company one however not a world wide one.

Our relationship with our partners was strained almost to breaking point. On the surface I was on a courtesy up date visit but I was in reality tasked with finding the source of the problem and offering a solution.

I landed, cleared immigration and customs, booked a taxi, and then called our local man on the spot—a basic, down to earth Aussie.

"Hi Pete," I said, "How are you pal? I'm here. On my way to my hotel in five minutes. It's late now. How about meeting me there for breakfast in the morning?"

"Oh, Den mate, so good to hear you. I'm going crazy here, these people. It's so good to talk to you. It's so long since I've seen or spoken to a white man!"

"What? Pete, are you okay?"

"I am now mate, see you tomorrow, eight o'clock in the coffee shop."

"Right oh, see you tomorrow, bye."

I was on the phone to the UK straight away. This was ten o'clock at night in Korea but only two o'clock in the afternoon in the UK.

"Human Resources? Joan? Yeah right. Found the problem in Korea, confirm tomorrow, will then advise solution, OK?"

"What, you've only just arrived haven't you? How can you know?"

"Trust me, I have. Call you tomorrow with details. Don't worry, no more problem than usual."

We said goodbyes and were to stay in touch.

I met Pete next day. The confirmation I needed was soon coming.

A stunningly beautiful, young Korean girl walked past in the lounge and I gasped and said, "Wow."

"What mate, what's that?" asked Pete.

"Her, you nut, look at her."

"That one, you mean her?"

"Yeah her, she's gorgeous."

"Den, what's the matter with you, she's black man, she's black for god's sake?"

There you go. Confirmation of the problem.

I made my report and faxed it off to the UK from the hotel's business centre.

While there I gave them my appointments list and they translated it all into Korean so that I could take a taxi and be sure that the driver knew where we were going.

We were in a partnership with Sungkyong Magnetic, a member of a giant chaebol.

The Directors were mainly called Kim, so we had MD Kim, Buyer Kim, Operations Kim and Manager Kim.

The older generation of senior managers were frankly a pain in the arse. The younger members of staff were frequently embarrassed at their peasant behaviour and were always apologising for them. The seniors were too arrogant to care.

A few times I had run ins with them and had to suffer the sulks and rudeness that resulted.

We had built and were running some of the commercial enterprises for them at the Sheraton Walker Hill as they lacked international credibility and could not compete with style and brands with some of the leaders in the same field in Korea.

Reviews were held once a month to evaluate results and progress.

We had received complaints from several major brands that their stock was appearing in discount stores in Japan that had been smuggled. This stock was upsetting the approved dealers and the supply had to stop.

We denied any knowledge. We were clean.

This particular review was tense.

Sales were down and there were no ideas forthcoming.

Operations Kim was raging at the staff lined up in front of him. He confronted one guy, shouted, and then started slapping him round the face—hard.

He moved on to the next, slapped him and then ripped off his glasses, threw them on the floor and stamped on them.

I had been so staggered at this that I was slow to react. I recovered, grabbed hold of Kim, dragged him away, caught hold of the collars of his jacket and shook him. He still raged—at me then.

I shoved him back in disgust and told him that if he tried to slap me, or anyone else and didn't calm down I would knock his fucking teeth down his throat.

He quietened down enough for me to tell him that his behaviour was outrageous and unprofessional. We didn't act like that and although we could and did get angry and frustrated we behaved in a more civilised manner.

We dealt with it differently. He would do so as well.

He muttered something about being his country and his people and I didn't understand—all the usual Asian crap.

I told him that I understood more than he would ever believe and that maybe they were his people but he and they were our staff so listen, learn and behave.

He complained that I had shamed him in front of the staff and I should apologise to him with the staff in attendance.

What was with this guy? Was he a complete idiot? It was his behaviour that had shamed him, not mine.

I refused.

He then turned his back on me, refused to turn round, look and talk to me.

So for a bit of fun I circled him trying to get in front but as I circled so did he. His back was always towards me. I changed direction, so did he.

The staff began to titter.

When he tired and sat down he did so showing me his back. If I pulled up a chair in front then he moved his chair round. I put four chairs round him and played musical chairs. He moved each time. We were circling in sync in different directions.

The staff had lost their fear of him and were roaring with laughter.

After a while I smiled and offered my hand, told him this was silly and that we should talk to the staff together and clear the air.

He refused and kept up this charade for two days.

I strongly advised his removal but the Korean hierarchy refused saying that he would be upset at the loss of face.

What about the staff and the loss of glasses.

Too bad, who cares? was the reply.

We did and paid for eye tests and glasses. We billed our partners.

I was always amazed at the behaviour of Korean business leaders. They completely lacked the charm, sophistication and know how of their Japanese and Overseas Chinese counterparts.

Young Koreans were something else. Let's hope they got their chance—they were worth it.

The lack of co-operation of Operations Kim enabled me to approach the supervisory staff more closely.

I asked them what the furore had been all about.

At first they told me what I already knew. The monthly sales were down, not just year on year but also against their competitors.

They were losing market share and hadn't taken the usual solution. That was why the manager was angry.

OK, the last bit was a new bit. What was the usual solution?

They contacted exporters, did a deal with surplus stock and put the proceeds into sales to boost results.

Oh, Oh, I didn't like the direction this was taking. Tell me more.

What stock, what deals and what was the final destination?

Africa and Japan, all branded and all in cash.

Jesus Christ, sorry for blaspheming, but this was bad.

Was it all the important brands?

Of course.

Bloody hell, we weren't clean, we were one of the culprits. We had been able to supply the stock in good faith because of our reputation for straight forward dealing and here we were involved indirectly in illegal trading.

After my report big meetings were held and we put a stop to it. Our partners didn't like it.

We were told that we should trade the Korean way, the Asian way, otherwise we wouldn't survive for long.

That bit they got right. We didn't renew our contract.

They crowed after our departure that they could then do it the Korean way.

They did and about two years later they went out of the business.

Pete was later returned to Australia. He was replaced by one young man from the UK and one from Australia. He wasn't disappointed, he was greatly relieved.

Before I left for Japan, my next destination, he decided we should go to a club he liked close to his hotel. Happy hour was cheap and the boys and girls were so friendly.

Sure enough when we entered they were all over us.

We sat down, with company, and the beer flowed.

Pete was giggling at the way the Korean men danced together round their handbags.

There was something I wanted to tell Pete but the music was too loud to talk and what I wanted to say couldn't be conveyed in sign language.

At last there was an interval of silence.

Pete was first. "Did you see that guy, he was offering his wife to you. She wanted to dance, he didn't, so he wanted you to take her. You should have danced Den. Been nice."

"Pete, she didn't want to dance, she was after something else, something else was on offer. You know?"

"Blimey, what a husband. Are you sure. He was offering his own wife, crikey mate?"

"She wasn't his wife, she's a pro."

"Why was he with her then?"

"To get in the club and to pimp for her."

"Oh mate, that's horrible. I don't like that."

"There's something else you won't like."

"What's that?"

"This is a gay club. They are transvestites Pete. The boys are girls and the girls are boys."

"Nah, not possible, they look all right to me. You've got it wrong. I come here a lot, they're okay."

"They're okay, sure, but they are gay okay. Are you gay Pete? You come here a lot. Take a close look. Stick your hand up one of their skirts, they'll love it but you'll be surprised what you get in your hand."

Pete took a close look.

He recoiled in horror. He looked at them all as though they had a contagious disease.

"Christ mate, I think you're right. We gotta go Den."

He climbed over the back of his seat, looking flustered and scarpered.

I paid the bill, contributed a few hugs and kisses, moah, moah, and followed him out.

Pete was in a state.

"Bloody hell Den, that was close. I wouldn't have done anything but some of those girls looked better than usual. Must have been the low lights. Phew it makes me shudder to think."

"I gather that you're a bit homophobic then Pete?"

"What's that?"

Yeah, right.

I left for the sanity of Japan the next morning.

Before getting in the hotel car for the airport my lovely assistant from the business centre came rushing out. She had organised me every day and done so well.

She was breathless, said she was pleased to have caught me, didn't want to miss me and would I spare her a few moments. No problem, what was it?

She blushed and said that she had enjoyed me very much and when I came again could I ask for her? She would like us to work much more closely together, not just in business hours.

Oh my god, she tells me this when I'm leaving. Cruel world.

I felt like cancelling the rest of my trip but managed to submerge my rampant libido and heroically decided to carry on. I promised to see her next time—for definite—but I never did.

I took a JAL flight and was charmed by the actions of the ground crew. As the aircraft started to taxi they lined up, stood to attention, bowed and saluted as the plane moved on. They then did a right turn and broke away.

Great.

We landed in Tokyo, Narita Airport.

I always got a bus to my hotel in the city centre. The taxis were beautifully kept, with fine lace seat and back covers. The drivers were courteous and wore white gloves. They were also very expensive. Totally different to most of Asia. There it was always a toss up between taxi and driver as to which was the most scruffy, smelly and rundown!

The bus was so well organised. You bought your ticket which had a time, bus number and passenger number on it. When you went to the bus stop with say a 12.15 ticket you were not allowed to queue until after the 12 o'clock bus had departed. If you tried to join an earlier queue then the uniformed attendant told you to leave—no ifs or buts—stand aside.

The exact number of tickets were sold to match the number of seats on the bus. No worry about grabbing a seat first and no one did.

The attendant escorted every passenger on board, assisting with luggage stowage.

When the bus was ready to depart, he stood besides the driver in the front, facing the passengers, bowed low, thanked everyone, and wished a safe and happy journey.

The Japanese are not Asian. Their lives and attitude bear no resemblance to the shambles and ill discipline prevalent throughout Asia.

No wonder they felt themselves to be superior. However this was no excuse for the barbarity they practised on their neighbours and others during the first half of the 20th century. A definite blot on their more recent history.

I had seen no signs of this on my business visits and enjoyed the lifestyle and the people very much. Let's hope the past is well and truly buried.

Addresses there, whether business or personal do not follow any clear known format. The mystery of where anything or anyone is can only be solved by the locals.

I would go into the business centre, the same as in Korea, and get my schedule confirmed, located and translated.

I was joined a little later by a colleague from our Japanese HQ.

Business had to be conducted formally and on time—no excuses. If you were late then you missed out because you had insulted the company directors you were meeting. It was better to cancel earlier, and reschedule than be late.

Courtesy was all important.

You bowed gently, carefully avoiding a who could bow lower competition, exchanged business cards and greetings and then took your place on opposite sides of a boardroom table. Business cards were kept on the table in front of you.

You were invited to state the reasons for your visit, preferably supported by a written text available to all the attendees. The document was distributed with due reverence and quietly studied.

While presenting your proposition you would scan faces to see what type of response you were getting.

Mostly you were met with polite, inscrutable looks, with only two or three more enthusiastic participants among the occupants on the other side of the table.

Naturally you fixed your attention there and focussed your pitch to them.

Big mistake!?

After you had finished all eyes swung to one elderly man at one end of the table who had said nothing and had remained totally still the whole time.

He was the big guy and you had missed out on him!

No matter what opinions they may have had, no one spoke and all deferred to his judgements. They offered no comments unless invited by him to do so. Anyone speaking was carefully listened to and acknowledged.

He agreed to us doing business and our proposal.

This put us into the dangerous guessing game of which yes it was.

It seemed we had done our homework well as he ticked off the sentences one by one with only minor and acceptable adjustments.

As we were breaking up one of his aides told us that the President had invited us to dinner that evening and if okay then we would be picked up at seven at our hotel.

Very kind, no problem.

The restaurant was at the top of a tower, exclusive, expensive and ideally appointed. The view was great.

We were asked what we would like to drink. I was gasping and wanted a long beer.

Which beer did I prefer?

"Kirin please."

This provoked peals of laughter, especially from the President.

"Why, what, isn't it okay?"

I was told, "yes it's okay but this is the Asahi main building and it is an associate company of ours. We own the place. Wouldn't you prefer an Asahi?"

Yep, I would.

I had accidentally broken the ice and we did good business for a number of years.

The Japanese dealt straight with you and expected the same in return—a contract was a contract. You were expected to keep your word.

I always made a point of trying to do a bit of culture so I attended a Geisha tea ceremony but found that although charming and well done it was a bit faded and touristy.

The Kabuki was something else. Superb piece of history. The stories could go on all day or longer if necessary and people would drop in or out to meet friends, eat or just take a break. It fascinated me that the younger generation had to use headphones for translation as they did not understand the ancient language being used.

It was very impressive.

I visited Rippongi district but found it very worldy and un-Japanese as I did other places recommended by expats.

Loved the Ginza though.

This was a time when the Japanese department stores were flourishing. Times were changing but they hadn't yet reached this prime shopping area.

The Japanese were on the move, less shy about travelling, more open to other styles and ways of living. The young had been the advance guard but now the older ones were becoming adventurous.

Standing on the corner waiting to cross Showa-Dory street I felt constantly under scrutiny. I could feel the eyes on me. They were analysing what I was wearing and how it was carried. You could almost hear the comments.

"Boss suit, Dunhill tie, Armani shirt, Gucci shoes and Mont Blanc briefcase.

I want that, I want to look like that."

Within a few years they did!

As I remember it Burberry led the way.

I decided to go Japanese and buy a few presents for family and friends. I chose the giant Takashimiya store.

I wanted a few traditional prints and they happened to be on the top floor—the fifth floor.

By the time I found what I wanted, selected, agreed, wrapped and paid, it was slightly past closing time.

As I turned round to leave I was embarrassed to see that all the assistants had remained at their stations and that the floor manager, with several supervisors were waiting besides the down escalators.

As I passed the manager, he called out a sharp command and the assistants left their counters. He and the supervisors bowed, clapped and thanked me for my custom.

This happened on every floor until the front doors.

There stood the Store Manager and his assistants. They bowed, clapped, thanked me and then saluted.

I was the last one out. What style—simply wonderful.

I understand that this practice faded away over the years along with other courtesies and pleasantries which was a great pity. Countries should keep what is good and dump what is bad—not the other way round.

I was fascinated by the Pachingko parlours, the constant noise, the colours and the actions of the winners.

They could not win money so they had to go to a concealed hole in the wall, hand through their token and collect their presents.

Very mysterious but I suppose it made sense to some one.

I used the metro during rush hour to go to the suburbs of Shinbashi and Nihonbashi. I enjoyed the experience of being crushed in by handlers with scoops on long poles.

There were well known discount stores there located near the train stations that were growing and flourishing against the traditional style of Japanese guaranteed quality shopping. These stores had added extra floors every two years and were busy with business people even during working hours. The range of stock was intermittent and unreliable but the lower prices on the most popular brand names was winning over previously reluctant shoppers. It was a trend that would continue, sound the death knell of many department stores, and change the way the Japanese imported, wholesaled and retailed.

I finished my trip with a visit by bullet train to Osaka gaining a fabulous view of Mount Fuji both going and coming back.

I returned to the UK with my successes, triumphant.

I found out a little later that I had to go back again. Not quite the total success I had believed.

Somewhat less eventful than before though.

More than One Night in Bangkok

I had been going in and out of the Far East for more than thirty years and had witnessed incredible changes. However most of the more visible advances were in the principle major cities so that much of the countryside remained as it had been for many decades.

This time I was not on a factory visit to Bangkok but was to meet Airport and other authorities to investigate the possibilities of Downtown and Airport Duty Free opportunities.

Most of the projects had already been taken up by "the usual suspects" but one or two people with good connections believed we offered originality and wanted to exploit a few openings.

I was meeting up with a colleague named Mark later.

No problems with immigration or customs. I have never had any interest in drugs, smuggling or contraband and so have never had any trouble traveling around the world.

During the taxi ride from the airport to the Sheraton Royal Orchid Hotel the taxi driver sized me up. He obviously judged me to be either a tourist or an immature up for anything businessman. I may have been at one time but I eventually grew up, although my ex wives would probably disagree with that.

He peered at me through his rear view mirror.

"You wan' woman," he stated, no question there.

"Nope not bothered, I'm okay," I replied.

"No okay, every man wan' woman, you wan'boy, rittle gal?"

"No I don't need a boy or girl, I'm just okay thanks."

He looked a bit knowing and said, "I leary, leary know you wan' woman. I saw you rooking. I saw you rooking a' her. She velly rubbery."

"Yep, she's lovely all right, but I don't want to know, I got already."

He said suspiciously, "You wearry alweady got woman? Who you got?"

This guy did not want to give up.

"I got."

"Who?"

"Come on man, what's it to you?" I exclaimed a little impatiently.

"You say you got, okay who you got then?"

"I got mama san."

"Young mama san?"

"Yeah, gorgeous."

"Where she is?" doubt in his voice.

Hoping it was still there from years before, I said, "Nancy's Night Club down the Petchabury Road."

Stunned silence, it was obviously still there and it was probably still a fairly high class joint.

We finished the journey in a sulky atmosphere.

Mark and I had to go back out to the airport the next day for the first of our meetings with an airport administrator and an existing concessionaire. We had several proposals for two vacant airside shop lots and we were looking forwards to viewing the sites. Our submitted business plans were basically approved. Our Thai colleagues obtained the necessary passes for us and we went through to the main airside terminal.

My eagerness started to fade when we passed all the good retail areas and kept on walking—and then still kept on walking.

"Whoa, wait a minute, where the hell are we heading?" I asked.

"Very near now," was the answer.

"Yeah, but near where? I've got to say I'm not a happy little budgie at the moment guys."

Our concepts were a very new and original perfume and cosmetics offer and a kit toy transport themed shop. They were good ideas but both needed to be in main traffic flow areas. Nobody was going to go looking for them off the beaten track and this track was not even beaten.

Then as a grand finale we went round two more corners before reaching the sites.

Hopeless, couldn't even be considered as our business plans flew out of the window. The rents weren't even that low.

Some one was flying a kite here but we were not going to play. Sorry.

As a last ditch plea my confederates pointed out that they were near the toilets and airport information. Yeah great. Mark and I did not even have to confer.

No thanks.

Well one down, two to go.

The next appointment was with a serious contender Mr. Verachai who had top level backing. He ran a very successful downtown Bangkok manufacturing and retail jewellery business. Tourist coaches were marshalled in and out of his factory showroom forecourt all day and every day. He had opportunities to expand beyond his core products and saw us as ideal partners.

I had to be vetted first so "OK, what's on guys?"

It was a case of "don't ask questions Denis, just go along with it. The how and why will be explained later."

Off we went in two cars, into the Bangkok suburbs, areas I had never visited before and didn't recognise. Any journey in Bangkok is long and arduous due to the traffic so there should have been plenty of time for talk and explanations. I got a bit nervous as it was clear no one wanted to talk, every one was just quiet with serious expressions.

I was told only that this was a big important man—several times.

Okay I believe it, so what's it all about.

I had to wait.

We turned off the road, through some gates into a short driveway leading to the outside of a huge glass lobby fronting a high level building.

We were ushered inside, passed bowing security guards and escorted like royalty by uniformed police to a bank of elevators. We entered the flashy one with only one floor designated and took in the luxury of the interior.

"Who is this guy?"

We went up 27 floors.

We entered a carpeted lounge but no longer so luxurious. It was sparsely furnished and occupied by three secretaries and four security guards who all looked like Oddjob from the early James Bond films.

We passed through without interruption into a large office with spectacular window views in three directions and not much else. I was quietly informed that this was in true Buddhist tradition. Worldly goods were not needed when so much of beauty and nature was on view.

We were met by a young man, tall, slim and athletic who came round from behind a large, austere empty desk and shook hands western style. He was friendly and accommodating.

He apologised for his father's absence. He was supposed to have met me, but had been called away urgently on other business. However he had been briefed so would I bear with him.

No problem I thought.

There then commenced what could only be called a thorough interrogation. He had my written history but wanted to hear me tell it. I had a break every ten minutes or so when the young man disappeared behind a screen and conferred with some one there for a short while. He then re-appeared and carried on from where he had left off.

This could have seemed extremely weird had it not been for the very pertinent questions being asked. They were relevant and not weird at all. My Thai companions looked comfortable and continued to smile encouragingly but you never know in Thailand. Custom requires them to be calm and polite even when in complete disagreement.

After about an hour and a half the young man smiled, excused himself once again and went behind the screen. This time he took a little longer before re-appearing.

He thanked me very much, appreciated me taking the trouble to attend a meeting so out of the way and at short notice.

Yeah, so?

He would like to know where I was staying and for how long as he was sure we would need to meet again. I gave him the details.

We were ushered out with profuse thanks, bowing and handshakes and shown the door.

"What on earth was all that about?" I exclaimed when back in the car. "What went on back there guys, tell me?"

"Well done," was the reply, "you did it."

"Yeah I know I did it all right but just what was it I did??"

"That was the office of the Minister who has all the petroleum and transport contracts sewn up. He was not allowed to meet you in person, face to face, not a good idea, so you met his son. The Minister has agreed provisionally that we should do business together."

"How's that, he wasn't there?"

"Yes he was, he was behind the screen!!!"

Oh, boy.

A few months later we reached an agreement. We would be part of the expansion with a management, development and supply contract, excluding jewellery products.

Mark in the meantime had been having a meeting with King Power Duty Free which went reasonably well for him and his design company.

We decided to go out and celebrate with a few other visiting business hopefuls.

In any evening out in Bangkok hopefuls always want to end up in Patpong. Patpong One or Patpong Two doesn't matter.

This is a typical Thai area with vice and respectability all mixed together. The authorities had clamped down on the sale of copies of branded goods in the Patpong markets but sex was still open house and on plain view. Anything and everything was available.

The girls took it all in their stride, developing friendships, relationships and an aloof attitude to their customers until springing into action along the lines of the latest porno video.

They were just making a tough living and lived a thousand times better than those left behind in the villages, which wasn't saying much. They all dreamed of some "Farang" coming to their rescue either temporarily or permanently and setting them up nicely. Sometimes it happened.

This was not for me any more but I did not want to be a party pooper so I went along for the fun but not for the sex.

Honest!

Mark knew of an executive level club so we headed for there after a heavy dinner. Thai food is pretty tasteless so to cover this up they lace it with red hot spice and then glory in any discomfort it may give to unsuspecting visitors. Well the Thais rightly love it but it doesn't export well.

For me there are only a few countries of the world who can understand the lifestyle needed to deliver a true combination of delicious quality foods.

They are France, Italy, India, Japan, Mexico, Greece and a number of Eastern Mediterranean nations, Turkey, Lebanon and Iran for instance.

Outside of them the others may or may not sometimes do okay but to me those few easily outshine all the rest. I refer to nations not individuals.

I didn't say this at the time of course.

Madam welcomed us with open arms. We were delivered to a bevvy of eager, nubile young ladies who rushed us up to VIP seats overlooking the stage and boxing ring.

Drinks immediately appeared as the girls sorted out which of us they thought had the most money.

We were told we were just in time for the sex spectacular. Without going into details as to how they played ping pong, pealed bananas or took the tops off bottles, the sex show ground on as usual. The boxing contest was between a boy and a girl with the winner taking the lead and the seconds and supporters joining in for a great orgiastic finale.

All good clean fun.

Our girls urged us to join in but as we were doubtful as to whether we would end up with a girl, or boy, or a boygirl, or all three, we decided to abstain. We watched. I could feel the heat building up in our girls and urged one or two of our colleagues to take some of the opportunities on offer. They did and returned rather too quickly. Oh dear, some more premature ejaculators and five minute wonders.

They seemed dissatisfied so I thought maybe we should liven things up a bit for them. I reminded them all of the film where, I think it was Meg Ryan, proved that women could and often did fake an orgasm.

"Let's prove it again but in the interest of gender equality the men should join in and fake it also." I suggested.

I had to calm down a few of the more enthusiastic ones and convince them that it could be done without undressing and exposing themselves. It was faking after all.

We lined up, alternating men and women, and commenced slowly and quietly at first, moaning, swaying and groaning in unison. We slowly built up to an uproarious climax, shouting yes, yes oh yes, at the tops of our voices.

We all felt so good we agreed we should do it again.

We did with a number of new recruits.

This time we were a little out of control, our ecstasy flowing beyond all bounds.

We brought the stage show and every other activity in the place to a complete stop as they halted to watch what had grown into a mass demonstration of utter bliss.

Someone went a bit over the top and said it was better than the real thing. Sad person!!

I thought we were sure to be evicted but the madam owner was delighted. She offered me the best girl in the house free of charge but I declined and said only she herself would do for me.

She very sweetly refused even after I persisted a little. Well it was only for fun and I was just a chancer.

As we had become part of the entertainment we were given a discount and a free entry pass for our next visit.

The girls were a little sad to see us go as it had definitely been fun but it had not been a great pay night for them even after we had tipped them well.

We all made promises we had no intention of keeping. The girls were always amazed if you did return as they usually had no memory of who they had entertained before—it was just how they made it all work.

Mark and I did a lot more research into prime sites and locations in the city and took a more detailed look at the airport's facilities and activities. We decided unless there were any bargains this was not the place to be.

A new airport was being constructed and although any South East Asian country rarely delivered a major project anywhere near on schedule it would be wise to wait before making an investment.

I remembered Bangkok when if you were up and about early enough you could see small convoys of overloaded elephants plodding along the main roads on their way to the city markets. The majority of klongs (canals) were open and used by local Thais in small boats to get to work or trade. So many of those same Klongs had been covered over during the years since and roadways built on top.

I had been lucky enough some years before to be in Bangkok when their much revered King was celebrating an important anniversary.

The turbulent Chao Praya river winding through the city had been cleared of it's usual constant through and cross river traffic for the important ceremony.

On this day the river was filled with colour, sound and pageantry. Brilliantly painted barges, with curved sides and Naga (a snake like dragon) prows cut through the water powered by paddlers working in perfect unison. All the entourage were clad in traditional civil and military dress with banners fluttering alongside.

These were only the outriders.

The Royal Barge was incredible, huge and bedecked with flags, banners and flowers. At the back was a magnificent drum which pounded out the rhythm for the dozens of paddlers down either side of the craft. It was designed to resemble a huge sea creature laying low in the water and absolutely leaped forward with each powerful stroke.

The king stood upright and impressive in his military uniform and royal headdress on a dais so that his people could see him.

Trumpeters sounded out a fanfare as they swept speedily down the river towards the famous temples quite close to the Palace where they were to pay tribute to the Buddha.

I had a grandstand seat on the terrace of my hotel and have never forgotten the marvellous scene. I got the video.

Ah those Bangkok days and nights!

We worked well with Mr. Verachai for some time and looked forward to the new multi purpose store to be built in Pattaya, a resort town a couple of hours car ride southeast of Bangkok.

A little outside of the town was a naval port. The port was often used by visiting ships from various countries paying courtesy calls.

It always amused me to think that officials viewed such visits as a courtesy. What the sailors saw was shore leave, girls, booze and more girls. If all that was not available then courtesy went out the window.

I've witnessed some wonderful fights when what was available was not enough to go round. A few times I had been the cause.

No worry in Pattaya.

The girls always flocked in like moths to a candle and the booze flowed like a river. The matelots were rarely any trouble if well juiced and well satisfied. If not the Naval Police were there to knock them unconscious and dump them in the paddy wagon to cool off.

Sex, alcohol and shows were open to the street and those unwary enough to stop and stare were soon roped in by unattached girls out to make a quick buck.

No doubt a bit tawdry for some but all in a days work for others.

Our major project was dependent on the success of the jewellery store.

This opened with a splendid ceremony.

I attended but didn't get much of the significance, as none of it was in English. Later Verachai gave me the video of the event and explained it all to me.

The front row was reserved for dignitaries. First to arrive was the local mayor and officials, then police and fire chiefs, then government officers followed by the Minister.

All stood up paying respect as the VIP's arrived, bowed and sat down. There was a longer wait.

Then all stood, including chiefs and ministers and all bowed solemnly to a well built, distinguished looking man who nodded back and sat down.

Verachai eagerly pointed all this out on the video as I watched, naming the people.

He then gleefully asked if I knew who the last arrival was. Of course I had no idea.

He was indeed very important. He was the East Coast Mafia boss. He arrived last and everyone stood for him.

Verachai told me he was his Godfather and he was very lucky as he looked after him.

Well I was glad I knew my job as these were not people you should disappoint.

Unfortunately before we left I did disappoint Mr. Verachai. He had arranged a departure present for us in Pattaya.

We went to a local hotel for a farewell drink as although we had planned to leave two days later we didn't want to inconvenience our host any further. Our business was done.

We settled down comfortably. Suddenly a group of girls arrived and Sawadeed Mr. Verachai. He made a small motion of his hand which led on to a lot of activity. The girls went to prepare themselves and we joined them a little later. They were all over us, two girls to one fella. After a short while they showed us hotel room keys. This I did not want. The fuss was fine but the fuck was not going to happen. I was in love anyway, but I had also outgrown the synthetic sex that comes from paying for it. No matter how much you pay and how acrobatic or hollywood rehearsed the pro is, for her it's just another job and you are just another Joe. Try not paying and see how much she really loves you!

Fortunately for me but unknown to our host I had had a message from the Malaysian Prime Minister's office organising a breakfast meeting for the next day. I had rearranged my flights for that evening and after the drinks had planned to be airport bound.

I had to make my excuses to Mr. Verachai but he was not convinced and not amused.

I was sorry but had to go.

"What do I do with the girls?" he asked.

Easy, I gave him a pack full of Tongkat Ali, the Malaysian equivalent of Viagra, patted him on the shoulder and wished him luck.

He was a great guy.

As it happened the new venture was not successful enough to proceed with the major project and we were allowed to just slowly fade out of the picture.

Great experience though and incredible people to deal with.

Communist China

Although Nixon had made access to China a little easier it was still difficult to get in. The more experienced traveller and businessman went through Hong Kong or Macau.

Applications for a tourist or business visa only took two or three days. Don't even think it from London or New York.

The Communist government was in the process of building industrial and entrepreneurial buffer zones between the mainland and the two colonies in the hope of slowing down the refugees flowing across the border. The Colonial governments were interested in slowing them down also.

I had to go to factories in Canton (Changzhou) and Shenzen. These were in the SEZ (Special Economic Zone) north of Hong Kong and the New Territories.

I took the early morning train.

Easy luxury up to the border. Then came the changeover.

Nothing wrong with attitudes from customs, immigration or the authorities. Just the difference in the concept of luxury.

Two officials joined me on the journey from the border to Canton.

One was from the factory and the other was a Party member.

We left the train at the old railway station and carried on by car.

We were in an official car. Except for a few battered ancient wrecks apparently operating as taxis there were no others.

The factory manager could only continually repeat one sentence, "how big is your order?"

The party member wanted to know what I thought about the economic miracle that was Mao's China. What a question. Mao was dead, so were millions of others, the Gang of Four were on trial and Deng Xioaping was just starting to make his mark so I suspected a trap.

"I am impressed by the official figures," I said carefully, "but I've learned to be skeptical about government published statistics."

"Aha, then. You are like me. You cannot believe the figures handed out by the capitalist, imperialist running dogs of the West. Communist Party of Democratic People's China tells it true. Everybody in China believes in them."

"Yes of course," I said, "it's very hard to dispute the facts when you are surrounded by the truth."

"Yes," he said, his eyes glowing, "everyone re-educated in China to know the truth. Those who false go back for re-training. Everyone soon will know the truth."

"I really hope so, perhaps I will be able to talk to some people, to hear the truth," I said, hopefully.

"No one speaks English now, Mao's revolutionary Red Guards exposed all Capitalist Roaders. All teachers, intellectuals were re-educated or destroyed.

New China now, cannot be corrupted by West."

"So I can't find out the truth for myself then?" I asked.

"No need, only one truth. Party truth." he said, strongly.

"So the West is wrong then?" I said somewhat sympathetically.

"Yes, they are imperialist swine, spread lying propaganda like dogs." he said very positively.

We arrived at the factory and the Party member said his goodbyes. He had done his job and handed me over to a tall young guy who would be my interpreter and guide for the rest of the trip. He would bring me back in a few days so that the party member would escort me to the border. I would be watched the whole time in case I wanted to defect to the paradise that was Communist China.

Once the Party member had gone I could feel everyone relax.

I was conducted on a tour of the factory.

It was as I had been told.

For years the Germans had made mechanical large, bold faced alarm clocks with a big double bell on the top. They could waken the dead, let alone deep sleepers. I had known one person who had to put the clock in a metal Mackintoshes Sweet tin to make it louder but he was rare.

The Germans were now into electronics and had sold all their old dies and castings to China. That was where I would have to buy my best selling alarm in the future.

I needed 5,000 white, 3,000 black and 1,000 each of blue and red. That was roughly the proportion in which they sold. I needed 10,000 all together and the factory manager rubbed his hands in anticipation. No problem.

We were both happy.

When?

He consulted his production charts and his operation manager.

They beamed, "immediately."

I couldn't believe my luck. My god, China had indeed changed.

Could I see samples please and did they mind if I did my quality control in Hong Kong before on-shipment.

No problem, and a sample was on its way up.

It came and worked perfectly.

"Okay," I said, "it's fine but this is green. My order will be as I asked, right?"

There was a hasty discussion. An anxious enquiry. Another discussion, then another enquiry.

"They're all green," said the interpreter.

"I don't want green," I said, "what about the colours I do want?"

A puzzled look, then, "they're all green. What's wrong with green?"

"It doesn't sell very well."

A short discussion, then, "it does in China, no one complains."

"That I can believe but I'm not selling in China, I'm buying for England."

"They don't want green?"

"Not very much, no," I said.

"Then we can't give you 10,000."

"How much can you give me then?"

"Immediately?"

"Yes!"

Short discussion, "none,"

"None?"

"No, yes,"

"When can you do my order then?"

"Cannot do in different colours. I have government quota. Say 20,000 clocks a month. All one colour is one straight production run, easy, can make quota.

If I stop production to change colour then cannot make quota. We loose merit marks and privilege. You can take 20,000 a month of each colour over a five month period. We make just for you.

"But that gives me too many of what I do want and far too many of what I don't want," I said quizzically, "can't you do the quantities I want and ship them to me because I'm sure that you can sell the others to other companies."

"No, because our production will slow for change over and I won't make quota."

"So you make things that people don't want but take because there is no choice just to look good statistically?" I said.

"So, what's wrong? Okay in China."

"That's because you have no concept of freedom, let alone freedom of choice. Sorry, no order. We can't do business like that."

Crestfallen the manager said, "no order, no order at all, no 10,000 clocks?"

"No, sorry, welcome to the free world and the free market."

We left the factory for Shenzhen after a brief canteen lunch.

We travelled by an old Mercedes bus. It was not meant for a journey of several hours so it was uncomfortable enough to keep you well awake.

That seemed to about sum up the whole of Communist China at that time.

Shenzhen was a vast work in progress.

On the journey my young interpreter conversed by means of a continual guessing game.

"You know who richest men in China?"

"No, who?"

"Farmers!"

"Why farmers, they sell their produce privately do they?"

"Yes, but not allowed and not reason."

"OK, so why then."

"You know one family, one child policy?"

"Yes, of course."

"Well farmer allowed more than one so he send children to study in America. When they get there they get jobs to help, send money to farmer. Farmer likes children in America. Americans very rich."

"You mean they are successful capitalist roaders?"

He giggled, "yes,"

He followed up with, "you know why apartment blocks only free stories tall?"

"No, but you are going to tell me aren't you?"

"Yes, I am. Only free froors because no rifts."

"I see," I said, "no lifts, that's considerate planning isn't it? Or is it because you just have no lifts in China?"

"No, we have rifts, you know why no rifts?"

"No I don't know, please tell."

"No rifts, no power. China Power, no power," and he chuckled away.

"Typical China Power, typical China. No power, no nothing!"

"You are not a member of the party obviously, are you?" I asked, "where abroad did you learn your English, it's surprisingly good?"

"Here, here in China, not allowed to leave. Not a farmer," he grinned "I am member of party, otherwise not allowed to talk to you. Students talk like me, but not at party meetings, not morons you know."

"Well, well, well," I said, "when are you going to dive across the border?"

"Will not. You Westerners don't like party, you would send me back and I in trouble, big heap of trouble. No more talk like this, hard labour and re-education for me. One day it will be different. Students have different dream for China. I listen to you in factory, when you talk to others, we know. We have leader now who will take us on different journey. We are ready. Old school going away."

"I hope you get your dream, Great! Considering all I came for were some bloody alarm clocks I can't get anywhere else and now I can't get them here either. Can I speak to a top guy?"

"Ha, ha, you know how to recognise senior official in China?" he laughed.

"Oh god, no. How do I recognise senior official in China?"

"Hair, grey hair. No bald, wear wigs. Now they dye black to seem young.

You see, all party officials have same black hair. Used to be grey. Used to be Mao uniform, now dark suits. No more old, still same party but new look."

The bus arrived at what I thought was the factory gate.

There were security guards who examined our papers before allowing us in.

Then we progressed a short distance to the factory itself. What the hell were they making there?

The factory manager met us as we got down from the bus along with several other officials. They all spoke English.

The first question I asked them was why the security and why the wire fences and border posts almost on the doorstep as though we had moved into a foreign country. The answer was simple.

The special economic zones were superior places to work for people with superior skills and who had a better life style. They were localised experiments close to capitalist Hong Kong. They were the first stages of China towards a more free market economy. Virtually the whole of China would move there if they could so the region had to be fenced off. It was easier to get in from Hong Kong than it was from the mainland.

There was also another reason.

The Chinese government had moved workers in from other regions who spoke completely different dialects. There were dozens of Chinese languages sharing a unified written text. The Party hoped that the newcomers would therefore speak a different language to the mainly Cantonese and Swatow in Hong Kong and not become infected by Western propaganda.

Tough shit. You just cannot fool all of the people all of the time.

My student interpreter told me on the quiet that the SEZ residents bought and set up illegal receptors and dishes to receive the Hong Kong programmes. Those cunning British sent out the programmes with Chinese subtitles that could be read and understood all over China even if the spoken language could not. Many people in the SEZ studied and taught themselves the language most used over the border.

Never look down on the workers. They are always brighter than the leaders.

They are just not so selfish, egotistical and power hungry.

This company was making metal souvenirs and jewellery. I was interested in the silver product. It was quite finely made and competitively priced. I told the production manager that it would have to be hallmarked in England to guarantee that it was sterling .925 standard silver.

No problem I was told, it was all pure silver.

That was good news.

Could I have a few samples to test initially in Hong Kong?

The answer was yes, no problem, but why bother as they exported all over the world.

I told them that I had found it paid off to always bother.

I placed an order subject to testing.

We returned in the late afternoon to the border.

I said farewell to my interpreter and wished him well and put myself into the hands of the party official.

He asked me how my day had been and told him it was a bit mixed.

I then jovially told him about the farmers and the lifts.

Whoops, he jumped all over me. He wanted to know details and who said these things. He looked very serious and concerned.

I flummoxed and flaffed a bit and was rescued just in time by the train being called. I hope no one got into trouble.

China may have been changing but it hadn't and still hasn't changed that much.

A few weeks later the result of the silver tests came through. It wasn't .925 standard neither was it pure. In fact it barely made 70%. We cancelled.

We did eventually do some business with the country but always using Hong Kong as a quality control centre. Not to do so was incredibly foolish.

After a few days of high pressure meetings in Hong Kong, quick, effective and to the point I was back in the normal world of business.

I had the approaching Sunday off.

I decided to take the Hovercraft to Macau and go into China from there. I wanted to see the home of Dr. Sun Yat-Sen.

No problem.

I had time enough to see the ruined Cathedral in Macau before crossing the border. If you didn't gamble then there was not much else to see or do in Macau at the time. It seems it's still much the same.

I managed to post some souvenir cards from Sun Yat-Sen's house, studied and came up to date on a bit of history and waited for the bus to take us to what was known as the Michael Jackson Village.

This was previously a commune, part of a disastrously failed agricultural system. Now the farmers could keep some of their produce for themselves and sell any surplus to supplement their income. Most of what they grew still went to the government however.

Some years previously Michael Jackson had paid them a visit arriving to a rapturous reception. No one had the faintest idea who he was but of course the marketing and propaganda teams raved otherwise.

He left caps, albums, t-shirts and other souvenirs behind as gifts. The villagers promptly found that tourists lapped up the story and paid a good price for the gifts they had been given for free.

They made their appreciation known and were resupplied several times. Michael, his hangers on and record company thought that he had a great fan base in the area and they were right. Not quite in the way they thought though.

I returned to Hong Kong not much older but a whole lot wiser.

Princess Diana Dies

We needed to put in some extra time and effort on one or two projects we had in the pipeline and also to bring our International President, who was visiting, up to date. So we worked in the office over the weekend.

Satisfied with ourselves and in a jolly mood we went next door to Chillies for a spot of lunch.

We ordered our drinks and food, dallied a bit with small talk and then glanced around at the various TV screens dotted above the tables here and there.

No sound of course as usual.

A flash of breaking news caught our attention and we yelled at the barman to turn up the volume.

He hesitated until yelled at again, tuned up and then screwed round to watch as well, impressed by our urgency.

Almost immediately every one in the place was watching.

The cameras were focussed on the wreck of a car, trapped and smashed, in an underpass. Then switched to ambulances with sirens wailing, police cars and bikes with blue lights flashing and hotel lobbies showing anxious personnel in urgent discussion.

What was going on? This looked serious.

The first announcements came in the hushed tones of the studio anchor men. Princess Diana had been involved in a car crash in a Paris underpass and was seriously injured along with her companion, Dodi Al Fayed, the driver and her bodyguard. All were critical.

Then the news came through that Diana, Dodi and the driver had died. Whatever opinions may have been held about the character, behaviour and lifestyles of the deceased, and much would be discussed over the years to come, this was a terrible tragedy.

Young people cut off in their prime, and children left without a mother. Awful.

A shockwave literally went round the world.

I called my mother in the UK. I was not popular. In my excitement I had forgotten that the UK was seven hours behind Malaysia. We were getting the live news hours before most of the western world had woken up.

I told her to switch on the telly right away, Princess Diana was dead. She didn't believe me until she saw it for herself, then she called my dad. "Elb, come and see this, Princess Diana's died."

I could hear it clearly as my dad was hard of hearing and my mum had to shout.

I left them to it after asking them to phone my kids in the UK.

Suddenly the UK Royals, Diana's family and Mr. Al Fayed were thrust into the spotlight.

Time to collect themselves and grieve with dignity went out of the window. Using, "right to know" and "public domain" as excuses the media, papparazzi and so called experts went into a disgraceful overdrive.

Although most of the criticism was directed at the behaviour of the Royal Family, quite frankly nobody came out of it well, except maybe Elton John!!??

Slowly everyone adjusted, redressed attitudes and behaviour and a degree of decorum was observed for the funeral. We watched the funeral on TV and was once more impressed with the British sense of ceremony.

It would have been wonderful if such a lovely, tragic young woman could have been laid to rest and remembered for her good works but it was not to be.

Controversy raged for so many years irrespective of the feelings of two fine young sons of whom she would most certainly have been proud.

When King George the Sixth died I was in the school Army Cadets, a corporal no less. I, along with hundreds of other teenagers, lined the route and had a front row view of the procession. It was to be the last funeral of a reigning monarch in Britain during the 20th century and was a staggering spectacle.

We first presented, then reversed arms, as the cortege passed by. The drums of the bands of the Brigade of Guards were draped in black and muffled.

Officers horses wore black plumes and ribbons, while the Horse Guards of course were mounted on their usual black chargers. Contingents of Army, Navy and Air Force, ceremonially dressed, passed by as did units from the Commonwealth and Empire. Yes, Britain still had one then. As it was winter, greatcoats dominated and so reduced the colour which would otherwise have had to be somewhat covered up anyway due to the solemn occasion.

The grandeur has stayed with me for ever. A year or so later I attended the Coronation of Queen Elizabeth the Second, standing outside Buckingham Palace. I was a member of the Boys Brigade and had been selected for a ticket.

Although it rained on the parade nothing could or did dampen the mood or enthusiasm.

A far greater spectacle than the King's funeral. All the Commonwealth turned out in full splendour. Everyone was amused that the Royal Canadian Mounted Police had to be taught to ride. The Queen of Tonga stole the hearts of everybody by traveling all the way from Abbey to Palace in an open carriage in spite of the rain but the star was the Royal Coach. Beautiful colours, prancing horses, liveried coachmen and a radiant young Queen waving gracefully to the crowds.

We waited for the special moment when they all appeared in turn on the balcony.

I cheered my heart out, along with the rest.

A policeman looked over at me and said, "Enjoy this young man, you are probably looking at the last coronation in this country. You're privileged. Regretfully this country could be a republic in the future. A shame, but enjoy it and remember how great it all was."

That was quite a general opinion at the time, not unusual.

Royalty everywhere was on the way out, not on the way in.

However the Queen and her Consort the Duke of Edinburgh did such a good job that within a few years any talk of republics or presidents had gone out of the window. It was rarely if ever discussed—so the House of Lords came in for criticism instead.

There were a few blips with Princess Margaret but nothing touched the Queen.

Then along came two silly young girls, destined to become Princesses but totally unsuited for the job. They would have been fine as anonymous "Sloan Rangers" married to chinless wonders "Hooray Henry's" but never as dignified Royals.

One would have been bad enough but two were just too much for the stodgy Royal Family to absorb and adjust to.

Of course a Prince was also involved who at times seemed to have lost his marbles and a sense of propriety so that within a short time good publicity was replaced by bad publicity and eventually by outrage.

Divorce, unthinkable for years amongst royalty, was becoming commonplace, and standards were slipping.

Could the Royals be human after all, and if so, why respect them as special?

I have never been a Royalist Cavalier, I would have definitely been with Cromwell, but I wish no harm. It just seems to me to be a little Disney like to play at Kings and Queens in the 21st Century.

However I would never think of shooting the Royals but I'm not so sure about the papparazzi??!!

If people want to call the Royals parasites, fine, but where does that leave the papparazzi?

Pariahs I hope.

After all the years that have passed, and all the changes that have come about and all the times I have moved house and home, I have only recently unearthed a 1947 Empire Youth Annual given to me by my parents as a 12th birthday present.

It's fantastic to read all the stories from around the world, lauding Britain as some great benevolent Mother country.

We lapped it all up and wanted to go out and save the world from barbarism and bring to it the benefits of British civilisation. We obviously failed??!!

PART TWO

Hard Livin'

The Not So Pampered Pet show

I had only been in Malaysia for a few weeks, staying at a newly built Hotel, when I resumed serious marathon training.

The hotel was ideally situated for this being close to the State Mosque, a truly beautiful blue and white marble palace of worship, surrounded by scenic parks and lakes.

During one early morning run I noticed a poster advertising a pet show, boldly proclaiming it to be no less than a State Pet Show in a nearby park.

I thought that this was too good to miss.

I don't know exactly what I did expect but I didn't expect to see very much. However I was surprised to see a well organised event covering a considerable area.

Five or six marquees were spread in a wide circle enclosing a number of small arenas. In between the marquees were stalls and side shows and the arenas were marked out for a variety of animals.

The parades and judging hadn't started so I thought I'd take an interested look around.

Many pets on display were caged because they were either of the vulnerable sort or of the potentially lethal kind. Some sensible person had kept the snakes and monkeys well away from the mice, hamsters, gerbils and squirrels.

Those considered more controllable were allowed to walk around with their owners but cats were kept away from dogs.

I was impressed. Everything seemed under control. Even the single wild cat on show lay fairly docile although still managing to look threatening while asleep in it's cage. After much initial "testing, testing, testing," and static interference, the tinny, echoing public address system burst into life.

After many apparently necessary pomp and circumstance style speeches the show was declared open.

As usual in Malaysia the egos of the organisers had been allowed to run well over the allotted time and the show was running behind schedule right from the start.

So everything had to be speeded up.

Instead of events running consecutively, they were being re-organised to run concurrently.

At first all went well.

Cute kids paraded with cute dogs. Cute dogs were behaving better than cute kids. The dogs were obviously better trained.

Many parents had decided that very young children were sweeter and cuter than older ones, which was true.

However the attention spans of the little ones was far less than the older ones. Inevitably their attention and retention started to stray.

A few were martial and stiff but some drifted way off course, others were in dreamland, while many waved coyly to their parents letting loose of their dogs. These dogs started to wander off tamely at first but then started to get territorial. This affected those dogs still being held and also their holders. Their holders soon became more territorial than their dogs so that an unofficial competition developed within the official one. Mummy's little treasures were snapping, slapping and stamping at other mummies little treasures. Dogs were snapping, yapping and jumping and the natural mixture of male and female dogs resulted in the usual sexual attraction. The very young paraders were not at all capable of dealing with horny hounds sniffing and banging away to the rear of the pretty receptive females and many started crying and showing signs of distress. Not the dogs though, they were enjoying it all.

The judges froze, so indignant parents charged in to try and sort out what was rapidly dissolving into chaos and eventually took over the parade.

Just as order was being established in the dog show arena, the cat show began.

This was immediately followed by other events in other arenas.

I knew they were running a bit behind but couldn't understand why so much had to be crammed together.

A fellow attendee told me that the show was a leftover from Colonial days, attendance was dropping and finance was short. What had previously taken place over four days had been condensed into one and a half. Hence the rush.

Pet owners paraded with that smug, self satisfied expression that all pet owners seem to acquire. The belief that only they and their pet warrants attention, whilst every other human or animal is either inferior or badly behaved, stands out a mile.

The smugness was shortly to evaporate into thin air.

Not all the dogs had been caught and brought back under control. There were still a number of dog owners frantically and vainly running around after their dogs. The dogs loved it!! Some dogs waited until their owner had nearly grabbed the lead and then shot away again. Red faced, unfit, overweight owners started swearing and sweating.

Then the dogs spotted better game. Cats!!

The dogs who were free sprinted into the cat arena, followed by strong dogs dragging weaker owners. Some just let go with a "what the hell" expression on their faces.

Pretty little kitties with pretty little bows suddenly bristled and turned into ugly spitting tigers.

I was in my element. This must have been just what the ancient Romans had seen at their games—history in the making.

Humans, cats and dogs were all mixed up fighting friends and enemies alike.

Announcements were spewing out of the address system at a rapid rate trying to get everything and everyone calmed down. They failed as frankly I doubt if water cannon and tear gas would have had any effect.

The adjacent arena starred the "Our Unusual Four Footed Friends" group. There were two chubby baby elephants, a few miniature ponies, a llama, a buffalo, three skinny cows and surprisingly a two legged ostrich. Somebody obviously hadn't counted the legs correctly.

The audience and animals were getting a little skittish due to the noise from the other two arenas. If a halt had been called immediately and this arena and others nearby had been cleared then the day may have been saved.

But the authorities decided the show must go on. Big mistake. The cat and dog fight knew no boundaries. It was pretty even as the dogs were of the pampered variety and saw it as some sort of baiting game. Cats only tolerate pampering on their own terms so this lot were up and ready for a fight to the death.

The cats were dictating the terrain due to their greater athleticism and could attack and defend at will from different heights. The dogs charged in at everything so it was inevitable that skirmishes would spill over into the Unusual Four Legged Friends lot. The domino effect took over.

The Four Legged Wonders took fright and flight. A number fled into the caged animals arena, knocking over and opening up a number of cages. The savage beasts, released at last, had been smelling lunch for hours from the vulnerable animals next door. They went straight for it.

Snakes on the loose were soon caught as they were found stuck in the cages of the mice and hamsters they had swallowed and were digesting. Monkeys were enticed back to their owners by bribing them with goody bags. Although getting calmer, tension was still running high, when some horrible little boy, I was told later, let out the wildcat.

This animal was so wound up from the bloodletting that it just went for all and sundry—no discrimination.

A number of people and animals ran away in panic all over the place. Pets were abandoned to their fate.

Order was restored eventually by brave participants, officials and police. Rumour had it that the wild cat was shot.

I have never seen an advert for a pet show since.

The Time that Greece invaded Kuala Lumpur

I called in the team. "We are going to be entertaining a Greek delegation," I said.

"Why?" came the less than enthusiastic response.

"Because it will help our International CEO and the company," I replied.

"Does it help us?" was the next key question.

"Maybe?" I said.

And that was the simple start that would lead us into a few months of total chaos.

The theme would be introducing Greece to Malaysia and Malaysia to Greece.

The plan was for there to be a fashion show, featuring a Hollywood Greek designer as the main act supported by a local Malaysian, who would go on first to do a warm up presentation.

Following the fashion show would be a Greek Orchestra, singers and dancers to further entertain the guests.

The anchor would be a well known Malaysian TV and Radio Star.

Underpinning everything would be a product exhibition and convention, accompanied by a trade delegation.

We were advised that a number of leading food manufacturers, with top directors, would attend together with several dignitaries and Ministers.

We were given a good outline but little detail and responses were slow and often contradictory which started to frustrate and quite frankly piss off our team.

We couldn't plan if we didn't know exactly what was wanted.

Our team were challenging me to call it off as they foresaw a disaster and some of this inevitably filtered back to the Big Boss. I got a phone call from Louis. Personal and private.

Our International Chairman and CEO was an extremely good man manager, he chose his senior personnel carefully, gave them their brief and let them manage. You then either sank or swam. He hired you to solve problems, not create them and if you were starting to go out of line then he would talk to you in a certain way.

"Denis," the voice was stern, "It is important that you and I of all people understand one another. This event is important to me and it will go ahead. I expect you to get your team on board and do a good job. I need these people and I need your help. Understand."

I understood clearly that I had better understand so I just said, "OK, no problem."

No problem, oh boy they were only just starting.

I immediately called a team meeting in the KL (Kuala Lumpur) office.

"Listen, it's on and we do it."

"No way, this is not going to work, neither we nor they know how to do this, it's crazy. Did you tell Louis?" They all replied, almost in unison.

"Oh yeah, I told him all right."

"And??"

"He then told me."

"So we get on and do it. If it gets complicated then step back and sort it, if it gets difficult work through it and if it seems impossible then you have to find a way. You can moan all you like but we have to get it done so shut up please. I will produce and co-ordinate a schedule that we will all keep to. Come on guys, we may not like it but let's show em."

Even I thought, "Yuk," at what I had just said!!?. So for better or worse we were up and running—oh the team did complain and often, but they were pros and they sparkled.

For a start April, our Marketing Director, shot off, hunting designers. Erik, our Operations Director, worked on required permits and licences for product and personnel while Johann, on loan from The Netherlands, set out to source designs, plans, materials and constructors.

Their results and actions mainly depended on the information we could get from Greece.

The orchestra was an excellent one, internationally known, and would need first class sound systems and facilities. Erik received a somewhat snobby communication implying that no way would they expect Malaysia to be able meet the standards.

True Malaysia apparently couldn't meet all of them but in order to complete them Singapore could, would and did.

They needed a white Steinway grand piano, which they didn't think would be available here but it was, no problem, in fact there were several in KL.

From our point of view things were moving but when we asked how many people in the orchestra, what their names were and what instruments they were shipping, we were fobbed off with, "not sure yet."

I set myself the task of organising food, tables, guests and invitations. Also finance and reviewing possible locations.

If the Greek government was involved, were they financing it?

The answer was, "probably, but can we charge entry money and sell tables?"

Not unreasonable actually but in Malaysia it produced howls of laughter and derision.

I was told that we were unknown, nobody here cared about Greece, so not only would people not be interested but they would expect a free show and gifts, if they could be persuaded to come at all. This was a blow that brought us down to earth but I was also told that to have any chance of success of anyone coming at all we would need a high royal or politician to attend who would expect a substantial donation to a favourite charity.

"Any recommendations," I asked. "Who would be the best."

"The best, well that would be the Agong (King) or the Prime Minister," was the chuckled reply.

I told Louis of the situation and he asked what I would do.

"Get the King." I said, and we both laughed at what seemed to be an impossibility.

Now for sure it was a huge problem but I soon had stroke of luck.

April, in her marketing endeavours and search for designers, had made a number of flamboyant contacts. They took to us and our project. We were invited to the grand opening of the Tower Records Showcase Store in Bukit Bintang, Kuala Lumpur.

This was a real show, with all the stops pulled out.

We went to a cocktail reception initially and from there we were taken in a stretched limo, to the store. On alighting at the red carpet we were blinded by spotlights, flashguns, camera crews and media interviewers. There were cheering crowds, craning to spot their idols, dramatically being announced by the presenters to sustained applause—until we arrived.

"And now we have"—nonplussed silence. A whispered, "who are they?" Puzzled looks.

Then relief because from the limo behind a galaxy of local stars emerged to great applause, which of course we acknowledged in a graceful and Queen Mother way.

The reception yielded a great deal of useful contacts, among one of whom was a Che Ungku (Princess), the wife of a Prince from one of the thirteen Malaysian States. The Tungku (Prince) just happened to be the son of the reigning Agong. The Princess, as we came to know her was lovely and charming. We talked to her about many things and discovered a degree of rapport and when we got round to explaining our project she clicked on to it immediately. She explained she would pave the way at the Palace and outlined the protocol involved. We followed the explicit routine, aided by her and the Palace Royal Chancellor.

Shortly I phoned our Chairman Louis and said, "Sir, the King and Queen will attend."

He, always the gentleman, said, "I never doubted it."

For Erik it was not at all plane sailing.

Try as he might he just could not get the details of product or personnel.

Finally he got a list of people totalling 97. Immigration did not like this at all and refused at first to separate the tourists from the workers and Erik was told to cut down to 60 otherwise entry would be refused. They could all come in as tourists or all as workers but not as both.

If all were workers then it would have to be 60 only. If all were tourists then they couldn't work. Erik was at pains to point out that one third of them were delegation and family. "Ah", said immigration, "so they are all workers."

There was nothing for it—an email went to Greece—"you have to cut back to 60, please let me have revised list."

Erik came storming into my office. "The bloody Greeks can't count," was his opening remark. "I told them immigration wouldn't give out 97 temporary work permits, only 60 so would they revise the list down to that number and advise me.

"So," I said.

"So they've sent me 83."

"Maybe something got lost in translation, try again."

He was back later that day.

"Did it work?" I asked.

"Yeah great, they've now sent me 89."

He finally solved the problem—60 would come in on temporary work permits and any others would come in separate from the main party on individual tourist visas. As there was an element of risk we had to make sure that the dignitaries were included in the 60.

This was only one of many problems for Erik. We had to differentiate between product coming in, either to stay as free samples or product for sale in Malaysia, or product going back out to Greece. No one was sure which was which and didn't want to commit themselves so Erik just guessed and made it up as he went along.

April was out designer hunting. They had to be good, relevant and Malaysian, able to stand up and not look weak against the visiting Greek designer. As in many fields in Malaysia good professionals were around but not in any quantity. Too many found that their talents were more appreciated overseas than in their own country, Jimmy Chou being a prime example.

She found three or four who could do the job and it was suggested that the Greek designer, Nigel Dukakis, should come and see who could gell with him and state his preference and choice.

There were two main contenders, Bernard, a more traditional Malay in style and Christopher Wu, a young and vibrant Chinese with a flair for flamboyance.

The meeting with Bernard didn't go so well. He was sensible and down to earth and was polite but not overawed by a man who had designed for Barbra Streisand, Cher and others. He wanted to make his own path. He was happily married to a former model, had children, was talented and could see a successful career ahead.

On the other hand the meeting between Nigel and Christopher went swimmingly well. Chris Wu was outrageously gay, had great style, vision, personality and vitality and Nigel fell in love. Chris was the chosen one.

Their behaviour together gave rise to misgivings but we went along with the decision although we felt that there could be disaster ahead.

Problems actually did arise early on but were smothered somewhat by all the other activities. April's initial amusement at all the boy/girl stuff going on soon gave way to many oh ohs and oh nos.

She had engaged the services of dressers, hair stylists, make up artists, models and assistants. Many were gay and soon got into the apparently accepted mode that being camp rather than serious was acceptable.

When I furiously read the riot act to them on a number of occasions I was accused of being homophobic. Not a good one to try on me.

I told them very clearly that I was not interested in their sexual preference, just their behaviour, which quite frankly was unprofessional, unproductive and unacceptable. I also said that their attitude was enough to make a saint homophobic, but they didn't catch onto the ironic humour.

One bright spark told me that perhaps I needed to get more in touch with my feminine side. "Okay," I said, "Which side is that? My upside, my downside, my inside, my outside, or my frontside and know clearly that I will kill anyone who says my backside!!"

Nobody did.

They did tone it down for a while though.

Johann meanwhile was having problems with the construction side of the event. Nigel emphatically demanded a catwalk so extensive we would have needed to change the venue and it would have taken the models far too long to reach the end of it and get back again. We succeeded in getting him to agree to shorten it just about enough to fit the ballroom we had booked.

This was important as the Greek visitors wanted dozens of round tables with guests being served dinner and it had been no easy task to find a hotel that could accommodate dinner, fashion show, orchestra, dancers and singers. They also had to understand and adequately handle royal and political protocol.

We breathed a slight sigh of relief, but not for long.

We had appointed event organisers and they wanted to know how many dresses, how many models, how many changes and how many accessories would be involved. They wanted a list of songs, dances and musical numbers and Johann wanted to know the space requirements for all this. We eventually got answers but it was like pulling teeth and absolute deadlines were approaching.

We began to realise that the problems arose not so much from incompetence but from cultural differences. Ours sprang from the North European preference for forward planning in detail, getting specifics settled early and moving as per plan. Southern Europeans and Asians viewed "manana" as too soon. Don't worry, no problem, it'll be all right. The fact that it was very often plainly not all right bothered us but not them.

We thought they were too relaxed, they thought us too serious. Somehow we all moved forward.

My Finance Director Kim, and I relaxed a little as both the Greek Tourist and Trade and Industry Ministries kindly guaranteed more than half the finance, prospective suppliers a further proportion, the Malay Tourist Board and Louis the remainder. We also had to guarantee a large sum to a Royal Charity which was chosen by the Queen—a good cause.

Johann had sorted out problems with the catwalk and other props with the various contractors who out of habit would supply inferior materials. They thought it was normal but with Johann it wasn't. So quite a bit of work had to be done again with Johann standing over them making sure that the usual bad habits didn't re-occur.

I was attending lessons at the Royal Palace, learning official procedures and protocol which I had to pass onto the team who were a bit miffed at not going to the Palace themselves.

"Yep," I told them, "It's tough at the top." Sometimes the old cliches if not the best just have to do!!

Louis visited a few times to check up on things and usually, as per Murphy's Law, when he came things were not going so well.

He must have thought at times that his key people in Asia were a load of frantic lunatics but he somehow remained convinced that we could do it.

We weren't to know that compared to what he was experiencing in Greece we seemed sane. We only found that out later.

On one visit our Malaysian partners decided to show off and entertain us to dinner at the exclusive Royal Selangor Golf Club. Louis came with a business colleague called Rayoush who had a business in Cyprus. Ray was always on the handphone and if possible he was on two at once. We reckoned he was actually calling himself to make himself seem important and in demand.

Our hosts were not very good. They suddenly found that there were some influential Malays eating in another room and they virtually abandoned us to pay attention to the others. Louis was polite and said okay but we didn't like it and it was very bad manners.

Then things got worse. Eating with our party were a couple from Hong Kong, who were also acquaintances of Louis. They were a Dutch guy and a Chinese woman.

They had various enterprises in China and we were frequently told, mainly by our partners, that she was a very important lady. We were always told this in a bit of a secretive whisper for some reason and so it became a bit of a joke among us irreverent lot as we whispered to each other, "she's important in China you know". I'm sure she was but we could have done without the drama and the hushed voices. They were actually very pleasant people.

They both went into an ominous huddle shortly after the seafood appetiser was served and then called a halt. Apparently the seafood was off—it should not be eaten. This was whisked away and fish was served but this was off as well.

Did they have nothing fresh in this restaurant? Apparently not!

We had all lost confidence by then and decided we should abandon the place and eat elsewhere.

But where were our partners Donald and Zulkifli? They had popped in to see us a couple of times but other than that they had left us alone.

Rayoush was angry and prepared to go to war. Louis, the gentleman, calmed him down a little and requested that when Donald and Zulkifli did eventually appear then he should be diplomatic and handle it with restraint.

By Ray's standards he did.

When Don and Zuhl popped in at last Ray greeted them with, "Do you hate us or something? Make sure in the future that you only bring the people here you hate and never want to see again. We're going, if you want to be sick then stay and eat this rotten food."

Very diplomatic.

We left.

The traffic in central KL was often at a standstill. The government was tackling a number of problems at the same time. They were widening and improving the road network. The Light Rail Transport and the Monorail were being extended and constructed and the constant danger of floods was being confronted. Consequently the benefits, which would certainly come, were in the future, they were not apparent then. So we were often stuck.

One time I had dropped everyone at the Shangri-La Hotel from the opposite side of the road so as to save time which was fortunate for them, unfortunate for me. It took me over an hour to get back due to one way systems, no u-turns, and roadworks. My colleagues were worried and thought of sending out a search party.

Another time we were faced with a similar situation when on our way to pick up Louis from the Istana Hotel in central KL. We were coming up on the opposite side of the road with a whole series of no u-turns and no right turns so Erik telephoned Louis to ask him to cross the road so that we would pick him from outside of a particular building. "What building," asked Louis."

Erik asked me, "Louis says, what building?"

"The one with the dwarfs on the top of the lobby roof," I replied.

April interrupted, "will he know it, will he know which one?"

I roared out, "How can he miss it? How many fucking buildings in KL have fucking dwarfs on top, for god's sake?"

That did it. We all had a fit of the giggles for hours, including Louis.

Everything was slowly and painstakingly coming into shape.

What we needed now were actual people and product, some of which were apparently on the way.

Erik was still tearing his hair out over the lists of both which seemed to be in a constant state of flux. At one stage if all the people and product on the proposed lists had turned up, Malaysia would have become very over crowded.

Pleas for reductions produced the reverse, the lists grew longer. How on earth did that country produce mathematicians of the stature and brilliance of Aristotle, Pythagoras, Euclid and Archimedes, to name but a few?

Louis had to intervene in Greece and he did. He brought everything back down to absolute essentials, goodness knows how, but he did, and Erik could get on and manage with what he had.

April had the event publicised and advertised and invitations despatched locally and nationally. The request for payments fell flat and was abandoned. If we had persisted we would have had the event empty except for Greeks and the Malaysian Royal Family and that was clearly unacceptable.

The show, food, drink and entertainment would be free and every one would receive a goody bag to take away. We were learning to talk the Asian talk.

At least we now knew it would be well attended.

Our so-called partners would attend although having nothing to do with the event and sadly it showed how far we were drifting apart.

They told me they were upset at Louis putting in a bill for services rendered as they had not allowed for it in their current budget. So I agreed that maybe the timing could have been better and that therefore I would re-date the invoices so that they could incorporate them into their next plan—no problem as long as they paid up. This went down like a lead balloon as they were used to another local bad habit—you give, we take and give nothing in return so let's go out to dinner, have a good time and tell each other what fine fellows we all are, but don't expect us to offer much.

Nigel Dukakis arrived, inspected the site, facilities and proposed personnel and was reasonably happy. We had the go ahead.

Louis had chosen the Palace of the Golden Horses as the venue he wanted, and it was a great idea.

The only problem was that it wasn't finished. We made an appointment with the Australian Project Manager.

He agreed that it looked like, and was, a typical construction site which didn't reassure us much as we only had six weeks to go to D-Day. For sure it would be ready enough by then, he reckoned, and we felt better for all of two minutes.

He suddenly excused himself, calling a foreman over. We were out front, looking at the facade steadily taking shape.

The conversation between manager and foreman went roughly like this.

"Can you see those three arches there?"

"Yes boss,"

"Not just yes boss, what can you see?"

"Three arches boss."

"No, tell me what do you actually see, describe them?"

"Oh, one big middle arch with a smaller arch on each side."

"Yep, correct, do they look right?"

"They look OK boss."

"Do they now, they look right to you, do they?"

"Of course boss, we built them, didn't we?"

"I know who built the bloody things, but are they right?"

"Yes boss."

"If they are right, why are they all different shapes and sizes?"

"Are they?"

"Yes they are. The middle arch should be bigger, ok, the other two should be the same but smaller, ok, otherwise all three should be identical, right, but they are not, so please tell me how and why they are not."

"Don't know boss, beats me."

"It might just come to that unless you tell me why on your shift you used different blocks for each arch instead of matching ones?"

"Oh, well see, we run out of matching blocks and we used what we had so we didn't lose any time. We think it looks better anyway."

"You bloody clown, for safety reasons arches have to be symmetrical with the keystone in the centre, these are all over the frigging place."

"But we thought—."

"That's the trouble, when you lot think you're dangerous so please don't think, just do the job like I say. Now stop what you're doing, strip it all down, the stonework above is not safe, and start again properly."

"But—."

"No more bloody buts, get on with it."

We expressed our concern to the manager but he shrugged and told us that this was common and all had been accounted for in the work schedule.

He seemed very competent so we took him at his word and left him to it but not without some misgivings.

It was finished before time—a superbly creative hotel and resort on a lake just outside of town.

We were soon able to gain access and begin setting up. Nigel had been busy, dresses and accessories had arrived and were being sorted, listed and put in order of selection.

Chris Wu had completed and delivered.

April, on seeing and assessing the length of the catwalk and the amount of clothing on the racks realised that unless there were at least four models on the catwalk at one time and the show was kept moving swiftly and effectively, we would not only run over time but it could go on all night.

She made the point over and over again, re-organised time after time but it was all falling on deaf ears.

She foretold disaster, so I added my comments to hers to no avail.

It was obvious that egos were swelling up, fuelled by the compliments of hangers on, and feet were no longer on the ground. Louis' team in Malaysia was starting to be brushed aside by newcomers who were self proclaimed experts on everything apparently and knew better than anyone else what should be done and how to do it.

To be fair a fresh look and added vitality was always welcome and a few of the ideas were good, but, and it is a big but, most of the intruders were just arrogant and the intrusions destructive.

In the interests of harmony we were prepared to be sidestepped a little but not blatantly shoved aside. So we started to dig in our heels which of course inevitably caused some friction and division. As the parties from Greece were now arriving we had laid on events and introductions for them with help from the local Greek community, the majority who were actually from Australia. In fact a totally different breed. Product had arrived from mainland Greece and several islands. Basically it was food stuffs, wine and olive oil. Frankly it looked delicious and the company representatives were knowledgeable, friendly and charming. We were confidant in presenting this to traders and consumers in Malaysia.

The Ministers, their aides and their wives were gracious, and although a little reserved and offhand they were mainly friendly and helpful.

The models for the fashion show were absolutely gorgeous and the singers, dancers and orchestra musicians were superb performers.

With such a fine cast how could we fail?

All important entourages are inevitably accompanied by fringe members and hangers on—if they stay on the fringe and enjoy the trip then that is fine. The problems start when they get carried away and start to interfere with an overstated air of self importance.

We had them and they interfered in abundance.

Mr. Yusus was just such a person, a bundle of energy with no official status. If he had directed that energy to our benefit then events may have turned out differently but for some reason known only to himself he wanted to compete rather than co-operate with us. He had never been to Malaysia, or South East Asia, before but within a few days he thought he knew everything there was to know, and more.

Yusus mistook our initial subservience and politeness as proof that he was superior and would soon be taking over.

He was too full of himself to see that we were taken aback at his foolishness and did not want to rock the boat out of loyalty to Louis. He was into everything, much of which was to have severe repercussions later, but the here and now was bad enough.

He had found a succession of characters, or they had found him, who latched on to his self proclaimed ascendancy, and started to involve themselves in all aspects of our business.

Uninvited, unwanted and unqualified they were appearing all over the place.

Greece had no Consul or official presence in Malaysia but suddenly out of nowhere came an individual calling himself, "The Greek Consul," a Mr. Popodopolus. Yusus introduced him as such to all and sundry and accorded him much ceremony.

Soon I was asked to afford him the use of an office and facilities within our own, and without further ceremony he claimed the office reserved for the use of none other than our International CEO and Chairman, Louis. He and Yusus claimed that they had the approval of Louis.

I approached Louis on this and other issues. I said bluntly, "Louis, I am a man, not a mouse, talk to me straight. I am here as your CEO, and I and others are being told that I and our team are out, finished, and they have taken over. For god's sake tell me what the hell is going on with this bunch of clowns?"

Louis seemed unperturbed, just slowly smiled. "Denis I employed you and your team, only I can replace you."

I rushed to interrupt. "but !!"

"No, no wait, just wait a minute. They can say what they like, I can see what is going on, but I need the influential people here for my possible future in Greece. Stick it out. Let the children play. They'll be gone soon. In the meantime sort out what you have too."

The sorting started almost immediately.

A delegation of all our staff, from top to bottom, arrived at my office door and almost fell over each other trying to get in and speak.

"If he stays we go. If they stay we go. If nothing happens we go. They are rude, arrogant, ignorant and useless and we are fed up with it all and the worst is Mr. Puffed Up So Called Greek Consul. Well?"

"I've got it, I'll deal with it."

"When? How?"

"I said I'll deal with it, and other issues, so that's enough."

They left but I could see the doubtful look on their faces.

A few hours later in came Mr. Puffed Up.

I asked him to join me in the board room.

"Sir, can you fly," I asked.

"No, why,?" he replied, naturally somewhat bewildered.

"Well we are on the 27ᵗʰ floor and if you don't leave, or greatly modify your attitude and behaviour, I am going to throw you out of the fucking window, so you'd better either go or learn to fly. You are just too rude to people. The staff don't like it and I don't like it."

Hardly a professional approach but he was so thick skinned he never responded to sensible hints. He left, greatly offended.

Kim, our finance director, was very amused as he never came back to collect his car parking deposit, even though invited.

That I thought was the end of that.—Wrong.

Two very well dressed Malay middled aged gentleman arrived at our offices and politely requested to see me.

They were Malaysian government officials, with the title of Dato'.

They voiced their concerns. The Greek party had visited the Malaysian Parliament, partly as tourists but partly also as officials as there were Greek Ministers present. This was welcomed and they understood about the trade delegation but that did not explain the behaviour of one or two individuals that had caused concern. One was stating intentions of huge investment plans, and the other was being introduced as the Greek Consul. When questioned on the investment plans and being told that Bank Negara had to be involved, the individual concerned said that was easily taken care of. Did I know of this?

Secondly, the Greek Consul. The Malaysian Government had not known such a position or person existed. Was this a change in Greek policy, because if so, then certain protocol was involved and certain official procedures had to be enacted.

I thought, "Oh bloody hell, what next?"

What I said was "no" to the first question and to the second I told them that to my knowledge there was no Greek Consul, and I was sure that the person involved would not appear again at official functions making such claims and I apologised for any disrespect.

They left, thanking me profusely for my assistance. So that I thought was that. Wrong again, but the fallout from it was to be sometime in the future.

In the meantime Yusus was up in arms.

I had told Yusus that overlooking and insulting Louis' chosen team in Malaysia would no longer be tolerated, we would be here after they'd gone, so would they kindly act as visitors and behave. Whether he even listened or understood I have no idea but he did seem to moderate his behaviour.

However he had gone underground and was saying and doing things quietly that he would have previously loudly boasted about.

He carried about with him a somewhat grubby piece of folded paper which he often flashed around, showing a small proportion only, which he claimed gave him access to $100 million dollars.

When I told him that many of us had received many such con letters from Nigeria he pooh poohed the idea and said his was genuine and it showed that they were serious important people. I let the issue slide and dismissed this as being just another silly antic—which was a big mistake and was to involve me in a serious scandal later.

He was also telling all and sundry that we were not important, he was, and people like him could easily cough up a million dollars as they carried little sums like this in their back pocket for interesting projects.

I didn't know it but there were some who believed him and started to do business—or so they thought.

This also was going to catch up with me later.

We, in the meantime, took back the reins and took care of our business.

The venue was ready with all the facilities in place so actual rehearsals could start. The orchestra did their sound checks, the master of ceremonies and DJ's did the same and we practised our parts. Louis rehearsed his opening welcome speech which he ambitiously decided to perform in Bahasa Malaysian—the Malay language.

After a few necessary adjustments the Malaysian and Singaporean equipment and technicians fortunately proved well up to the standard demanded.

April had decided that we should have a publicity preview at a well known restaurant in the centre of KL. This was a largely open air venue so we would be taking a risk with the weather. April set it all up with her usual thoroughness and invitations to press, media, advertising, star personalities and PR companies were sent and accepted. Between her and Ogilvy and Mather it seemed that the whole of Malaysia became aware of the event.

I was still worried about the weather. We were in the middle of a period of violent tropical storms so I looked for a plan B.

Short of changing the venue, which was not an option, I jokingly said I was turning to prayer. If that was the case, I was told, then I should consult a Bomoh. (A sort of shaman cum witch doctor).

A few days later we were attending an art gallery's promotion of Malaysian Painters and after throwing in a few pieces of our inexpert opinions we sat down with a group of people to eat. During the course of conversation my weather situation arose. Well who should be seated with us but a well known Bomoh. Was this going to be a fortunate coincidence?

The Bomoh anticipated no problem and for a reasonable fee was prepared to ensure fine weather during our PR exercise.

We decided that first we needed to talk more so we asked him about his life and operations.

He explained that ordinary people needed faith and hope and when all else had failed then he provided just that.

Yes, he did supply love potions, bad luck and good luck potions. They were actually the same thing but worked differently with different people and circumstances and he also used natural herbal medicines. When challenged he did admit to preferring doctors and hospitals for his own medical problems but this didn't put us off him too much.

He looked us over and told us that all humans were in fact just a part of a universal cycle and we all evolved from earth, through rock, water and animals, finally arriving as humans.

However humans had to evolve through a part animal cycle too until arriving as a total human. When he looked at people on a bus for instance he saw few total humans but lots of part tigers, snakes, elephants and insects.

Linda asked him what alcohol and drugs he was on as she would like some, whereupon he told her that she had a long way to go to be a full human and that she should stop torturing herself. He smiled at me and told me that I had already arrived. Linda reckoned that was only because I had agreed to employ him.

I had, and asked him if he needed to see the venue. No need apparently as he knew it, visited it often, so just needed the dates and time. These I gave him and without moving he said it was done. We had found a middle class Bomoh.

When we told Louis he rather good naturedly went along with it but I'm sure he had as many doubts as us.

Every day prior to the event it didn't just rain but poured.

To put it mildly we all looked nervous and apprehensive.

On the big day sure enough it poured all morning, then amazingly stopped and dried out.

The event was a great success with all the guests getting connected, very merry, and well plied with food and drinks, always the main reasons for attending.

Just as we were finishing clearing up, yes, the rain came down again.

We received a tremendous amount of positive publicity and viewed the Bomoh fee as money well spent.

It was a pity that the fashion planning and rehearsals weren't going so well.

The two designers thought it was 24 hour party time and some of the staff took the opportunity to join in and enjoy. The few serious dedicated personnel were a little overwhelmed. Chris Wu was determined to look enticing in his own female creations rather than sorting them out and planning the much needed orderly routines. He was camping it up far too often. Nigel seemed mesmerised by this sparkling display and couldn't get his act together at all.

April took all the fashion team out to dinner one evening in an endeavour to get them together, bonded and focussed but it failed as they thought it was yet another opportunity to play the fool. Bonding took on a totally different meaning!

I looked in towards the end and if I hadn't had deadlines to meet I could have been amused. Basically I was watching supposedly grown men acting like giggling schoolgirls but unfortunately in my position I couldn't find it funny even if I wanted to. I sympathised with April having to handle it all evening.

This was getting us nowhere so April and Erik roped in the more responsible members and took on the responsibility of the catwalk flow and order.

They assisted in the choice of clothes, shoes, hair, make up and accessories for the individual models.

Malaysian and Greek models co-operated wholeheartedly as did hairdressers, stylists, and make up artists. This approach succeeded in gaining the intermittent attention of the designers and assistants and we began to see progress.

In the meantime we needed to set up the trade exhibition so we turned our attention to that area. The product stands were to be set up in two or three smaller halls beneath the Great Ballroom where the main event was to be held. Yusus told us that we were not needed as they had brought the best and most famous display practitioner in the whole of Greece, in fact he had no equal anywhere. Not one for slight exaggeration was Yusus. Always full of bullshit.

Well we thought, great, we would watch and learn.

We watched with increasing trepidation as we realised that he was not only too slow but he wasn't that good either. He looked more than somewhat bemused.

We decided to rescue him. We told him it was his lucky day. He could take the evening off, have an early night and rest easy. So we bundled him off with little resistance.

He obviously said something to Yusus as that man arrived very quickly, huffing and puffing with indignation. We bundled him off also without any ceremony. We'd taken enough of his crap. We were not particularly the best of anything but we were good enough and worked all night.

When Louis and the Ministers arrived to inspect in the morning we got the seal of approval. Even Yusus gave a nod. It did look good. Some hours later, all the dignitaries were on parade. The opening ceremony and speeches went off superbly, tapes were cut, hands were shaken and the exhibition was up and running.

Several factions and cliques had opened up amongst the visitors but fortunately open warfare did not erupt, only a bit of bitchy sniping. The worst result of this, thank goodness, was just a tendency for one clique to be extra early, trying to embarrass another clique, who tended to be late. It did cause some bad feeling with locals who were inconvenienced but damage limitation was not too difficult.

As the big date approached I was checking and double checking on food, beverages, tables, chairs, ornamentation, yellow carpets (yellow being the Royal colour) and working with Palace officials to ensure that every one involved was acquainted with, and understood the protocol. We all went over the routine time after time so that the previously unknown became normal.

After the reception and entry of the Royals, dinner would be served with music from the Greek orchestra.

The fashion show was scheduled for after dinner.

April was constantly drumming home the fact that the fashion show had to run with fluidity, and four models had to be on the catwalk with two more waiting in the wings at all times. Music had been synchronised for this, rehearsals showed that it was feasible and the designers appeared to understand and go along with it.

The contracted event organising team appeared to be happier and more relaxed especially when it seemed that the need to keep to a set schedule and timetable had sunk in to all concerned. The orchestra, singers and dancers would follow the show and then the King and Queen would tactfully withdraw to allow every one to join in the party and dance.

The principal players from Greece and our team were to greet the royal party on arrival, be introduced, and then follow the Royals to a beautifully decorated ante room for light refreshments and conversation. The King and Queen and other members of the Royal Family could then become acquainted with their hosts.

After a suitable period of time a courtier should arrive, knock on the door, request entrance and humbly inform their Majesties that all was ready. Erik was chosen for the role of courtier.

He had spent the better part of two days practising and going over the few words of address which caused no end of leg pulling.

Yusus was also coming in for a bit of leg pulling. He was in love, he had found a girlfriend. He had been introduced to her at a meeting, a lovely Malay girl, and was swept off his feet. He had sent flowers with a note, apparently a little suggestive and wanted a clandestine meeting.

Yusus confirmed this rather self consciously and said he had also met one of her relatives, a Mr. Syed Mahomet, or something like that, and he was very important. Being busy and distracted I did not pay as much attention to this as I should have done. I would pay dearly for this lapse of attention a little later.

Another character had appeared after the Parliamentary visit called Charles. Charles was a short, dapper, beautifully turned out Malaysian Indian who said he was a government aide. Which government he aided I never did take the trouble to find out as he was actually very useful. He gave me an insiders crash course on Malay culture and habits, official behaviour, the need for the right connections and how to behave generally. "Be gracious, not ugly," was his favourite catchphrase.

He reminded me of the lawyers in the USA who listened out for accidents and arrived on the scene offering their services to those involved. I felt that Charles hung around Parliament in much the same way.

He did make a number of introductions at the highest levels but mainly with industries with which we were not involved.

We could not open up and run car dealerships in other countries, we did not weave cloth or process palm oil, neither did we make televisions or micro chips.

We designed, built, renovated and run retail projects internationally in every way you could think of—we were into development—but Charles was not, so eventually we parted company.

He disappeared as quickly as he came.

During our time together he gave me some degree of insight into Malay politics. He told me that "the old man" (Prime Minister) would retire in a few years, but he still hadn't found a successor he was happy with. He had built up Anwar, his current deputy and given him openings to shine but instead Anwar had played to an international gallery.

This made the P.M. worried as he wanted some one to put the country before ego. The international currency crisis would help the PM to assess Anwar as Anwar was also Finance Minister.

The PM also had some deep holes he wanted to plug first and would not want dug up later. He kept personal and confidential files as well on all personnel he felt necessary, said Charles.

"Hmm, very interesting," I thought, never realising that I would soon be involved myself with many of the well known names being bandied about in the media.

This was late 1997.

At last the big day. We were ready but still nervous about the schedule as we were requested to keep right to time by Palace officials who said that the King and Queen did not want to stay late due to a tight calendar of events.

Then treachery—I was the victim of some last minute sneaky political manoeuvres. A few nasties told Louis that I should not sit on the top table, they had people much more important to sit with the King. Louis told them that if it wasn't for me there would be no Royal Family present, no table to sit at, our team had made it all possible and what was more, on arrival, in the absence of Louis' wife, April would introduce us to the Royal ladies and he would present us to the Royal gents.

They seemed taken aback. Why I don't know. Perhaps living in their lofty, self centred universe they thought it had all happened with the wave of a magic wand.

It grew dark outside the Palace of the Golden Horses, it was time.

You could feel the tension and excitement throughout the whole building. Aides and special branch had searched every nook and cranny and examined us and anything that looked remotely suspicious. Police lined the entrance and driveway dressed in best uniforms along with ceremoniously dressed guards.

Suddenly senior officers became ultra alert. The Royal party was on the way—they had left the Istana (Palace) and would soon arrive.

Suddenly it came to us. We had been so busy organising and so continually, deeply involved that we hadn't had time to relax and look at what we had achieved.

Only at that moment did we become aware of the great honour afforded us. We would be hosting the Royal Family of Malaysia, who had kindly agreed to grace our event.

And here they were.

Looking out, at first we could only see pitch darkness, no lights.

Then it happened.

First we heard the great roar of dozens of escort outriders, with flashing hazard lights slowly coming into view. Then came the motorcycle body guards, black leather clad, followed by an open military vehicle occupied by straight backed military guards holding swords upright at their sides and dressed in colourful ceremonial uniforms.

Behind them came the Royal limousines, Rolls Royce of course, plus another military vehicle, bodyguards and escorts, and then support cars and ambulances. To the roar of the engines was added the shouted commands of the officers of the honour guard, the police and those lining the route. They all snapped to attention, crashing boots, slapping weapons, presented arms and stood motionless while the National Anthem (Negara Ku) was played. As the King alighted officers saluted and formed a channel through which the King and Queen could proceed to the entrance.

Wow, we had the whole works.

It was a terrific spectacle and we all had goose bumps and chills down our spine. Marvellous, but now we had to collect ourselves for the introduction.

Louis and April salaamed, were introduced and then introduced all of the entertaining parties to the Royal Family in turn. Then the principals followed into the ante room while the remainder took their places in the ballroom.

The King and Queen always had to sit higher than any one else, with suitable positions for other Royals according to status. Then normal mortals sat within easy conversation distance, without turning their backs at any time on the King.

The current Agong (King—the Sultans of Malaysia rotated the position every five years) normally ruled the state of Negri Sembilan. In his absence, while occupying the position of Agong, a Regent ruled the State.

All of the family were English educated to a very high level and many were or had been leading sportsmen. They were relaxed, friendly and interested and made conversation easy.

Soon came the knock on the door. The door was ceremoniously opened and there stood Erik, tall and elegant in a tuxedo requesting entrance. He was welcomed in. He salaamed, bowed low and started to enter. Erik was very tall, but the door wasn't, so he had to bow lower, but still not enough so he had to bow lower still. So very low he nearly fell in.

This was supposed to be a solemn moment but every one was grinning, including Erik, who could hardly get his carefully rehearsed words out. He managed the invitation but then had to back out. This was harder than coming in. To everybody's amusement he was safely assisted backwards by a pair of helpful bodyguards. We went first so that we were in place when their Majesties arrived at their seats to great applause and fanfare.

All was suddenly a hive of activity. Food was arriving, in strict order of status of course, and we were gently serenaded by the orchestra of Georges Yanin. Louis was seated besides the King while April and I were seated at opposite ends of the slightly U shaped top table. I sat next to a Tunku (Princess), and considering all the noise and activity made easy and light conversation. Louis was then called upon to deliver his speech of welcome with his introduction in Malay. He had been concerned about pronunciation and accent but he needn't have worried—he did very well but even if he hadn't he gained respect for doing it. He was loudly applauded.

When the food was cleared the lovely Malay MC moved the proceedings on and introduced the fashion show and it's theme, "Greece to Malaysia, Malaysia to Greece—A tribute."

Cue lights, music and models. To thunderous rock music the models of Chrisopher Wu moved on stage and proceeded down the catwalk. Every one gasped. Colour, style and flamboyance hardly described the scene—it was a great display but soon I could see April becoming agitated. She looked at me and signalled with her watch—it was too slow. Soon she was sending messages down backstage, which resulted in a speed up, but the first show over ran by more than 30 minutes. At that time no one cared, except April, because Christopher came on stage with his models to thunderous applause. He deserved it, he was a great success, but I noticed that April had requested a runner to be permanently by her side. She had never been psychic but she certainly had a bad feeling about this now. I decided that I had better have a runner also.

Now came the star event. Gracious, splendid, Greek models moved confidently, aggressively and arrogantly down the catwalk, turning to approach the King and making an elegant bow when level. Nigel had made a successful mixture of Greek and Malay, actually fine, but far less spectacular than Christopher and it showed.

So Nigel decided to make up with quantity, what was lacking in quality. He was also putting only two models at a time on the extra long catwalk he had himself requested. He continually refused all requests to speed up and put more models on the catwalk. The requests steadily became orders, which were also ignored.

The audience began to get bored and restless, which was temporarily interrupted somewhat by a succession of models in low cut see through dresses bowing low to the King. Nigel had decided to spice it all up a bit in order to try and recover a degree of prestige. Some were amused and enchanted except for the royal aides and many who were horrified. This was a Moslem country!

His Majesty had to take a short break causing one of the aides to say to Erik who was running between April and Nigel, "where did you find this lot, why are you associated with them?" Fortunately the aide rushed off before Erik could reply otherwise god only knows what else he may have said!!

April was going ape shit and I was by now joining in, which meant that we were neglecting our royal guests,—unforgivable. Complaints were arriving all the time and we were told very seriously that if we didn't move everything on immediately then the royal party would move out. This would create a scandal.

April sent down the message, "pull the plug officially now or I will come down myself and do it." Again she was ignored.

Eventually she had to do it herself and the plug was pulled amid great resentment without a grand finale. The MC did a professional cover up, the orchestra took over, singers and dancers performed wonderfully and the dust started to settle.

Georges and his Orchestra hammed it up in front of the King and Queen for far too long until April sent down another message, "Great, but cut it short now as you're losing the audience, move to get every one dancing." To his credit he did.

The King and Queen retired, and many, including the royals moved onto the dance floor. Others were leaving, saying their goodbyes. I received a message that the aides and royal palace organisers were worried that they would be in trouble and blamed for what they regarded as a fiasco.

Before I could properly digest that my dancing was interrupted by another message. Nigel was depressed, disturbed and upset and friends were worried he would kill himself.

April heard and said, "Kill himself, if I could get my hands round his throat I'd do it for him."

Frankly my sentiments exactly.

However he was asking for me. Evidently he was of the opinion that I might be sympathetic and would try to be of help. I wasn't but I would.

He was in his room, behind a locked door with cronies outside looking as though they were auditioning for a Bollywood movie.

They told me in over dramatic voices that Nigel was distraught at what had happened and that they thought he had been badly treated. Actually he had but only a few of us had known of the real drama taking place and the trouble the two designers had caused and brought on us and themselves.

Nigel knew of course, and when he heard my voice he weakly asked me to come in. I don't think he expected any sympathy and he didn't get it.

However what I hadn't fully realised was that a Greek TV team was filming the whole event of which Nigel was a central figure and they hadn't been able to film a glorious finale because there hadn't been one.

Now this I could understand and try to do something about. I had little sympathy for him but a lot for the situation. We called up the crew, explained the situation, sent messages to every one left in the ballroom asking them to stay there, and recalled the Greek models and organisers and briefed them.

To their credit, and my relief, everybody agreed to do it and do it as well as possible.

The TV crew were pros and could make a smaller crowd act up and seem large and noisy.

I explained to Nigel that he had to put on a brave triumphant face, replacing the pained deflated look he was showing to the world.

"Hang in, not hang dog," I told him.

No matter how he really felt he had to see this out to a successful end as this was purely for his benefit. Most of us were tired, worried and just wanted to get home.

OK, he was a bit of a wilting violet but he agreed, started to perk up a little and we left his room amid a few cheers and plaudits from the cronies.

Everyone in the place who were involved had been appraised of the situation and their role in it and were enthusiastic about helping out. They all rallied round and showed great character.

Nigel and I stood in the wings as the finale took shape. He turned and said to me, "Denis, whatever you do don't leave me. I don't know if I can or want to do this because it's not the real thing is it?"

I agreed in a way and sympathised a little but the muck up was not of my doing and I just wanted to get on with the frigging show.

"Nigel," I replied, "I am glued to your bloody shoulder from now to the end and believe me I will shove you up those bloody steps for the finish whether you want it or not. All these people have turned this on for you out of sympathy, respect and friendship, so don't cock up now. All these boys and girls are professionals and you are too. Make 'em proud."

He did and got his finale.

Early morning, a day later, I was at the Palace talking to the Lord Chancellor and making my peace.

I promised to make a written apology, taking the responsibility for what I called over enthusiastic creative people allowing their egos to get the better of them without concern for others. I exonerated the palace staff which went down well and was appreciated. I managed to regain some degree of self respect. As the apology was generously given, the Lord Chancellor responded and praised the efforts and professionalism of all concerned in spite of the problems.

I shot off as soon as possible to the Palace of the Golden Horses wishing to catch all the Greek performers before they left. I arrived just as they were boarding the buses and was able to pass on the Chancellor's comments. I thanked them profusely for their efforts and was loudly cheered.

There were still a few days of exhibition left and of course constant analysis of what happened during the fashion show.

People took sides as always and made their opinions known, but no amount of jaw, jaw could change anything so it was all academic anyway.

Chris Wu had exceeded his brief, managing to press all Nigel's buttons, but he was young, saw his chance and took it. Nigel was foolish in his response, he had acted like a big girls blouse, but had been a little betrayed and naturally felt it. He was actually a nice guy.

Neutral opinion was in favour of Chris Wu, but with the local press in both countries mainly favouring their own countrymen. The Malaysian press though actually panted madly over the Greek models.

Finally all our visitors had gone. We wished them well, but far as we knew there were no positive results from the trade exhibition, which was a pity as the product and companies were excellent.

Now we could get on with the real work or that was that I thought. However.

Azilah, our receptionist, told me I had a visitor. He didn't really want me, he had asked for Mr. Yusus, but when he heard he wasn't there he reluctantly accepted Azilah's suggestion to see me instead.

Azilah showed him into my office, very humbly. I saw why.

My visitor was a short, slightly built Imam, with a wispy goatee, dressed in all white robes with a kepiah on his head and sandals on his feet.

(a kepiah is a small white oval ornamented cap).

He was very polite, gracious and self effacing.

He told me he represented the syriah, (religious police) and also an important religious leader on a delicate matter. He apologised for disturbing me and asked when Mr. Yusus would be back. He had been made to understand that Mr. Yusus was an important man and that he knew my name as Mr. Yusus had mentioned that I worked for him.

I really wanted to shout, "that fuckin' Yusus," but my visitor was far too refined for such an ugly outburst.

Instead I politely but firmly told him he had sadly been misinformed, Mr. Yusus (I nearly choked on the Mr.) had been no more than a Greek visitor at a convention and had gone back to his own country, and had no plans to return.

"Could I be of help?" I asked tentatively.

He hesitated. Obviously he felt that this could be difficult to explain to an Orang Putih (white man) from the liberal, somewhat debauched Western World. However he explained.

A very young, sweet and naive young lady's modesty had been offended by propositions and suggestions of a very inappropriate nature. Her reputation was at risk and he wanted to know the intentions of Mr. Yusus whose unwelcome and uninvited attentions were the cause of all this trouble. Her uncle was a very important religious leader and the young lady was from a strict family who were extremely upset.

I thought, "oh bloody hell," but said instead, "What options, what actions are necessary to put it all right? Can it be put right?"

There were a number of ways. First on the list was a marriage of convenience and conversion to Islam, the second was a huge payment for restitution and the third was to submit himself for prosecution under Malaysian law. The syriah had no direct authority over a non moslem unless committing khalwat. (An unmarried couple caught alone together in intimate conditions).

Again I thought, "oh bloody hell, what's to do lah?"

I told him my main concern was for the young lady. I thought she had been an innocent participant in a ridiculous ego trip by a very ignorant, selfish foreigner and shouldn't suffer any more humiliation. We, as a company would issue such a statement in letter form to the family and the syriah, along with an abject apology and state that no blemish should be attached to the girl's character.

He considered this, looked at me kindly and shrewdly and agreed that this course of action could be agreeable.

Would I however contact Mr. Yusus and obtain his opinion? I said I would think it over and try to contact Yusus. After he left I told Erik and April, who thought it was hilarious, but I didn't. Well it was me in the firing line.

I didn't intend to contact Yusus as I couldn't rely on a sensible response so I tried the written apology approach. I accepted responsibility again for the behaviour of ignorant visitors who just blundered in without due consideration for their actions and others. I explained the difference in cultures and that no insult had been intended, only a compliment to her beauty, and that no blame should be attached to the girl.

The wonderfully forgiving Malays accepted.

All this reminded me of one of the lines of the great blues singer Buddy Guy, "Where is the next one coming from?"

I didn't have to wait for long.

A few days later four Malay men of assorted sizes and ages arrived at our office and demanded a meeting with me.

"Demanded, not requested." oh oh!!

They were polite but firm and acted with relaxed authority.

A complaint had been made by Bank Negara (Bank of Malaysia) and they represented the Bank and the Malaysian Anti-corruption Agency. "Did I wish to make a statement?"

"About what?" I asked, more than a little bewildered.

"Why $100 million dollars entrusted to me had not been paid into Bank Negara," was the reply.

"What ??!! Listen gentleman, I don't know where you get your information but I don't have, nor have ever had one million dollars, let alone 100 million.

I wish."

"We must tell you Mr. Denis that fraud and embezzlement are serious offences, we advise you to co-operate."

"I'm well aware of that, but come on help me here, you've got to give me more information, I honestly don't have any idea what you are going on about."

But in the back of my mind there was the glimmering of something. $100 million, could it just be a co-incidence?

They explained that on a visit to Parliament, in the presence of some Minister's aides and a couple of Bank Negara managers one of the Greek party had introduced himself as someone of importance. He had flourished documents advising of $100 million credit facilities. This sum, he had said, was intended for investment in Malaysia. When told it would have to be deposited in Bank Negara he had replied that it posed no problem and it would be done immediately. He had referred to me, one of his employees, with relevant company name and address.

I couldn't help it, I just blurted out, "I knew it, it's fucking Yusus again."

The officials were tough cookies but even they were startled.

I started to explain, at first it sounded a bit lame, but as I got underway it started to sound more convincing.

I ended by saying that perhaps they would like to pursue the subject with Mr. Yusus in Greece but it would go nowhere as unfortunately the man was just full of bullshit. A bit rough but I was losing patience.

I made a statement under oath, which was reluctantly accepted and they went away unhappy. No arrest and no $100 million.

I was absolutely fuming but relieved.

"Mama Mia, what next?" I thought.

It wasn't long in coming. A week later I received an invitation for dinner at the Istana hotel in KL from an ex Chief Minister of Mallaca. I accepted and took April with me.

When introduced I recognised him immediately as a guy who had a bad reputation, short temper, and vicious bodyguards.

We had dinner and he was most courteous. After dinner, over coffee, he waived over a couple of aides who spread out plans and documents in front of us.

Very interesting but what was it to do with us? We had only met the man briefly once before.

He startled us by saying, "right these are the islands you have bought from me. They need some development, so I thought it would be helpful to you if I brought along some suggestions we have. We could work together as partners."

"Wait a minute sir, what purchase, what islands, what development and what on earth are you talking about?"

April looked equally as puzzled.

"You know, the islands your agent bought for a million dollars a couple of months ago. You got a bargain by the way."

"Sorry, I'm not being deliberately difficult but I don't get this at all," I said." We have no agent, and we haven't bought anything, let alone islands we have never seen or heard of. That's just crazy. What lunatic would do that anyway?"

He looked more than a bit put out at this and April, very sensibly, flashed me a warning glance. Tread more carefully.

"Sorry sir, apologies, forgive me, but we have no idea what is going on here, can you explain?"

There was an atmosphere, tension, and a feeling that he wondered what sort of a game we were playing.

He told us that he had met some officials from Greece some weeks before. They explained they were eager for investment opportunities and had the cash.

When he told them that he owned some islands in the Straits of Mallaca, just offshore, that he wanted to sell and develop, they jumped at it. He told them the price was one million US dollars. One of the men told him he was lucky as they were serious, important people and they carried small sums like that in their back pockets. He was told it was a done deal.

When he wanted to finalise he came to me as they had said that I worked for them.

I said, "don't tell me, one of them was called Yusus, and also don't tell me that they bought sight unseen."

"Yes and yes."

"Also don't tell me that they are really just small sandy desert islands with one palm tree."

"No, no, not at all."

"Well thank god for that."

"No, they are just a series of rocks that are uncovered at low tide."

"Oh no, who is stupid stupid enough to do this?"

"But they do have potential."

"Yes, to drown the owners at high tide!"

I then followed up more respectfully with, "I'm really very sorry sir, but we don't work for or with Mr. Yusus and never have done.

This is not our deal and the people concerned are back in Greece. They were only here for a short while with a Trade Delegation. I can give you details if you want. Why not go to Greece to see them?" I felt like adding, "please do," but refrained.

To say he was miffed was putting it mildly.

"What about you," he said, "are you interested."

"No, no way I'm afraid, it is not our line of work at all."

"So, I've been wasting my time."

"Unfortunately it appears so sir, I'm sorry, can we pay for dinner? It's the least we can do."

"Not necessary," he said very abruptly, "that's already taken care of."

He motioned to his aides, swiftly cleared up, and left without another word.

April and I breathed a sigh of relief and ordered two large brandies.

We still had to calm down a few other situations. One of them involved an Australian Greek chef, Pauline, who owned a restaurant in a KL suburb of Bangsar which was then a thriving area of nightlife. A media team from a local TV station had agreed to film her cooking a Greek meal, Malaysian style, in front of an audience which would include the Greek Trade Delegation.

We had arranged transport from the Palace of Golden Horses hotel to the restaurant but only half of the delegation was ready. The rest sauntered casually down eventually making us arrive nearly two hours late.

In the meantime phones had been ringing, and pleadings and queries had given way to anger. Most angry was the chef. She was a tough, capable cookie who had made it the hard way and was not amused.

Preprepared food had been spoiled, and had to be done again, but once underway she turned out to be a real trooper, and made it all seem easy and successful.

We took the full brunt of her anger and frustration afterwards.

April settled it by arranging a recorded dual between Pauline and a Malaysian Chinese chef who was just making his name and was later to become famous on TV.

I managed to take a couple of CD's of the Greek Orchestra to the Lord Chancellor who was thrilled but another gift was not so gracefully handled.

I received a message that representatives of the Greek party wished to send a crate of wine to their Majesties, should they do so?

I replied in the affirmative and told them to send it to our company and I would do the necessary in a proper manner. Could they do this simple thing? No.

Some bright spark decided to cut me out of the equation and send it direct. They received a receipt and thought they were such clever dicks but didn't understand why I was in a mood.

I think they thought I had wanted to take the credit away from them. I hadn't wanted anything of the sort. I didn't want any more problems that's all.

The King was the protector and leader of Islam in Malaysia and the consumption of alcohol by muslims was banned by law in the country. More embarrassment.

Some people never learn do they?

It took another few months before we were finally free of the episode we called, "When the Greeks came to town." ??!!

Louis, reading my report later, just smiled and said, "well it kept you busy, didn't it?"

Yes it certainly did, didn't it?

A Very Greek Wedding

O ur big boss had sorted through a host of marital problems. He was divorced and ready to remarry.

The girl of his choice was one of the party at the Greek festival and was now number one in his life. She was typical of so many European Mediterranean women, stylish, passionate, practical and equally at home in the company of men or women. They well understood the advantages enjoyed by men in most societies but just try telling them they weren't equal!! They had somehow mastered the knack of sometimes being overbearing and out of order and yet charming and attractive at the same time. This was something that American women had never mastered and other European women were losing.

We were invited to the wedding.

We were told that our chief had converted to Greek Orthodox in order to be properly wed and also to be allowed to marry in the Greek Church.

The church chosen was famous even in a city like Athens which was packed with famous buildings.

It was situated on top of a hill with an avenue of trees leading up to it.

It was about the size of a royal family's dollhouse or the size of a kid's toy house in the garden.

Wonderful.

Of course we couldn't fit in it, so the impressive religious ceremony was mainly conducted in the open air. The priest was dressed traditionally, and conducted the songs, prayers and chants in a resonant pleasant voice. The bride had arrived in an open horse drawn carriage looking as splendid and radiant as all brides do on their special day. Well it was their day, their last day of freedom and it was supposed to be their last day of innocence—so they should enjoy it to the full.

The best man was the Greek fashion designer, who had recovered well from the debacle in Malaysia and become firm friends with both the bride and groom.

He was glowing just as much as the groom.

The happy couple, grinning from ear to ear, drove off in the carriage to cheers and congratulations amid bucketfuls of thrown rice.

The reception was held in a first class hotel, great food, superb wines and appropriate speeches. All the beautiful people beautifully turned out.

The view from the hotel balcony was spectacular. Athens is one of those cities that defies description and has to be visited.

It really was a day to be remembered.

Before the wedding however we had been to various receptions, parties and meetings.

At one of these meetings Louis introduced me to a tall, somewhat rotund, genial looking man called Hans. He had joined the company apparently shortly before but I missed exactly what it was he did.

He suggested we went somewhere quiet to talk. I agreed as Louis had told me to see if I could get on with him.

We started off with smalltalk but then took a change of direction.

"Wait a minute, this was seeming more like an interview and an interrogation rather than a friendly chat about getting on together," I said to myself, "What gives here?"

I thought this a bit off but what the hell. I went along with it.

Well Louis always played somethings close to his chest, dumped you in it and then either let you shape up or shove off. I decided to shape up.

Under cross examination I explained what we did, what we were doing and why we were doing it.

Much to my surprise Hans enjoyed it, embraced it and contributed to it all.

He saw possibilities for our company to open up, spread out and expand further.

Louis joined in later and we decided to seek contracts in areas we had not contemplated before with a range of products that suited the contract, not just the company.

A whole new horizon had opened up and we were going to go for it.

In doing so we were going to get into situations with people who belonged on a movie set except that if it was movie you wouldn't believe it.

The day after the wedding was spent sedately touring and eating in secluded places.

We decided on a bit of culture. We booked for the English translation of "Son et Lumiere" that night.

We took our seats on a hill overlooking the Acropolis set high up on the hill, recently restored and bathed in a few floodlights, looking magnificent.

Suddenly the lights were dimmed, drums rolled, trumpets sounded and the temple was bathed in varied coloured floodlights. A tremendous spectacle.

The French directors should have left it at that and quit while ahead.

Instead using lights and music they started to act out a piece of Athens ancient history at war. The music wasn't so bad although somewhat over done. It was the dialogue, delivered by a blaring, tinny, inferior public address system, which had us grinning at first, then laughing and finally groaning.

It was a French producers idea of how the ancient Greeks may have conversed and communicated—it was pompous, pedantic and ridiculous.

"Ho Tomatos, what seeth thou? Seeth thou mine enemy?"

"No Humous, but wait, I seeth Dolmus approaching in haste. Ho Dolmus hast thou grave news?"

"Aye, Meze, grave indeed."

Cue flashes of floodlights, thunderous drum rolls and strident trumpets. etc, etc, etc.

This was not culture, history or beauty—it was piss taking.

We left early.

The next day we wanted fun.

We wanted breakfast, lunch and dinner at places that offered good food and great music.

We were told it was not possible.

What! Not possible in Athens—no music, no food?

No, it was the combination that was impossible. If the music was great then the food was crap and vice versa.

So eat first, sing, dance and smash plates later.

That's what we did.

Except that there was no more smashing of plates. Why? It was a great Greek tradition.

Yep, but people had got drunk and stupid, particularly tourists, got out of hand and used the plates as frisbies. People had been injured.

Now you threw roses. Sorry, not the same.

I had been to celebrations where a guy had sliced dramatically through a pile of plates in seconds, where dancers leaped over plates thrown between their legs and others where the plates were piled up, bottles of whisky poured over them and were set alight.

We all danced around the flames.

The Greeks knew how to party. But not anymore apparently.

Why not stop the idiots instead of stopping the activity?

The whole developed world had become over protective that was why.

The only risks taken were by directors and financiers with other peoples money!!

Why ruin one person's health when you can ruin a whole economy?

After dining well we followed the music right into the heart of the old town. We were put off as everything was too commercial, all set up for tourists, with souvenir shops selling the usual crap. The stuff you wonder why you bought it when you got home.

We followed a friend who said he knew where to go where it was more authentic, but not too authentic, it was Athens after all.

He was right. The Taverna was full of Greeks, drinking, shouting, dancing and mixing everything up.

We were welcomed and joined in.

I loved the sheer joy of Greek life and enthusiastically pranced, rather than danced, the night away.

It was only when I was tired and collapsed on my chair did I notice that my colleagues were giggling and wriggling. They were looking at the band.

The band consisted of four old guys and one young fella.

The young fella was the incredible bouzouki player. The others were the drummer, bass and back up bouzoukis.

The drama, excitement and tension in Greek music is infectious and I find it hard to concentrate on anything else when a band is playing.

Suddenly I focussed. The old musician on the extreme left of the band seemed sound asleep, although still playing, and was about to fall off his chair.

Just when he seemed about to go over the edge the drummer, just behind, gave him a sharp smack on the head without breaking rhythm. He jerked awake, sat upright, looked around with a startled expression and picked up the melody. It was then I noticed that he was cross eyed and was staring at a sheet of music perched on a stool in front of him, very intently with his tongue sticking out of the side of his mouth. He looked at his friend with a puzzled expression. His friend picked up the sheets, turned them upside down, flicked over two pages and pointed out where they should all be. The sleepy guy didn't bat an eyelid, he just kept on playing the same as before. Goodness only knows what he was playing because a few minutes later we saw that he started to sag again, leaning right over, until taking another crack on the head from the drummer.

At the start of the next number the drummer started to sing in a loud rough voice. So what was wrong with that?

Well the rest of the band seemed startled, stopped playing, and frantically started to search among their sheets of music.

All except one.

Sleepy just kept on playing.

There was one big difference. There was no sound. He was not plugged in.

He noticed, awake at last. He stood up, searched around and about, found a lead, followed it, plugged it in, struck a chord and nodded his head. The rest of the band had found the right song sheet and were getting ready to play again.

The drummer had never stopped playing and singing through all this and nodded his head in a smug satisfied manner when the rest of the band joined in.

Sleepy however had become disconnected when he walked back to his seat and was shoving his way between the other musicians carrying his lead. He had plugged in, walked back and promptly got unplugged. The lead was too short. He did this a few times until he gave up with a shake of his head and carried on silently playing until he finally fell asleep and fell of his chair with a loud crash. The rest of the band ignored him—apparently this was normal.

This was real entertainment—our sides ached. Back in Malaysia a few days later we were still talking about it.

An Unusual Millenium Celebration

A New Millenium was approaching and needed to be celebrated. We had no idea that our choice of venue was going to lead to a constant round of laughs.

By the time December 31st 1999 finally arrived pretty well everyone knew that the existence of a Millennium bug was bullshine and the biggest con of the century. Planes would not fall out the sky, traffic lights would not fail and ships would not run aground. To nature, computers and those humans who had a degree of common sense it was just another day. What an intellectually drab way to end a momentous hundred years.

I have always been amused at what people believe or don't believe.

Humans are strange animals.

So what the hell? Let's celebrate anyway.

The day before New Years Eve we loaded bags into the car and set off for Lumut, a port north of Kuala Lumpur. Here we would take a 45 minute ferry ride to the island of Pangkor and stay at the Pan-Pacific Island Resort. (since renamed Pangkor Beach Resort).

We took the North South Expressway, an excellent standard motorway and made good time in spite of heavy traffic. The towns we reached and passed so swiftly such as Sungai Buloh and Tanjong Malim had seemed so distant before the coming of the expressway. We passed the exit to the Genting Highlands and crossed the Slim River before turning onto the old highway going through the small town of

Bidor. The town hadn't changed much, with its dusty main street and ancient shophouses on either side with cafe tables spilling over into the road selling pre cooked Malay and Chinese food. Repair shops operated mainly in the open with spare parts giving the impression of a junk sale rather than repair and renewal. The authorities had recently installed traffic lights where the old north south coast road intersected the main street and the exit road from the expressway. Just outside of town we turned off onto the Lumut road and crossed the river on a brand new two lane bridge. This had recently replaced the ancient single lane British Army Bailey Bridge that had been well past its safety date for years and had been shored up with sandbags. The old dusty, narrow lanes full of holes and bumps, treacherous in the dark, were being replaced by well paved roads that bypassed the towns of Teluk Intan and Setiawan where there had previously been long traffic jams and delays.

We were concerned at first at some of some of the stubble burning in the paddy fields which were giving off large clouds of smoke blowing across the road. Fortunately we eventually left this behind motoring between rows of overhanging palm trees and the leafy branches of numerous Palm Oil and Rubber Plantations.

This is a fairly flat part of the country but you are never very far from a view of the mountain ranges which run like fertile green spines north to south down the middle of the peninsular.

We reached Lumut at last after three hours solid driving. We had been lucky with the weather, at times a bit drizzly and overcast, but mainly sunny and bright. We drove up to the Jetty Esplanade, collected the ferry tickets, made sure we had the right vessel, unloaded the luggage and parked the car in the long term car park. There was no public car ferry. The top heavy old passenger ferry lay just offshore chugging its way laboriously to the jetty. It was reminiscent of an old diesel tug that had been converted to two decks with a canopy covering part of the upper level. None of it was very clean. It showed clear evidence of much saltwater usage and none of it gleamed in the strong afternoon sun. A few years later this old ferry would be replaced by large, modern, sleek, speedy cruisers, much safer but completely lacking in character.

Two workers from Indonesia swiftly secured the ferry and the gangplank was lowered.

All the luggage was thrown over by hand, shore to ship, to be stowed on the deck in front of the wheelhouse, covered with plastic sheets and secured. Then I was amused to see small motorcycles being handed over in the same way, together with their riders, to make the crossing up front. Everyone seemed to view this as normal and not in anyway contrary to safety rules and regulations.

The Malay captain came out of the wheelhouse looking unhappy. He was barefoot, wore a t-shirt and khaki shorts, the only hint of rank being his battered naval cap set on one side of his head. He conversed, with dramatic gestures and much emphasis with two Indian attendants dressed in oil stained blue overalls and threadbare trainers who merely looked down at the deck and shrugged their shoulders. An announcement was made over the tinny tannoy. The ferry was overloaded—fifteen people would have to get off otherwise the ferry would not move.

All the passengers were suddenly pre-occupied with so many important things that had just occurred to them and nobody moved. Stalemate, virtual checkmate unless some one gave way. Nobody did.

So the captain surrendered, muttering that if people wanted to drown then it was no business of his—he and the crew had life vests and rafts and there wasn't enough for any others.

No one appeared anxious about drowning, only about not going, so we cast off and got underway.

It took a while to clear the river estuary, the port resting on the southern side of the river.

Outside of Lumut we passed the large Royal Malaysian Navy and Coastguard base, capable of refitting large vessels, which occupied much of the southern banks of the estuary.

Once clear of the base and the lighthouse situated on the north shore, the densely forested hills on the Island of Pangkor came into view, the channel between island and mainland being only a few miles.

The ferry ploughed its way over mild seas, rolling and bucking a little, manoeuvring between fishing boats of all shapes, sizes and colours but all seeming to possess identical, powerful, deep sea boat engines. The fishermen frequently acknowledged the waves and shouts of hi from the ferry passengers but of course we didn't know whether they shouted back greetings or insults.

Probably a mixture of both depending on their luck that day.

There were also several on-sea fishing villages. They took no notice of us at all. The fisherman lived simple lives and frequently lived on their fishing boats while the sea village people usually stayed put in their homes whatever the weather. Their huts were covered by skimpy thatched roofs. The floors and walls were supported by bamboo poles with little extra protection. They cooked, washed, slept and lived their basic lives on the sea. They farmed fish in enclosures surrounding the village in much the same way a market garden operated on land.

We rounded a woody headland and saw straight ahead the weed smothered concrete piles of an enclosed jetty. This jutted into the sea on the far side of a sandy bay overlooked by hills covered in dense jungle.

At the end of the jetty we could see the ancient, open sided bus that would take us over to the other side of the narrow isthmus on which the hotel stood. The bus belonged to the Pan Pacific and as all the passengers were bound for there, except for the motor cyclists, then there was no need for any complicated sorting out. The motor cyclists and bikes were a little extra cash bonus for captain and crew.

The baggage went ashore the reverse way it went on board and was loaded into a trailer. This was attached to the rear of a golf cart that set off for the resort with some bags bouncing precariously beside and behind the driver. Not all the luggage would fit into the trailer.

Unfortunately not all the passengers would fit into the bus.

The driver loaded as many as possible for the first run—he would come back as soon as possible for those left behind. We were among them. We were actually the lucky ones.

Those who had joined in the mad scramble to be first on board found that the driver squashed people up two to a seat, squeezed two in a row standing and had some frantically clinging on to the sides.

Off went the bus rocking and rolling accompanied by a mixture of yells of complaint and shouts of delight by the passengers.

We relaxed, and enjoyed a few cold beers served up by a chubby Malay woman in sloppy T shirt, baggy track suit bottoms, scruffy trainers and full tudong. (Malay scarf style head covering). She had an ice box full of Carlsberg. I was a bit surprised that a Moslem Malay was serving alcohol but who was I to judge someone making a few bucks from thirsty tourists arriving on the island?

About twenty minutes later the bus came back full of departing guests, followed by the luggage trolley. This was timed to catch the same ferry back to the mainland.

We kept well out of the way of busy, bustling, over fussy people making sure their luggage was safe going aboard the ferry. We waited and climbed on when the bus was free.

We arrived at reception about thirty minutes after the other guests. We received a VIP welcome, apologies for delay, were swiftly checked in and found our luggage already delivered to our room. That was style.

We enjoyed the welcome cocktail in the open plan reception area, which looked out over a deep blue sea, with a beautiful golden beach, surrounded by rocky cliffs covered in dark green jungle. This view once caused my son in law Gregg to exclaim that it was the closest to paradise you could get. Refreshed we went to our room which was the House on the Rocks. These were rooms, separate from the hotel, built on stilts partially on the rocks and partly over the sea. It was relaxing to sit on the verandah as the waves rushed below and crashed onto the rocks behind.

We had dinner, slept well, breakfasted next day, swam and sunbathed and then got ready for the Millennium Party.

We had booked a table at what passed for the hotel's posh restaurant, in the outdoor section but under cover.

We and others experienced in the tropics were taking no chance on the weather.

However many were holidaymakers and quite a few were honeymooners. They were in no mood for practicalities, they were into excitement and adventure. So they booked beach parties, barbecues and tables in the sea. They looked a bit scornfully on us pessimists. This was a new Millennium so just go for it.

The hotel organisation for the actual arrival of the New Year was a little open ended. They had planned the countdown to be led by the band on the reception floor, phasing into Auld Lang Syne and other songs.

The DJ however was of the opinion that he should be MC of the whole affair and he should lead everyone into the celebrations.

There was also an outsider. This was Hermann the German, who together with his wife Nelda, were frequent guests at the hotel.

He had acquired a device that was programmed to count down to the Millenium and according to Hermann, gave split second accuracy, as it was German made. Therefore he was the only one who knew for certain the exact moment of the arrival of the New Year on Malaysian time. Hermann had also booked a table under cover but close to the edge of the canopy. He wanted to keep an eye on everyone.

By eight o'clock everything was in full swing.

Ladies were dressed in flowing gowns, wispy and short or flowing and long. Hairstyles were perfect, jewellery gleaming and finger nails all the colours of the rainbow. The men were more casually dressed, shirts open showing nearly as much cleavage as the women.

Those on the beach and in the water were showing how macho they were, carrying the women to tables in the water, bringing cases of beer to cool in the waves and generally flexing everything they had.

They all cast superior glances in our direction indicating that at least they were having fun in the spirit of the Millennium Party.

The fact that a sharp breeze was springing up and there was a dramatic storm out to sea only added to their sense of bravado and excitement.

The staff started to make early warning gestures and suggested to the beach and water folk that they should come up and establish themselves under cover around the pool.

They were brushed aside. The sea air, party spirit, cleavages, bare legs and alcohol had boosted egos and inspired an air of recklessness.

The wind picked up, staff moved in but the revellers waved them away, almost contemptuously, and didn't budge an inch.

Well at least not until the first big waves rolled in. At the same time the heavens suddenly opened up, lightning flashed and thunder crashed all around. Then they didn't just move, they panicked. Tables and chairs were knocked over and swept up the beach, followed by not so macho guests, wet and disheveled, making for the pool. Too late.

The hotel staff were great, clearing and saving everything and everyone, getting them to safety in a short time.

Hermann and those on the edge of the restaurant had to move sharply further in as a mixture of rain and spray was blowing in almost horizontally from the sea.

This was a disaster. Surely nothing else could go wrong?

But it did.

All the power failed.

The hotel managed to get some emergency lighting going and depressed spirits started to recover. The food and beverage manager got a great round of applause when he awarded free glasses of champagne to everyone.

Soon the restaurant guests were singing, "When the lights go on again, all over the world", and the drowned beach party people around the pool linked arms and swayed giving a rousing edition of "Singing in the rain."

Shortly after the power was restored, the kitchens re-opened, the storm passed, the beach party were found tables, the band started up and every one settled down for the approach of the New Year.

We charged our glasses in anticipation.

The band announced "The Final Countdown", meaning the song and broke into the intro', 10, 9, 8, 7, 6 etc. As the band completed the count and swung into the verse so the audience, who had joined in and mistaken the introduction for the real thing started shouting "Happy New Year" and singing Auld Lang Syne, dancing, hugging and kissing.

They soon realised what had happened and were getting sorted out when the DJ chose that exact moment of confusion to burst onto the stage and launch into his countdown.

The guests, startled at first, loved it, topped up glasses, gleefully joined in and celebrated for the second time.

Then enter Hermann, who for sure had the real Millennium time, shouting, "Nein, nein." (no, no).

Wow, the guests all joined in yet again, "Nein, eight, seven, six, Happy New Year, Auld Lang Syne," fill up the glasses and sing away once more. What a fantastic Millenium.

Everyone was rocking, dancing, cheering and singing to such an extent that the staff joined in and got carried away. They were keeping the booze flowing in more ways than one. They were overflowing glasses, tipping it over themselves and their friends formula one style and bursting beer cans. Some got so excited they jumped in the pool and dragged others in after them.

The supervisors lost control and called in the General Manager. He was not amused at being taken away from his own family celebrations.

He got his bedraggled, now downcast staff, all lined up and gave the whole lot verbal warnings.

One unfortunate wag couldn't resist saying, "don't know what's wrong, it's the cleanest we've been all week!!"

He got a written warning as well. Great party though.

The next day everyone was somewhat hungover but had to pull themselves together for a prize event organised by the hotel.

The management sponsored a one kilometre beach run every week. The winner got a free family weekend stay at the hotel.

There we all were, gathered at one end of the beach, ready for the off. All those hard bodied aerobic women were prancing up and down in their designer sports wear, twisting and turning into bone crushing positions to warm up.

Male runners wore their souvenir runners T shirts, lycra shorts and specially made running shoes. Myself, the old guy, and all the young kids just wore baggy shorts and would run in bare feet.

We all lined up with me behind a crowd of the youngest ones.

I told them, "I'm a marathon runner kids so just stay out of my way and we'll be okay."

I needn't have worried.

As soon as the gun went off so did the kids—like rockets.

They left everyone behind in a cloud of sand and sea spray.

The first ten finishers were all under fifteen years old.

So much for warm ups and fancy clothes—there is no substitute for youth.

Sometime later the hotel abandoned the event due to complaints from embarrassed adults smelling a bit of corruption. It appeared that some older unattached smart arses had paid fast young kids to go and run for them. At least that was the rumour.

Whatever the truth, it all came to a halt.

After the race we decided we should see more of the island and hired a motor bike or what passed as a motor bike in those regions. The engines were more like hair dryers.

I had passed my motorbike test years before in the UK and had owned some great old bikes such as the 650 cc BSA Gold Star and the Black Panther, 1,000 cc HRD Vincent in my youth.

These were nothing like those bikes, they were more like my 50cc NSU Quickly of later family years.

However these little machines raised problems of their own. They were severely underpowered, frequently overloaded, and we were about to test them to the limit. Two heavyweight westerners were not ideal for tackling the hills on the island.

My feet were too large to fit properly on the dual gear change pedal. It was not the normal up down single pedal but a rocker front and back type. My foot was too big to get leverage so I had to lift my foot up and down and backwards and forwards. Consequently I was slow.

We all set off steady and comfortable.

Steady and comfortable was not good enough to get up the first hill. Half way up we stalled and fell off. We remounted, hit the throttle, shot sideways, stalled again and fell off.

We pushed the bike up the hill, over the top, got on, coasted a little way, put it in gear and we were off again.

We made sure we got a very good run at any other hills and although on some it was a close run thing we no longer fell off.

We ran through small fishing villages, visited an old Dutch fort and some other ruins of which little was left.

We stopped for lunch and fortified ourselves. We reset off on our tour well fortified, perhaps a little too well, but we told ourselves we needed it to face the unknown reverse side of the island.

We were full of confidence and when we approached a narrow wooden bridge we were not at all put off. It seemed a simple construction of wooden planks but once I was on it I realised that no one plank went all the way across. I had to wriggle and jump the bike across from plank to plank with two feet dragging on the ground.

When I successfully reached the other side I was so cocky and fortified that I turned around and went back across again.

I made a splendid skid u-turn, roared back onto the bridge only to come face to face with a small truck nearly halfway over.

We both stopped and glared at each other giving the famous Asian "look."

I stared at him and he glared at me, neither being intimidated. I thought I could outlast him as he needed to work. This was a wrong assumption as this was Malaysia and no one worries about things like that. "Sorry late lah, traffic bad lah, OK?"

I backed off and when he was safely out of sight I gave him the tosser sign.

We made it back to the hotel without any further hold ups.

In the hotel car park April amazed us by saying that she wanted to have a go and ride around.

She re-assured us by telling us very forcefully that she used to ride her brother's trial bike over rough ground from a tender age. These little futt futts posed no problem to a veteran rider like her.

OK, go girl, and she did.

She roared off very impressively.

So impressively that two couples decided to stand and watch from what they obviously believed to be safe places.

April streaked ahead, too fast, suddenly veered left and then shot straight towards one of the couples. They fled for their lives shouting reprimands almost incoherently in English and any other language they could think of.

The other couple, clearly in a panic, were saved by April mounting the curb, ripping up a small grass lawn and finally crashing into an ornamental rock just before a brick building.

April, rock and bike emerged incredibly unscathed with April looking a little confused and muttering "its not as easy as it bloody well looks!"

During my early morning training runs along the beach I frequently disturbed lizards and monkeys who seemed to resent my intrusion without too much fuss but one morning I was in for a treat. A family of sea otters was having a parley on the beach just ahead of me. They calmly observed my approach which they clearly thought was too pedestrian so they sprang into action.

They jumped over each other, under one another, turned head over heels and performed cartwheels on the sand and then charged for the sea where they did the same thing under and above the water. Those wonderful athletic and agile creatures left me spellbound and totally entertained. They were cheeky, bright, intelligent acrobats—truly one of mother natures marvels. The little show offs succeeded in making me feel inferior.

The monkeys were sometimes entertaining, sometimes not. It was difficult to tell which mood they were in at any one time. They were certainly scavengers who didn't like to be frustrated.

One particular time they were on the hunt in packs and were harassing guests for food.

Most guests just threw down whatever snacks they had and moved swiftly on leaving the monkeys to it. I was carrying a plastic bag containing swimming gear and sandals.

One large old greybeard had decided it was food and kept on attacking the bag and he was soon joined by several adventurous youngsters. I just kept on walking so he started hissing, baring his teeth and snarling. That was it.

I turned on him, flailing the bag, shouting and stamping and rushed at him, staring fiercely into his eyes.

"You want it, well here it is."

Animals do not want to get hurt or damaged. If threatened and there is an escape route then they will usually take it. To be damaged is to be vulnerable. I wasn't challenging him for leadership, territory or his females, only food which he could get elsewhere more easily.

Just don't back them into a corner.

The youngsters beat a hasty retreat, leaping around and hooting.

Not old greybeard. He decided to stand his ground. For a while. Then under constant attack from me he backed off but when I turned away he came back.

"Okay, you don't get it, then I'm really going to hound you." I flew at him and he yelped, jumped in the air and ran for it. On the way he started to take out his frustration and humiliation on the young ones who had seemed to be observing and enjoying.

They all sped away across the grass, screeching, fighting and jumping around.

Unknowingly I had created a spectacle and an audience who had unfortunately misread the situation. From a distance they thought it was a typical crazy European having a bit of fun with a group of cheeky monkeys.

They joined in the fun.

For the monkeys this was the last straw.

They turned nasty and turned on the humans as a pack.

The usually peaceful grass lawns were changed into a mass of fleeing people chased by enraged monkeys.

The next day the hotel management posted warning notices regarding human and animal behaviour. I wasn't sure into which category I fell.

Eating outside the hotel could best be described as an experience, usually not good.

Most of the so called towns were little more than one road villages boasting a couple of fish restaurants.

Uncle Ho's was one not to be missed.

Uncle Ho did not want customers, did not like customers and hated to serve customers. Going there was a challenge. Uncle Ho sat in a back corner watching an old black and white TV which had to be bashed heavily on one side every so often to stabilise the picture. He had a great choice of beers, just Tiger and Anchor, both from the same brewery just off the Federal Highway between KL and Port Klang. This brewery along with another one further up the same highway had been the subject of a one time feeble terrorist attack. A couple of grenades had been lobbed over the surrounding wall into the main car park which was totally empty at the time due to it being a weekend. The damage was so slight and the car park so rough that if it hadn't been for shrapnel lying around then no one would have known about it.

We figured it was a dissatisfied customer of Uncle Ho's who had had to wait too long for his beer.

It was a trial. We shouted at him and got shouted back. We went to the large fridge and helped ourselves and got a bollocking for our pains and finally got the bottles opened by banging them on the edge of the marbled tables, and got another bollocking.

If you were persistent then his wife would appear, tally up the number of beers and offer food. The offering was fish.

Grilled?? no.

Steamed?? no.

Only barbecued, Sweet and sour?? no, Ok then barbecued please. Rice??

Yes, sticky white rice, chicken fried rice, seafood fried rice, pork fried rice or egg fried rice.

OK, chicken fried rice with a fried egg on top, easy, sunny side up.

Huh, what??

I repeated.

Huh, what??

Oh for god's sake, chicken fried rice with barbecue fish five times.

OK. I do egg on side, no can cook egg on top, OK??

Yep, how about vegetables?

Many veggie, all bean sprouts.

Can you cook in butter.

Cook in garlic.

Garlic is good, garlic please.

OK, I repeat order?

No, no, it's all fine!!

Just at that moment Uncle Ho, without moving an inch, shouted out to his wife, "telephone."

She ignored him so he shouted louder and they then argued for a good five minutes in what one of our friends told us was Cantonese.

The telephone solved the problem—it stopped ringing.

The wife went to the kitchen and we raided the beer fridge again for the fourth time.

On the way back we stopped off with Uncle Ho and asked him why he was such a miserable old bastard. That got his attention.

He told us that difficult customers and high overheads had made him depressed. We expressed our sympathies and understanding with straight faces until we sat down back at our table and then burst out laughing.

The customers weren't difficult, they were in short supply because of him and as for the overheads—well. He owned the building and lived upstairs. The restaurant itself consisted of three plain whitewashed walls, food and insect stained and absolutely inviting graffiti with a plain grey concrete floor and a pull down grill out front. The tables were metal with marbled tops and the chairs were bendy red plastic. Lighting was supplied by over bright fluorescent tubes hanging haphazardly from the ceiling with wires falling down all over the place and electric plugs hanging off the walls. Two flickering "blue ray" insect killers hummed frantically on opposite walls bursting occasionally into life as an animal was zapped, the victim joining the decaying pile underneath.

A damp cloth and broom would have been useful additions too.

Never mind, two years later he was the victim of progress when the buildings were bought out, upgraded and modernised. Unfortunately the quality of service and food remained the same.

I would like to have said that the food was worth waiting for, but it wasn't.

Even so we returned to KL refreshed and ready to face the next hundred years.

Goof Up in Guam

Mark and Louis had discovered an opportunity with a duty free operator with stores in Guam and Saipan. It was a Japanese owned company that had not adapted to the new Japanese "FIT". They were the "Free Independent Travellers."

Previously the huge money spenders had been Japanese businessmen with company credit cards and large expense accounts. This enabled them not to lose face when doing business with the foreign barbarians. The medium earners, but still substantial other spenders, were those in tour groups.

Catering for these had been the pattern for over 20 years.

The shopping habits were still very much the same, brand names, quality and bulk buying so as to give gifts to friends on return to Japan but it had become more fragmented rather than in bunches. Also independent middle class honeymooners and young backpackers were making an appearance, a previously unknown phenomenon for Japanese.

Marketing had relied on targeting airlines, tour groups, tour guides, cab companies and hotels and this approach still had a great deal of merit but tourists, especially the young, were increasingly breaking away from set routines and making up their own itineraries. Basically they were setting out to find you rather than you setting out to find them so your stores had to be more attractive and user friendly.

Hakasaki was a family company and they had already unsuccessfully tried one partnership. It was possible that we could be a better fit—in fact we were sure of it.

Apparently the father could not face failure so had run off to Japan leaving his wife and sons to sort it all out if possible. Mark had performed a favourable overview earlier and he and I went to do the first more detailed survey. First impressions were good. The Guam store was not on the seafront strip with other duty free operators but was still quite well situated on the tourist map.

It needed a very thorough overhaul of stock, display and renovation.

We also looked at other sites.

Next of course was due diligence. The young American educated son in charge on Guam was named Soki and was a very likeable, capable young guy. He was a little out of date on Japanese behaviour and was prone to state that the Japanese didn't buy candy because they didn't have a sweet tooth when duty free stores all over the world sold chocolate to Japanese by the bucketfull. He was also under the impression that the Japanese didn't buy shares on the stock market. There were many other indications that he would have to have a period of retraining if he was to fit in with us. He had got used to conservatism whereas we were all about innovation and change.

During this visit Mark and I had an out of world experience. We had drunk the Hilton Hotel bar out of Beck's beer and had retired a little merry and squiffy for the night.

We were just sorting ourselves out and had entered our rooms when the earth moved. Wow!!

I thought, "Jesus, that was great beer."

I got on the phone to Mark.

"Did you feel it Mark? Bloody hell that was some beer!"

Mark said, "yeah, what happened?"

"The earth moved mate, I haven't felt the earth move for ages, woah, it just moved again."

"Yeah, I felt it too, I gotta tell you though it's never moved for me before," he said.

"You poor old bugger, you a married man and never felt the earth move, you are such a sad specimen."

"You don't know the half friend," he laughed, "it's taken Beck's beer and an earthquake to do it."

We had experienced our first noticeable offshore earthquake and aftershock on the island but later found out that it was quite a common occurrence.

Just in case it wasn't the earthquake we made sure the Hilton stocked up on Beck's and I decided Mark needed a woman, not a good one but a really bad one.

We had to find a Karaoke!

We found several and I'm glad to say that by the time we finished up in Guam a year or two later it may have been a bit too much to say the earth had moved for Mark but it had certainly shifted a lot!!?

Stock revisions, designs, renovations and contract outlines were proceeding well but due diligence was not. There seemed to be a stumbling block on obtaining audited accounts. Management accounts, yes, but audited accounts, no. Also current bank receipts, debts, stock take results and cash flow details were very blurred to say the least.

These obstructions were worrying and I deliberately stalled on proceeding with any contractual agreements. Although Guam and Saipan were run separately there were financial overlaps and responsibilities so that they had to be treated as a whole package. Saipan may have been the more financially stable of the two but if one went down the other would go too.

Saipan was a smaller operation, beautifully situated along a beach road with the whole island being more rural and far less sophisticated than Guam. It suffered a similar malaise to Hakasaki Guam but was more transparent and obviously handled with a lot more care and attention to detail. It was run by two of Soki's half brothers.

They did not welcome us as wholeheartedly as Soki and were just as friendly as they needed to be in order to appear co-operative.

Guam and Saipan along with the tiny island of Tinian were "Protectorates" of the USA.

This was a wonderful modern word for "Colonies." They were policed by US Customs and Immigration and had American style Governors and "First Ladies."

Tinian had, for reasons best known to the US Airforce, been selected as their prime Pacific airbase during World War Two but had been largely neglected since. It certainly wasn't the prime destination for Japanese honeymooners that Guam, Saipan and Hawaii were. However most flights between Guam and Saipan did a stopover there. One or two people occasionally got on or off.

Ironically at the same time that I was dealing with young generation Japanese fifty five years after World War Two the film Pearl Harbour was released. The whole family decided to go and see it with me on Saipan.

So there I was sitting between five young Japanese men explaining what it was all about as they honestly hadn't got a clue. World War Two did not feature anywhere near their horizons and as far as they were concerned it was fought by nutty men donkeys years ago who valued conquest more than business.

They seemed to enjoy it though but found it difficult to see why the Japanese were doing what they did and it didn't bother them one bit whether Japan or America had won. As Soki said, "Its just old history man."

Fascinating for me though to see the whole thing from a different perspective.

I had read in newspapers, magazines and periodicals and also been told in any number of earnest conversations that there were no birds on Guam. This was due to the accidental introduction of a tree snake that raided birds nests and either ate the birds or their eggs. Knowledgeable, learned experts regarded this as an ecological disaster and used it as a great example of human irresponsibility.

One day I decided to explore a little and walked up the hill road leading out of the strip near to the Hilton. At the top I saw an old rusted barrier, partially collapsed, with an overgrown roadway leading into a forest. I explored. The forest was alive with birds and not a snake in sight. I felt like shouting out that I must have been seeing and hearing ghosts. Didn't they know they were extinct? Obviously not. They were victims of human irresponsibility all right. They were the victims of second hand, second class experts with an agenda and also gossips who tried to appear learned without checking the facts first. Subsequently I saw and heard thousands of birds all over the islands. God save us from the experts, especially those drummed up at a moments notice for TV news comments.

I have been "the man on the spot" so many times who could debunk most of the myths that are periodically dragged up and regurgitated. "Sabah and Sarawak along with most of North Borneo have been turned into deserts through uncontrolled logging."

"Oh yeah. I have flown over these "deserts" many times and they have definitely invented a new colour for deserts. Green."

Logging should certainly be better controlled but it serves no sensible cause to be caught out in a blatant lie. It results in lazy slipshod reporting.

Effecting due diligence at Hakasaki was becoming a little like attempting to renovate an old house. As fast as you pealed off one layer of paint and wallpaper you found another layer in worse condition underneath. I pushed harder for the facts and pulled back on agreements. Slowly a bad scenario emerged. There were unpaid business loans, unsettled personal loans, outstanding court cases and banks breathing fire. The hardest hitting of these and first in the queue was Citibank.

The building, ostensibly owned by the family, was in fact mortgaged several times over and Citibank's patience was exhausted. The local branch handling Hakasaki was in the care of a zealous new young manager who was over anxious to make his mark. He was headhunting to make a reputation and saw the settlement of this as the way of achieving his ambition. In many ways I couldn't argue, it was bad, but we were intent on providing a solution. He was in no mood to listen and perhaps because of his stubbornness we had a lucky escape.

He was pushing for a court case to get Hakasaki declared bankrupt, or unable to conduct further business. He wouldn't necessarily get much out of it for his bank but he was on a crusade.

This was not the time for any new players to emerge but they did.

First on the scene was Arnie. Arnie was a successful business man in Guam, a well connected Indian Indian, not a North American misnamed Indian. He also ran a restaurant upstairs in the Guam store but his main claim to fame was his contract for a meals on wheels scheme for old people and the disabled.

Soki arranged meetings with Arnie who was suggesting a solution. The solution was that he would buy the building and rent it to us. This appeared a great solution to Arnie and Soki and it wasn't too bad a suggestion. Except for us. In a steadily worsening situation we would no longer be a partner in a business with sizeable assets but a tenant. If we were going to be a tenant then why confine ourselves to the current location, why not find and rent a better site?

I made my concerns known and Arnie complained to Louis. Next on the scene was Hans who came from Amsterdam charging in like a bull in a China shop. Things were in a mess according to him, Louis was angry, did he have to do everything himself, and what the hell was going on?

Where the hell did all this come from? I had, as always, kept Louis informed verbally and in written reports, yet here was Hans, usually positive and supportive, with hardly a smile on his face and a dagger in his hand.

It was a mess all right, but it hardly needed a genius to work that out. The mess was uncovered by us, not created by us.

Anyway I was prepared to step back, take another look. Perhaps I had got a little too close and absorbed in the detail.

So go then Mr. Bossman Hans.

Hans involved himself with the main players and came up with an almost immediate solution.

We would take over completely, finance everything, rent the building from Arnie, pay a lot to rent the Hakasaki name and recoup the investment from profits.

Yeah good one Hans, just about everything I was trying to protect our company from. We would have none of the assets and all of the liabilities.

Modesty has never been one of my strong points, however who was I to judge, so I kept my head down for a change and waited to see which way it would go.

I did do a bit of crawling by telling Hans's son, who had come with him for some reason, that his dad was very clever. He sort of agreed so I suppose the irony may have been lost on him.

We didn't have to wait long. Citibank foreclosed so Hakasaki no longer had a building to sell to Arnie.

Meetings with local tour companies, hotels, cab companies and tour guides had resulted in us agreeing that although now virtually extinct it would be better to revive the Hakasaki name than trying to build a new brand from scratch.

The problem was that the name had been devalued yet again so Hans's scheme was in tatters as was just about everything else.

Soki then blotted his copy book with me. He suggested that we take out a loan to cover everything, really everything. Business debts, personal debts, capital necessary for revival, all would be covered. I pointed out to him that it would have to be repaid and did he have any sensible projections to achieve that?

He asked me why I was worried, it was not my money.

Uh oh, not the right answer, that was not the way I thought or worked.

I also asked Mark what was bugging Hans. Hans was not my boss, but he was influential on the board, and we had previously worked well together in harmony.

Hans had rather petulantly remarked that the company was experiencing financial problems due to having to keep Louis' new high society wife in royal style.

To say this to me was inappropriate to say the least.

Mark said that Hans had problems not connected with me and he would tell me more about it later.

Okay, I would cool it.

Hans decided to go and leave me to it. Very smart as he would not then be associated with failure, which was where this whole thing unfortunately seemed to be heading.

This could have been a worthwhile project but everyone previously involved had had more than enough of Hakasaki and several so called rescuers—they didn't want to know anymore. Sadly we were being tarred with the same brush.

We decided we should go to a sleazy strip joint we had found and chilled out in when things went a bit apeshit. As this was often then we were frequent visitors.

That was our excuse—at least we were watching people more unfortunate than us. Pathetic.

The club was situated on a hillside on one end of what passed for the Strip. It was in an older building on the first floor, reached by a rickety staircase along an ageing verandah. Ancient posters sagged off stained walls that hadn't been painted for yonks.

It was really a dump but we thought it had character.

We took our usual places in the front row, right up against the stage. We liked this as we were so close we could clearly see the cellulite, stretch marks and appendix scars. This made the performers almost human.

The rules were simple, the girls would show and manipulate everything they had but there was no touching, no rough stuff and no insults. Approval could be shown by stuffing dollar bills wherever they could be stuffed or wherever they could be thrown.

Not exactly elegant but effective.

The women would never have won any beauty contests at any time in their lives and gravity was clearly winning. They sagged all over. For us this added to the enjoyment.

Other services were available if required but we didn't require.

The performers always started to look better as the evening wore on even though the only beer available was Budweiser. Definitely not Becks, Stella or Kronenburg. Pity, because then the performers would have looked even better eventually.

Hans was not the most relaxed, man on the town type of person, but he seemed eager enough to enjoy what was about to happen. Things were swinging along nicely when suddenly there was a bit of a commotion, a stripper was recoiling from Hans with tears running down her cheeks. What!!

A stripper reduced to tears on stage—what was going on.

She shuffled past Hans's son and Mark and deposited herself down in front of me, legs apart, trying desperately to appear sexy and composed. She failed and rocked backwards and forwards crying her heart out.

Oh for goodness sake, what the hell?

"Hey, tell me, what is it?" I shouted. The music was loud.

"It was him, him, he wouldn't put the money where I told him." she cried, pointing at Hans.

Jesus, I didn't want to ask where he wanted to put the bills but I had to say something.

"Where did you tell him to put the money?"

"In my mouth."

"So?" Not so bad but what did Hans want to do? I couldn't wait.

"He refused, he said no one tells him what to do with his money."

"And that's it?"

"Yes."

"He didn't tell you his preference?" Oh boy I was just dying to know. "No."

"Okay, but why so sensitive, why the tears?"

"He insulted me, my intelligence and my art."

She got me there, what else could I say?

"I apologise for my colleague, he obviously didn't appreciate your skills, I will go to madam and sort it, okay?" This was becoming necessary and urgent. Madam at the front desk had been joined by two heavies, built like tanks and looking our way with serious looks on their faces.

I shot over to the tough old bird and got my explanation out like a rapid fire machine gun.

What was the solution?

Easy, fifty bucks to the girl, fifty bucks to the house and get the stupid prick out pronto. Agreed?

Agreed. I paid.

Suddenly the heavies evaporated, madam was all smiles and graciousness and I was invited to stay longer—no hurry.

No way man, we were going, otherwise I could see a few more bites out of our cherry coming up.

Hans was totally unaware of the close shave and was still protesting that he had to be the one who decided what to do with his money an hour after we landed on the street.

Well they called him a prick, I didn't.

Mark and Hans's son thought it hilarious and would break into chuckles every time they thought of it.

No mean trick to made a stripper cry.

Not one to take home to mum either.

"Hey Mum, Dad reduced a stripper to tears while she was shaking her tits and pussy in his face and nearly got us beaten to pulp. We had a good night though!"

Hans and son departed the next day and Mark and I started what we thought would be an attempt to salvage a lost cause.

I contacted HSBC Guam.

This arose from a lucky co-incidence a month or so before.

April had spotted a newspaper report that the Governor and First Lady of Guam were visiting Malaysia and resourceful as ever had found out the name of their hotel in KL.

Still more resourceful she sent flowers, chocolates and a welcome note to the First Lady and she got us an early appointment.

The Lady was charming, appreciated the welcome and although she had a busy schedule was interested in our project. The Governor just had time to look in and they made suggestions as to who could maybe help with finance and legal details. Their secretary gave us his card and we were told to stay in contact.

They had pointed out that HSBC USA was one of the later arrivals in Guam and had made it plain they were looking for investment possibilities—why not give them a try. Why not?

So I did and got an immediate positive response.

We hammered out an agreement along the lines of gaining a loan to cover building rent, restoration and renovation costs split between ourselves and whoever eventually owned the building, possible share holding in the building, stock and start up costs and payment for the Hakasaki name.

Security would be the business itself and a lien on the building jointly with the owner.

On the strength of this Arnie bought the building. I told him not to do it for that reason. To own it fine but he shouldn't count on our agreement being finalised, nothing was settled.

Hakasaki would have to settle its own debts. We started serious planning.

I decided that it was time to involve our KL team.

We took the only available connecting flight from KL which unfortunately left us with a long stop over in Taipai Airport, Taiwan before catching the overnight to Guam. Taipai was not designed for long stop overs, in fact it was not designed for anything much at all really.

To be fair you couldn't find many that were. Singapore was the best by far. It managed to combine shopping with relaxation and points of interest. BAA airports were the pits. At a meeting some years before at Heathrow we were told of plans for more and more shops, even to the point of taking out some toilets.

"Bloody hell," I exclaimed, "they're the only places that are left where you can sit down!"

I have never managed to win a business popularity contest.

We arrived very early morning in Guam just as the sun was rising.

I had a typical Malaysian mixture with me, Malay, Indian and Chinese, all young women. All professional, all qualified and smartly dressed, although a bit bedraggled from fourteen hours travel.

I went through immigration and was joined by three more at the baggage hall. We waited for our other two. We waited and waited.

Only one customs officer was left in the hall and she called us over. She told us we could not wait around like that, we would have to move out.

We told her our problem.

She asked the usual, how many in our party, why were we there, how many were missing etc.

She made a call and found that they were detained by immigration.

What the hell, why?

She asked about passports. No they had them and had also filled in landing cards. No they weren't self declared criminals nor drug addicts and they were just business people like us.

She was puzzled and sympathetic. She told our girls to take all the luggage through and get cleared.

Me, she told to wait.

Then she said go back up and see what's what.

How? There was only one down escalator.

Easy, press the red stop button at the bottom and walk up.

So I did.

The immigration hall was totally empty.

I made my way to an office section and explored.

I found our two Chinese Malaysians seated uncomfortably before a desk looking very concerned and bewildered. So was I, what was going on?

Suddenly a stern voice broke in behind me very severe.

I turned to face a six foot three, blue eyed, blond haired, pink skinned, uniformed immigration officer. Very corn fed.

"Who are you, what are you doing here, you have to get out immediately or I will have you forcefully removed."

What question did he want me to answer first, if in fact he wanted me to answer at all?

He didn't.

Before I even started he told me again to get out.

I didn't say another word, I just pointed over his shoulder. Facing me was a notice stating the Immigration code of behaviour.

"At all times to be helpful, considerate and polite."

He looked, didn't get it so I walked over and stuck my finger on the relevant sentence.

He got it. He was big but not very bright. He calmed down a bit.

I stood my ground and stated my case but this guy just didn't listen. So I told him to eject me forcibly as per his threat, I would not resist, I told him to deport me but not before giving me all his details so I could make formal charges of obvious prejudice and racism against him. I told him a previous generation had fought a war against Nazis, didn't he know that?

Somewhere in the dim dark recesses of his brain something started to work. He told me to wait downstairs and he would send a senior to interview me.

I went.

I waited about twenty minutes when a Mr. Five by Five, African American in civilian clothes approached me. Thank god it wasn't another uniformed white Nazi. He introduced himself and quietly and politely asked me what this was all about.

I told him the whole story and why we were there. I said we were doing due diligence but such a long word was obviously beyond the vocabulary of the upstairs guy. He listened, asked a few questions, told me to be patient and wait a while. I was patient.

He shortly came back down with our two girls and a slightly red faced immigration officer.

The immigration officer escorted the girls to a taxi and off they went to our hotel. The supervisor smiled and said, "Sir we attempt to staff our borders with our brightest and finest but I'm afraid sometimes we fall a bit short. Sorry for the delay. Good luck with your business."

We shook hands and I went to join our staff.

We set to work and stuck our noses into everything we should and could.

During one particular excursion the differences in walking speeds emerged. There is a European speed, a Chinese speed, an Indian speed and a Malay speed.

We had to walk about one and a half kilometres slightly uphill.

After about five hundred metres we were well spread out, exactly in the order above. The English and Chinese got plenty of rests while waiting for the others to catch up. We all had a good laugh about the fact that compared to a European a Malay doesn't seem to move at all. Must be the climate.

We still maintained a relationship with Soki and his brothers but the fact remained that they didn't like being left to pay their own debts and so things were a bit tense.

Soki was worried his mother would lose her home and other property and to be sure the vultures were circling.

I sympathised but they had led us a dance trying to obscure and cover their tracks and we had done our best to sort it in spite of that.

Soki's mother was a great lady. Charming, sweet and elegant and even at an advanced age she was a beauty.

One night she had been out to dinner with a man friend and we met them for drinks. I noticed that Soki was amused and was teasing his mother. I looked at him and he whispered, "I don't believe it, she's pissed, my mum is pissed." So we discreetly decided to leave them alone.

Arnie would meet us in his restaurant at night but after a while he would drink too much of his own cellar and the business aspects deteriorated to such a degree that we would rather have talked about other trivial things. But Arnie wanted to talk business.

Not a good idea. He not only talked rubbish but also got a bit offensive. Even Mark, who has more than ten times the tolerance and patience that I have, got exasperated and annoyed.

We still pushed on but then came the final curtain.

Due to lack of real progress combined with a downturn in business in the region we were informed that HSBC was withdrawing from Guam.

That was it, we started to wrap up and leave.

It was over.

So what's this with Hans I asked Mark.

Hans, in a way, was not really a member of staff, he had his own IT company. He had attracted the attention of Louis. Hans had sold him on the idea of financing his company in producing a comprehensive computer programme that would encompass and combine all aspects of the business. When launched the system would be put on the market and sales would recoup the high cost of research and investment.

For some time Hans and his staff were flying high, in fact too often making comments on other areas of business that they were clearly unqualified to do.

A while previously Hans had misrepresented our agreement regarding our salaries and allowances and blamed me. We had negotiated everything in Sterling and agreed on the new deal. Then he asked if I minded being paid in Euros as it was easier. No problem, I thought. But there was. When my salary came through, the agreed amount of English pounds had morphed into Euros. I was now earning less than three years before. Why on earth would I do that? It didn't make sense. He argued but I had recorded it accurately in a report and got my way but a bad taste remained.

To my mind something was wrong. This was not the Hans of old.

Now questions were being asked as to when actually his project would be complete and ready. When would the miracle, devised by geniuses, come to fruition? Answers were very woolly and frustration was growing.

Hans was under pressure and so was not feeling as charitable and accommodating to others as he used to be. To me this was a pity as Hans on his day was very good and he had been helpful and supportive in the past.

So I had to watch my back but it was to be a few years before I found out just how much.

In the meantime we had plenty to do.

Where was I on 9-11?

We had finished our meetings at the Company's HQ after a working lunch and travelled into the centre of Amsterdam. Being early afternoon we fancied a beer and popped into the nearest bar. We sat on stools by the window and ordered a couple of Amstels. We talked a bit about the business and then, realising that the other customers were staring at the TV above the bar, turned our attention there.

Oh God, yet another disaster movie from the good old USA.

At least this one didn't have King Kong climbing up the Twin Towers after a helpless blond. Just a fire to put out on one of the towers. When will the All American hero appear?

Well now this bit's original, a jet has just flown into the other tower and burst into flames.

Suddenly, to our horror, we saw the CNN sign at the bottom of the screen and a banner appeared saying "Breaking News". This was not a movie—it was real and it was now!!

The commentators had been so stunned that for some time there had been little commentary. When they did comment you could hear the anguish, shock and pain in their voices.

We watched silent and spellbound as the towers crumbled to the ground. Sadness was not an adequate description of our feelings as we thought of the human lives that were being lost before our eyes. Destroyed buildings can be rebuilt, destroyed humans cannot.

Then came scarcely believed reports of a plane crashing into the Pentagon and another highjacked plane crash landing into a field, thought to be headed for the White House.

Unbelievably America was under a surprise attack.

The whys, whats and hows that followed would consume miles of paper and hours of film time. It didn't matter to me what opinions I or others may have held about the USA. No matter how propagandists wanted to dress it up, this was murder. I watched with disgust as TV channels showed footage of people in some countries dancing in the streets, celebrating and cheering. I listened to and read completely ridiculous conspiracy theories. Did the authors really believe the often contradictory crap they were writing?

All sorts of unlikely unqualified people were dug up to substantiate the most silly stories. One of them was a beauty. Some nutcase somewhere put together yet another team of doubters. They viewed the whole scenario with great suspicion, particularly the way the towers collapsed. The towers looked so substantial that they must have been sabotaged by explosives they said.

Completely ignoring the planes full of highly flammable fuel smashing into them at high speed flown by terrorists clearly identified later as Arabs they tried to convince people that it was all a secret plot by anyone and everyone except Arabs.

They toured the world promoting such garbage. (who paid for the tour—now that's a more pertinent question?). No explosions of such a precise nature were ever recorded. No remains were found, and no explanations as to how any group of people could have entered unnoticed over an extended period of time with huge amounts of explosives. They then had to place them unseen with expert precision over many, many floors, time bombs perfectly synchronised to explode when the towers were hit high up by public airliners in a surprise attack. Well as my old mum said, "there's one idiot born every minute!"

The star of their show was a latin american janitor of one of the towers. He was sure the towers were blown up.

Well that's it then—ignore all the facts from TV coverage, experts, on the spot participants, firefighters and common sense, just consult a janitor!!

So presumably if a disaster happened to the Petronas Twin Towers then there's no need to bring in all sorts of knowledgeable people—just ask the Bangledeshi toilet cleaner.

Sickest of all were the completely untrue rumours such as Israel's Mossad knew of it and probably planned it, no Jews went to work that day and the American Government were behind it all anyway.

To me this said more about the mental instability and bigotry of the perpetrators of the stories than it did about what really happened. And that was quite another story in itself.

Sadly the world changed more in that one day than in many years. Osama bin Laden had succeeded in making the whole Moslem world seem a threat to peace and prosperity.

The non moslem majority of the earth's population were reduced to either condemning that religion or making excuses for it while moslems themselves appeared muted and soft in their responses.

Footage of Bin Laden entertaining Middle Eastern Mullahs in his hideaway, all gloating over the event and praising Allah and the Prophet added to the disgust. I watched on Al Jazeera as Osama outlined how he planned it, how he had studied the plans, how he knew where and how to strike with maximum effect due to his engineering and construction knowledge. He and his accomplices were also hiding in a country that had wantonly destroyed ancient Buddhist statues. So tolerance, understanding and the will to live peacefully with others had gone down the drain.

Completely forgotten was how the western allies stood firm with Saudi Arabia and Egypt when faced with invasion by Saddam Hussein and together with Saudi forces swept Iraqi forces out of Saudi and Kuwait. They were in Saudi because they were invited by the government and lost lives in doing so.

It rarely occurred to anyone that perhaps the majority of moslems were just as shocked and staggered by what had happened and didn't know exactly how to respond.

So they felt threatened but not nearly as much as the rest of the world.

Then there were those who claimed not to know what a terrorist was—shouldn't they be called guerrillas or freedom fighters? If they genuinely couldn't tell the difference then they only needed to apply a bit of common sense and look at history. Guerrillas and freedom fighters worked to secure the freedom of their country or people from inside or outside forces that intended to conquer and rule them illegally through cruel oppression. They usually represented the real wishes of a frightened people.

Terrorists did not. They wanted the power to impose their rule and further their own ambitions frequently against the wishes of the majority. They wanted to enslave, not set free. They spread their terror beyond boundaries and freedom.

If you start a war, invade another country, and you lose, then you have to be prepared for the consequences. If you are not then don't start the war. This is something that Hamas, Al Fatah and Hezbollah Palestinians seem incapable of understanding, especially as they are spurred on by irresponsible neighbours and others who can't seem to mind their own business, urging them on from a safe distance.

I feel sympathy for the Kurds, Palestinians, Israelis and others who just want to live safe within their own borders.

Of course propagandists distorted the terrorists true aims and actions so as to make them appear heroic warriors for a noble cause. I have always failed to see what is noble about terrorist leaders hiding themselves away, protected as much as possible from harm, while sending out young kids to die and commit suicide on their behalf.

Osama bin Laden and others like him called themselves men of god and said they were not afraid to die, they were in god's hands.

Strangely they then refused to rely on god's hands and surrounded themselves in secrecy behind dozens of human hands, all sworn to protect and die for them.

So much for their faith and trust in god!!

My problem with Osama and others like him was that they made the issue one of religious differences instead of political, educational and economic inequalities.

Nothing of course is so totally black or white but the world has had plenty of wonderful freedom fighters in recent times including Ghandi, Martin Luther King and Aung San Suu Kyi none of whom advocated murder as the right course of action. Even Nelson Mandela who advocated fighting Apartheid refrained from revenge. He really had a case for taking retribution. Of course, in my opinion, the advocates of the terrorist/ freedom fighter question are mainly being deliberately obtuse.

Their sympathies really lie with the terrorists but they are too cowardly to admit it.

The results, on millions of lives, since 9/11 have all been negative, none positive.

Well done Osama.

Jungle trek—Sabah

Eldest daughter, and her husband planned a visit from the UK. They said that they didn't want the usual touristy bit of a few days in Kuala Lumpur, followed by the beach in the comfort of a resort hotel—they wanted adventure.

They wanted the jungle, the real jungle, the deep jungle.

Okay, but we thought this a bit reckless for beginners. We had built up our expertise slowly and had gradually come to enjoy it, but it was not for the fainthearted.

However, we thought, "let's do it!"

We met them at KLIA, put them up over night, and set off next day.

We took the MAS flight to Kota Kinabalu in the East Malaysian State of Sabah.

We rested up for a few days to enable our visitors to recover from their jet lag. While there we took advantage of the time to take a trip on the North Borneo Light Railway. This was not quite as simple as it sounded as the train only ran at certain unscheduled times and then only if it was nearly fully booked. It was possible to turn up and have to wait a few days until the administrators decided it was economical to do the return run—almost the full distance of the old Colonial commercial line.

We were lucky. The train was running the next day and we bought tickets. The officials seemed to take an over the top delight in the unpredictability, telling prospective passengers that they could be disappointed even at the last minute. What is it with some people?

Anyway after a bit of pomp and exaggerated performance we got underway. Most of the scenery was interesting but not spectacular with a few stop offs of minor cultural importance. There was one fascinating section as the train ran through mangrove swamps with the water lapping well over the wheels but the view was not the main point. The emphasis was on the Colonial history aspect with lunch being served in traditional tiffanies by uniformed attendants in rolling stock that had been restored and decked out in the original livery. The coaches were walk through with an open air viewing balcony at the rear of the last compartment. The track was in the old narrow gauge.

A very nice worthwhile experience just low key enough to relax every one for what was to come.

The next morning we took a taxi to Kota Kinabalu International Airport to catch our flight on a light aircraft into the interior.

We jokingly asked the taxi driver why we and anyone from Peninsular Malaysia had to have a passport, even the Malays, when visiting Sabah and Sarawak in Eastern Malaysia on the island of Borneo.

He took it seriously, maybe a bit too seriously.

"It's to keep those mad, mainland Malays out," he exclaimed vehemently.

"Ever since Union when it was agreed we were together but also apart, they have been trying to take over with their religion and politics.

They're just Sumatrans and Javanese who took over Malaya and now they want our land too. Well they won't get it!! We have our own culture, history and religion, much better than theirs. The British knew it, and respected it but this lot respect nothing. So we humiliate them by making them visitors, ha ha ha!"

"Woah fella," we thought. We had read and heard bits and pieces like this but never anywhere near as strong. We changed the subject.

Check in and departure was as near normal as possible from a major airport allowing for the size of the plane. Luggage was stowed at the front, behind the pilot, using a small baggage van equipped with a small conveyor belt. Passengers climbed up a narrow set of mobile steps and entered the aircraft through a lift up door at the rear. There were about twelve of us and the plane was full. We were the only tourists which should have told us something.

The plane was an old German made Fokker Wolf with wood panelled windows and flowered curtains. The seats were a mixture somewhere between an armchair, director's chair and a deck chair in a single row each side of the aisle.

The uniformed attendant handed out peanuts and bottled water as though to relatives and friends, as no doubt some of them were, and chatted away covering all the local gossip.

We were largely ignored.

After an hour we slowed, circled and dropped down sharply. I have always loved the sound of turbo prop aircraft as they feather the props and vary the revolutions. Then even when the engines are cut right back the planes seem to cling to the air until the last second. They just want to fly unlike their jet big brothers who drop like stones and hardly conceal the fact that landing is just a barely controlled crash.

We taxied in and came to a stop as the flight attendant lifted up the exit door and said, "mind the step."

The step was two boxes of different sizes, not quite together, and shifted position every time they were stood on. We knew then why the locals rushed to get out first. By the time it was our turn the boxes were well spread out, but we didn't care. This was part of the adventure so we jumped almost spritely from box to box onto the ground.

We then found out a second reason why the locals moved quickly.

The luggage was loaded onto a handcart and pushed into the shed that passed for a terminal building. Arrivals and departures were the same.

The trick was to grab your luggage promptly from the trolley because at the same time as you were removing yours, the departing passengers were chucking their bags onto it. If you weren't quick enough then your bags would be going back onto the plane.

This was a vital escape exercise as the flight was an immediate turn around.

We exited the terminal and were fortunate as we were met by a young guy who, after looking us critically up and down, welcomed us with a wry smile. He led us to a rather ancient looking five seater pick up truck which unfortunately looked even more used up inside than out.

We loaded up with me in front with the young driver.

At first we travelled along a metal road for about an hour, then turned off onto a stoned, uneven road for another hour and eventually turned onto a dirt track. We had been surrounded by jungle for most of the way and now it was closing in more tightly around us. We went deeper and deeper each different surface causing a variety of disturbing sounds from within our vehicle.

During the journey the driver acquainted us with details of the lodge where we were to stay. The style was that of the Malay Longhouses, common to the area, and was raised on stilts connected by boardwalks. It was situated on the banks of a river the size of which varied not just day by day but hour by hour depending on the level of rainfall in the nearby mountains. The river could vary in a matter of minutes from 30 metres wide and swift flowing into a raging torrent 100 metres wide sweeping everything away.

He told us that the deteriorating track we were using was the only way in and out and they did the journey about once or twice a week.

The jungle was a part of a huge, natural game reserve and was policed by well trained rangers and wardens who would also act as our guides.

Any animals seen were wild, unused to humans and were extremely dangerous and unpredictable—unlike Africa they were not used to seeing loads of trucks filled with tourists clicking away with expensive cameras. All species of flora and fauna were protected and we should leave the area as natural and unspoiled as we found it.

This was okay with us and my daughter had that eager, let's get at it look on her face until the guy told us about the green leech socks that we should always wear.

He told us about how to detect and remove the Tiger Leeches before they gained a hold.

That was shock number one which was quickly followed by shock number two. With a loud bang the front offside tyre punctured.

We found out that we had to change the wheel ourselves. The driver had to keep an experienced eye out in case of approach by hostile animals or reptiles. The track was narrow, the ground potholed, the jungle dense and our nerves were strained as we gingerly climbed out of the vehicle.

However the change, although awkward, was made without hindrance and we set off once more. This was not without some trepidation as the spare was not much of an improvement on the damaged tyre.

We wound up and down, round about, on a seemingly endless green journey, when we came to the bottom of a gently rising hill giving a clear view along the track for over a hundred metres up to the brow.

We suddenly stopped dead. The driver turned off the engine, motioning us to be quiet and very still.

Shock number three was about to happen.

Just at the top of the hill was a huge bull elephant straddling the track, ears flapping (not a good sign apparently), tearing at the foliage and dusting off his back with branches. He lurched backwards and forwards seemingly without noticing us but fortunately our driver was very experienced and not fooled by his apparent nonchalance. This wonderful big fellow had spotted us.

We were then told the good and bad news.

The good news was that this was rare. We were lucky to see it. Many visitors frequently went days without seeing any animals.

The bad news was bad.

The elephant was fairly certain to be a rogue bull, chased from a herd by a dominant male or males and rejected by the females. With any human or animal this would be an unhappy situation—with a huge frustrated bull elephant it could be suicidal. He would interpret any interruption as an irresistible challenge and the disturbing bit was that on this terrain it could easily outrun our vehicle. The track was too narrow to turn around in and difficult to back up.

So we waited.

After a while the elephant moved off a little into the forest, making a small clearing as he went. The destructive power of this specimen was awesome.

The action encouraged our driver to start the engine and edge up the track a little.

This seemingly innocent move caused Jumbo to swiftly back onto the track again, sideways on, curling his trunk, flapping his ears and letting out a loud bellow with loads of steam.

We stopped.

Seeing this he went forward into the trees again so the driver crawled up a way and then shot past as quickly as the track would allow. Not quick enough however as the animal spun round unbelievably fast for its size and charged.

This was the last split second scene on my video as the truck shot forward, catapulting me backwards and bringing an abrupt end to my filming.

We went over the brow of the hill at a fair lick as the driver threw all caution to the winds and then stopped about 70 or 80 metres down.

Waiting to move at a moments notice the driver asked me to pick myself up and tell him what the elephant was doing behind us.

This magnificent creature was standing still, 50 metres away, spread legged, in the middle of the track, trumpeting his triumphant victory over us mere mortals. After having established his undoubted supremacy he turned and lumbered away into the forest.

I then turned round excitedly telling my family what an incredible thing they had witnessed only to see them clinging to each other, trembling with white faces. They said that they had never been so frightened in their lives, we could have been killed or injured. The driver confirmed that the elephant could have made a mess of us and the truck if it had wanted to. That particular comment did nothing to console or reassure them.

This occasioned my partner to remark that she had thought that they were a couple of Crocodile Dundees only to find out that they were a couple of Waltzing Mathildas??!!

We reached the lodge soon after as the driver was in a hurry to report the incident to the other rangers.

Almost immediately we were on the way back in a truck equipped with floodlights and other gear. They said that they believed that the bulls always stayed close and never strayed far from the main herd and that there was a good chance of us catching sight of it. As the light was fading we reached a point on the track where two herds, not one, were crossing in different directions. A few of the matrons in each herd were acknowledging each other with soft sounds and lightly touching trunks as they ushered the young elephants into a narrow track in the foliage. Absolutely incredible.

We watched from close up with no problems until as darkness came we switched on the floodlights. A group of females, concerned that we and the lights were disturbing the babies in the herd, turned to us and in unmistakeable elephant language told us to clear off.

We did.

What a remarkable end to an incredible first day.

I never failed to be amazed at the difference between animals in zoos and safari parks compared to animals in the wild. The wild animals were so sharp, attentive, fit and muscular compared to the others. They were free, in charge of their own lives and environment and they knew it. They lived with real danger every day. Nobody spoon fed them.

On arrival back at the lodge we finally got ourselves checked in, filled out all our documents and permits, and purchased our green leech socks, sticky tape and a few other items. We settled in and then retired to the small bar in the rather sparse indoor recreation area and treated ourselves to a few beers before going to bed. The indoor recreation area was necessary due to frequent cancellation of treks due to heavy rainstorms and flooding.

The next morning we were introduced to our guide, who was both eastern and western university trained in agricultural science. He was a mature young man from Sabah who had returned to his roots. His knowledge of forest herbs, roots, drugs and local medicines as well as western science was copious. His grandfather had been a tribal witch doctor and had passed on much of his knowledge and experience.

He told us that these old guys had been very smart and tricky, they kept close secrets, held people in awe and fear through superstition and were the ultimate con artists.

They could make people ill, or hallucinate, or whatever, by sleight of hand and then miraculously cure them to great acclaim. If the patients died they claimed it was because the ancient spirits had been too upset to relent, or were possessed by immovable demons or because the gods loved them so much that they had to take them. It was win win all the way.

They could make love potions, hate potions, hypnotize or induce as well as carrying out all sorts of ceremonies to enhance their reputations.

Many of the stories he told were humorous but some were horrific as although anthropologists love to romanticise the lifestyles of primitive tribes, the infant, child and mother mortality rates were terrible. Deafness, blindness and skin diseases were rampant and animals and reptiles took a high toll.

His advice to anyone who was ill was, "forget the mumbo jumbo" and find a good doctor and get to a first class modern hospital.

We kitted ourselves out, pulled on our leech socks, tucked our jeans into them and made them secure with the tape.

We were wearing long sleeve shirts, buttoned at the wrists and at the neck, and stuffed into our pants. The idea was to show as little bare skin as possible. This was not due to excessive modesty but a means of reducing attacks by insects and leeches.

We set off for some ancient burial grounds built high up on a mountain side some three hours or so away. The rainforest scenery was spectacular and initially the trek was leisurely but became more exacting as we made progress towards the mountain.

The jungle was full of rustling noises and loud animal and bird calls, but little was to be seen except foliage, trees and bushes. Until you looked closer.

The animals may have been shy and not in evidence but the floor was teeming with insect life.

Furry centipedes, shiny millipedes, horned cockroaches, green geckos, millions of ants and termites were scurrying all over the place completely oblivious to our presence just getting on with whatever it is they get on with.

Not one of them, not even the lizards, messed with the soldier ants. Neither did we.

The secure clothing protected us from many of the floating, flying and waving would be intruders but not quite all. The normal leeches from rivers and field were no threat as they needed low level prey but the Tiger Leech was a different proposition. They used various hosts to climb up plants and trees and when they sensed warm blood they would try to drop onto an unsuspecting victim. We actually teased a few we spotted on plants by going very close and circling around driving them crazy.

They frantically waved their bodies this way and that trying to find the source of all that wonderful heat and make contact.

We frequently inspected each other and usually found one or two successful attackers working their way down a sleeve or a leg trying to find a way in. We quickly learned the trick of removing them. They attached themselves first at the opposite end to the bloodsucker. They then curled their bodies over to change the attachment from one end of their bodies to the other. In this way they worked their way along the host, literally turning somersaults. For a while, during this manoeuvre they had no firm contact and could easily be flicked off if you timed it right. We usually did.

Details of the people who made the burial grounds were largely unknown. The area had not been settled for a few hundred years and there were no surviving written or verbal records. Any habitation had long been taken over by the jungle as nothing had been built of stone. The coffins survived because they were hollowed out from very hard wood and were placed in holes cut out of the mountain at a level inaccessible except by a tall ladder. Tests on the remaining bones revealed that they were several hundred years old and although one or two artifacts remained most had been removed by robbers long before.

None of our party wished to shin up the rickety long old ladders to view the coffins, artifacts and bones in situ so it was left to me to hazard the climb. The ladders were made from the branches of local trees, stripped, with the steps cut to size and then tied with twine to the two supports. This would have looked precarious enough but some steps were missing and some of those remaining were hanging at an awkward angle. I struggled up and produced the necessary photographic evidence.

On our way back we were caught in a torrential tropical rainstorm with thunder and lightning booming and flashing back and forth between the mountains around us making an intimidating yet spectacular scene. In a rainforest it is impossible not to stand beneath a tree during a storm—that was number one safety tip gone out the window.

We just kept moving.

We arrived at a river that we had crossed easily by stepping stones earlier only to have to wait for more than two hours after the storm for the waters to subside enough to facilitate a safe crossing.

The previous slow low level stream had been transformed by the rain into a wide swift flowing deep river—we were patient.

We then made the discovery that trying to dry out wet clothes in a rainforest environment was not easy.

Later that evening I had my first ever encounter with a truculent wild boar.

Towards nightfall a couple of adult wild boars frequently came down to the village to forage for scraps.

They also, for some peculiar reason, found the kitchen waste water more desirable than the river water—they probably saw it as some sort of a rare cocktail—in this case though "well stirred but not shaken".

Due to weather, wild animals and flooding most people lived in the longhouses built high up on stilts. The animals therefore had become very territorial on the ground.

I rather unwisely decided I would take a close look at this underworld and came down from my lofty perch to take eye level photos and videos.

One of the boars immediately transfixed me with both of its icy glaring eyes which is not easy as the eye of a boar is set more on the side of its head than the front. Either he managed it or I imagined it because as I moved around so did the boar keeping me in his sights all the time. It was obvious he was spoiling for a fight and just wanted an excuse to charge me so I started to move discreetly backwards. The boar moved indiscreetly forwards, shaking its head and snorting.

Fortunately the other boar was content to enjoy his "Happy Hour" otherwise I might have got caught in a crossfire.

They were ugly, hairy brutes with flat snouts, short tusks, heavy bodies and stocky short legs. The hair was matted, tangled and dirty and their hoofs were covered in mud and waste. Not one of nature's prettiest sights.

As I retreated so the boar advanced.

I decided to climb back up onto the elevated boardwalk and carry on my observations from there. Of course the boar could not physically follow me but he did with his eyes and his obvious intent to attack or intimidate did not waiver.

I played little tricks and games. I would stand behind a pillar and then suddenly re-appear, I would crouch down out of sight, move along and then spring up or I would stand behind a door for a while and then come out of another one further down. No matter what I did I found him to be still ready and waiting with a look of disdain whenever and wherever I emerged.

He was not impressed or deterred.

His determination to get me reminded me a little of my ex wives.

This led me to conclude that there was only one course of action— head for the bar and some cool beers.

Early the next morning we had a walk in the skies. We climbed up on specially constructed rope ladders to walk along wood and hemp suspension bridges slung across the roof of the rain forest. From this swaying viewpoint we got an idea of the various diverse layers of rainforest ecology from the top down instead of from the more usual bottom up. We were at times more than two hundred feet high amongst trees that were more than two hundred years old.

The overall feeling was of an impressionist painting with multi shades of green and brown, slashed with red, yellow and orange splotches. No blues, blacks and purples there.

Almost on cue we were fortunate to see a performance from a large group of Gibbons who are the most athletic of the ape and monkey species. They stayed high in the sky and staged the most talented and daring show that would have put the most able of circus artists to shame. They leaped, swung, twisted, turned and defied gravity with their tricky somersaults crashing through the branches. The noise, physical contact, both tender and aggressive between them plus their constant activity made us tired just to watch. After about thirty minutes they moved on and so did we.

On our way back down we managed to catch a short glimpse of an Orang Utan, the only time I have seen one in the wild. He was partly squatting, chewing a leaf and fanning himself with a leafy branch at the same time. He had a doleful expression on his face. They tend to be quite shy, lonely characters and this one just ambled away from us as though we didn't exist.

The Rangers never tired of telling us that the variety of wildlife we had seen was exceptional and unusual. The animals did not come out to order, in fact sometimes did not come out at all as they wandered over large tracts of the forest.

The lodge position had been carefully chosen but nothing could be guaranteed. You needed some luck and we had it.

Many visitors had seen little all day and had to be content with the night tour. This was straining it a bit as you could only hear so many frog sounds, imagine so many eyes shining in the dark and spot so many night owls before becoming bored and thinking the bar offered more fun. We did see a Nail Snake though. This was a long, threadlike, elegant reptile which glided with head held high. The head was the shape of a nail head, hence the name. During our previous jungle treks we had seen plenty of snakes but this was a new one.

The following day my family insisted on a rest day. My daughter wanted to clear her room out of ants, cockroaches, lizards and mosquitos and asked the Rangers to help. They fogged it so thoroughly that they decided it was time for the recreation room. My partner, although not bothered so much by the intrusion of insect life took the same option.

I was still raring to go and got a lucky break.

I was invited to accompany one of the guides who promised a surprise.

We travelled a long way back down along the entry road in his 4x4 until we turned off along a track, obviously well used and rutted, but surrounded by dense jungle on all sides.

After about an hour of tedious bumping, slipping and sliding we burst out into a huge area of cleared land.

On the edge was an old style single story colonial house, built on stilts with a verandah surrounding three sides, fans revolving and punkahs swaying above rattan furniture, behind which were shuttered windows.

This was previously a colonial rubber plantation, now owned by a Malaysian company with varying business interests including forestry, rubber, palm oil and fruit. The manager was a friend of my guide. They had been at college together.

We were to join his friend who was with a small party of rangers, police and environmentalists, complete with a mobile film crew.

They had been out trying to track down a tiger that had been seen in the area. They had not had any success but a tapper had caught a glimpse that morning close to an area of newly cleared land. It had not attacked any local humans but had certainly scared the living daylights out of them and it was of the utmost importance to catch it and relocate it before it had the chance to become a man eater. The plan was to tranquilize the animal and move it to a more remote location. The tiger however would be alert and more interested in hunting and killing for food than in being put to sleep which made the whole operation somewhat hazardous.

We drove into a large parking lot set amongst warehouses, silos, buildings and processing plants a little way from the house finding a convenient spot amongst a group of military type vehicles already parked there. The hunting party was nearly set so after some brief introductions and raised eyebrows at my presence we jumped into one of two beat up old Land Rovers. The film crew occupied the other one while everyone else climbed into converted pickups and we roared off onto one of the tracks crossing the plantation.

The manager explained that he loved his Land Rovers, left behind by a previous administration, because they just went on forever, particularly in rough country. Just as he said that we careered off into a lane between a forest of palms. The ranger in the Rover with us was on the phone to two trackers who had been out since first light following up on a previous sighting but had changed to pick up on the latest one that morning.

The were guiding us in as they were sure they were in the vicinity of the tiger and advised a slow, quiet approach in the vehicles.

We joined the trackers on the edge of the trees before a large area of cleared land, a field intended but not yet fully ready for any planting.

We all alighted and the rangers, trackers and camera crew seemed naturally to fall into a much rehearsed routine. I, together with the environmentalists, stayed out of the way.

They would only go into action if the tiger was subdued and caught. They would arrange the humane treatment and transportation.

No one was looking at the ground for tracks, no need for that. The tiger was close. They were scanning all directions seemingly at the same time.

Almost immediately everyone of them became super alert because a ranger was pointing to the opposite edge of the clearing about 150 metres away. We could see nothing but were told to get back into the Land Rover and watch carefully.

A few minutes later we saw the tiger—a large adult male we were told—slowly working its way along the edge of trees in our direction. It looked menacing as it sometimes crouched lower, tail swishing and head moving from side to side taking everything in, and then lifted its head and body giving little sniffling snarls as it came. The different shades of black and brown on tiger and forest showed how well the natural camouflage worked in these surroundings. The team were not too worried—or so they said—as tigers usually attack lone creatures from the rear after careful stalking. They were hoping it would come close enough for them to get a clear shot causing the tiger to fall unconscious fairly quickly and for a decent period of time. They could then call on the support team so that the tiger could be tagged, caged and transported without any injuries.

Anything less than a full dose could be dangerous for both tiger and humans.

When the tiger was less than a 100 metres away it suddenly accelerated towards us, its back legs skidding sideways with the terrific push forwards, kicking up a small cloud of dust—the speed was incredible. It was an absolutely riveting and fantastic sight as the whole of its body became fluid and every muscle rippled with effort. It seemed to just scream into action.

The Rangers, police and trackers didn't waiver.

They lined up their weapons, both drug pellet delivering and live bullet delivering (the bullets were the plan B back up just in case) and waited.

The camera crew bravely did the same.

However just about 40 to 50 metres away the tiger swerved into the palms and disappeared. That was it for the day we were told.

The method and plan had failed but it was a first attempt—previously they had not got that close and were not sure even that it was still in the area. Now they knew for sure.

They also had some important pictures that could be studied in order to identify the animal along with some of its characteristics.

A few days later the tiger was caught using drugged bait in a lair and eventually ended up deposited somewhere on the Sabah and Indonesian border where it would be tracked for the rest of its life with scientists studying its movements, mapping its territory, and recording its state of health.

All involved hoped it would survive as such a fine specimen was becoming increasingly rare. This was only partly due to hunting. It was mainly due to the narrowing down of suitable environments.

Wild animals needed to roam over large areas in order to find sufficient food and shelter, particularly elephants, who had large appetites and could deplete substantial sections of forest in a short time. Huge, natural, wild places were becoming less and less, not so much from destruction, but from settlement. Animal life, plant life and human life would go on but wild life would not.

We all noted the irony that humans were regarding savage dangerous animals as creatures that needed to be preserved while the animals still regarded humans as prey that needed to be eaten.

Once again I had been fortunate to get so close to a wild animal but the guys said that if they had known it was going to be that close then they may have thought twice about me being there.

After two more days of trekking, flora and fauna spotting, flicking off leeches, dodging the wild boar, navigating at night and insect spraying we had drunk the bar dry and found it was time to move on home.

During the flight back to Kota Kinabalu we had a clear sighting of Mount Kinabalu, the highest peak in South East Asia, and I stuck a note in the back of my mind to organise a climb one day.

We had time to visit a reproduction of an old native village with its activities and lifestyles preserved. It was built around an ancient graveyard which reflected the animalist religious beliefs of old. Borneo has never completely embraced Islam and many of the North Borneo peoples look back with nostalgia to the rule of the White Rajahs. Although politicians here vehemently deny it many Malaysians say that education, organisation, freedom of religion and way of life was far better under the British than now. Perhaps they are just being kind and polite to us.

Close by were the preserved remains of a cannibal headhunter's settlement complete with a houseful of human skulls. We were glad times had changed.

As we were boarding the MAS flight back to KL my daughter let out a great gasp of air. She told us that she had been an absolute bag of nerves the whole time and could not relax for an instant. She was glad she had done it but was glad it was over. Only now could she believe she was safe.

Obviously jungle trekking was not for the inexperienced or faint hearted.

A sort of sequel to this came about two years later.

My grandson's school heard about the adventure and in co-ordination with other schools, the UK Ministry of Education and Authorities in Malaysia organised a trip cum project for UK 14 year olds. My grandson, along with a number of other young guys and gals attended camping, trekking and basic survival courses in Britain and then came out to Sabah to live and work in an Orang Asli jungle village. There they stayed, did trekking, attended nature classes and with some adult technicians they built an all weather bridge across a river that had been promised to the people for years. The project was completed in six weeks—a fine example of international co-operation and goodwill. All the participants grew in stature and confidence and matured significantly.

Bali before the Bomb

We had seen quite a fair bit of Asia because although mainly on business trips we had taken advantage of days off to explore and tour the areas we were in.

However whenever family or friends visited we took time out to just be tourists.

We had been to various Malaysian holiday locations on several of the family's previous visits so we decided to branch out.

First up was my son and daughter, both from my second marriage, along with a young man son in law to be.

Daughter and young man were students at Hull University and were a couple. My son was two years older and working.

We went to Bali and stayed at the Sheraton in Nusa Dua.

This was a luxury hotel resort area and everything was priced accordingly so many gravitated to Kuta, a back packing centre, and Denpasar a shopping district, where prices were more reasonable.

Kuta beach was justifiably famous for its sunsets, but there are some beauties in Malaysia also. Perhaps the Malays are just too modest about their country. Malaysia is stunning.

However Bali really knew how to extract the maximum from tourists and as this was before the horrendous and murderous Bali bombings the place was very busy.

We did the standard jungle bungy jumps and I tried the surf board bungy as well. Good fun.

We then went up through Monkey Forest to the high hilltops for the start of the White Water Rapids Ride.

We stripped to swimming gear, grabbed helmet and flotation vests and attended the customary briefing. We were the intrepid trio. Dad, son and future son-in-law.

Six of us crew had to spread around the sides of an inflatable raft with the guide at the rear. He would pilot us through the rapids, steering, controlling and instructing as we went.

If anyone went overboard then the pilot would slow as much as possible by making us paddle backwards against the current and the nearest would lean out offering an oar to the swimmer.

Safety rules were simple—don't fall out??!!

If snakes were spotted then the call was, "snakes in the water."

If a crocodile was seen then a gun was fired, not at the croc, but in the air as a warning.

In both cases the cry was, "get out of the water," or, "now is not the time to fall in."

However it is Bali and the river was wild so many fell in.

The initiation to danger was swift. Within 30 metres of the start the river hit the first rapids with a sharp right turn.

Casualties there were high with the whole crew frequently being dumped in the river and the pilot having to resort to grabbing life vests where possible and lugging people unceremoniously back into the dinghy. Those negotiating this phase successfully, often prematurely, stood up to celebrate, only to go overboard or be bounced into the back of the raft with legs inelegantly flailing up in the air.

Modesty and caution were the key to survival.

As we possessed neither qualities then we could expect to get wet. We all lined up and at the word, "go" we raced for our dinghies.

We were third away, Australians and English against the world. A Middle East crew, who were second, missed the turn coming out of the first rapids, and all spilled into the river. We were so close behind that we couldn't miss them bouncing off the river wall and went right over the top of them turning their dinghy over in the process. They did recover but were out of the race.

We should have been concerned but we weren't—sadly we were jubilant. We were now second—only a Japanese crew a fair way in front. We just kept going hard but couldn't seem to close the gap. In fact a Chinese dinghy was slowly catching us.

In front and behind us the crews were finding ways through the rapids fairly successfully, few hold ups. We were getting desperate when we reached the falls at the halfway mark.

Here you take a break, jump into the water and shower under the falls.

Young man was a bit nervous due to snakes but suddenly said "oh what the hell," and jumped in. Even when we helpfully shouted out, "crocodile," he didn't turn a hair.

The river was in full flow, due to heavy rains, so at the urging of our pilot we scampered back up the nearest rapids, locked hands above our heads, crossed our legs, slid into the turbulent, crashing surf and did a human torpedo down through the rocks. We came out at the bottom like a cork out of a champagne bottle. This was exciting so we did it a few times until our pilot told us to lay off as it was quite dangerous and we shouldn't push our luck too far.

It was time to resume anyway. We set off again in the order we arrived but rather like after the safety car in Formula 1 we were bunched closer together.

We were all hurling good natured abuse at each other and it was tactical to break off and attack another dinghy that came too close in by drowning them with splashing paddles.

The Japanese pulled away with us close behind but no matter how we tried or manoeuvered we couldn't get past.

Then just before the finish we got lucky and took our chance. They momentarily lost attention and ran straight up on a rock at the last rapids. These were pretty formidable and they were falling all over the place as they tried to paddle and pull off.

Those in the water could hardly keep their footing on the rocks and barely succeeded in hanging on let alone wrestle the craft off.

We took another route through and passed them, gloating unashamedly.

They were further delayed picking up crew from the fast flowing river. You had to finish with a full boat. The video showed us celebrating just before the finish with the Japanese crew looking on in disarray behind.

I don't know why I felt so clever as I looked most unsteady. However we won.

Then you have to throw yourself in the water and go with the river flow over to the arrival landing stage. The dinghies were hauled out of the river, loaded onto trailers behind Land Rovers and driven back up the mountain to the start line. Your clothes and towels came down in the same truck so you could get dried off and dressed up in the facilities provided. We were certainly clean.

The next day I had booked up for a days diving off a northern beach. I am an experienced certified Padi Open Water Diver so was looking forward to it. I had told the hotel booking clerk not to fit me up with a cowboy outfit. Teaming up with irresponsible guys is bad news as they can be silly, dangerous show offs.

I was assured that this company was fine.

A converted Land Rover picked me up and I loaded my gear in the back and joined two other couples on the benches fitted along either side. They had never dived in the area we were going to so it was a new location experience for all.

We met our dive guide, kitted up and checked each other out. Being on my own I was to buddy dive with the dive leader. We were in a sandy bay with a reef about 100 metres out. The bay was enclosed on three sides by rocks filtering from behind down into the sea. I looked for the dive boat but was told that we didn't need one, we would be wading in for a few yards after which the bottom dropped sharply away down to the reef, a fall from 30 feet to 90 feet. Two atmospheres down to four.

Stay close and watch out for each other was the only other bit of pre-dive briefing. We waded in, snorkeled out and then submerged. Our first shock came seconds later when we saw dozens of deadly sea snakes rummaging through the rocks only feet away from us. They were the black and white banded type, highly poisonous but usually not aggressive. One or two curious ones came our way but fortunately decided we were posed no danger nor had any food value and sheered away.

The dive leader signalled us to follow him which we all too willingly did—obviously not very happy with him though.

We headed obliquely towards the reef placidly through shoals of fish, not of the exotic type but more like the fried dinner variety.

I just had time to notice a spot of turbulence ahead when we were caught up, spun round and shot along at a speed that we found difficult to control. This was our second shock.

Two of our party banged against rocks and were grazed while another had a bloody hand from fending himself off a jagged piece of coral. We all fought to stabilise ourselves but bumped and rubbed against rock, coral and each other.

One of our party traced a gap in the coral and we broke through into the sanctuary of the open sea. Boy were we relieved. We signalled to go up and when we surfaced we exploded. The guide was nowhere to be seen.

We were safe but sore. We had hit a powerful underwater current and would have to negotiate this on our own to get back to the beach. We had no further use for the Indonesian Dive Leader. We agreed he was either a complete clown or an utter dumbo or both.

We dived slowly back through the reef and went much deeper down. This did the trick. We went below the current and followed the reef on the inside of the lagoon, until we reached the other side of the bay. We worked our way into a 30 foot depth, surfaced and then snorkeled back towards our start but ending well away from the snake pit by the rocks.

When we emerged there was our guide, as large as life, looking a picture of innocence accompanied by an air of reproach.

"What's going on, what happened to you, what on earth did you think you were doing? I was worried when you went your own way, you mustn't do that."

We just stopped our big Australian surfer from smashing him in the face and instead gave him a piece of our minds. We were all experienced divers and had managed to handle the situation but a rookie would have been in very serious trouble. The lack of accurate pre-dive briefing was scandalous and the dive leader should have been banned.

We demanded our money back and threatened to sue but hey it's Indonesia, what do you expect? So we just dressed and went on our way determined to dive anywhere in the world but not Bali.

The Cameron Highlanders

Back in Malaysia the gang wanted to go Jungle trekking. They hadn't been before so we decided that the Cameron Highlands would be a good place to start.

This used to be a summer retreat for Europeans during the extreme heat of mid year, escaping to a higher altitude and cooler air. Parts of it had changed and others hadn't.

The Olde Smoke House was a replica Tudor style country house converted into a hotel and restaurant, relatively expensive but worth it for its charm and service. It was placed at a Y junction and on approaching it looked as though it was situated completely in the English countryside.

The town as such boasted a couple of hotels on the outskirts, a central bus station, some very poor restaurants and a number of second class souvenir and gift shops along with a drug store, masseurs and clinics. Not really a place to stay for long.

The road up was hairy, with landslides, hairpin bends and steep drops alternating with sheer rock sides. Halfway up were the Iskandar Falls dramatically roaring over the cliffs and thundering under the road bridge which carried the old highway to the top. This was a well known tourist spot and was a good place to take a break. We climbed the track beside the falls and at times edged our way out onto the slippery wet rocks. Many visitors came equipped with swimwear and dived into the various rock pools making sure the water didn't flush them over the edge or down some of the sink holes. We were not equipped.

The road did not go through to anywhere, just went up and down. On the way it passed Orang Asli villages and roadside stalls selling seasonal fruit.

The Orang Asli are made up of many indigenous tribes who were left behind in both the Colonial and Post Colonial eras. Most lived in a combination of bamboo, rattan and thatched huts without running water or sanitation. They found it difficult to maintain school attendance or regular work but of course still wanted a TV, motor bike and hand phone. They felt that they had been let down by government and representatives, which was mainly true but it was also a fact that many efforts to improve their lot failed because of their resistance to change and all that it meant.

We passed through the only town on the way up, a semi industrial place for logging and mining interests.

Higher up we visited the tea plantations that clung to the mountainsides on either side of the road. Here we got a great cuppa and did the tour, got the video and a few souvenir mugs.

The British didn't just take from their colonies, they also introduced many products when it suited themselves and the climate.

Malaya got rubber, palm oil, tea and pineapples as well as other flowers and vegetables. Not such a bad deal as they were all left in good enough condition after independence.

At these altitudes we always switched off the car aircon, otherwise it would blow up, heat up and steam up.

We checked into our hotel on the upper side of town and consulted our jungle trail maps. There was one particular spot north of the town which was a useful starting point for a number of treks. It started off on an easy path and after passing a waterfall it branched out into a selection of tracks of varying degrees of difficulty. The choice was yours.

There was one which led almost straight up the mountain with a sign that said, "not to be attempted." The jungle there was very dense.

Of course, as per my worst feelings, our two young men choose this one.

I never entered the jungle without a map, a compass, water, nutritional bars, slicker, backpack, first aid kit, walking stick and parang. None of it weighed very much but all of it was essential. The number of people who got lost, injured or panicky was high and the newspapers carried far too many stories of calamities brought on by lack of simple preparation.

Up we went, straight! We had to cling on in places, grabbing hold of bushes, trees and rocks in order to pull ourselves up. The heat and humidity was stifling and we were sweating buckets. There was no opportunity to use the parang to cut a way through. If we had stood up at all we would have fallen backwards, it was that steep.

We eventually reached an easier path which wound up a gentler slope to the crest. We broke through into a clearing, looked around but could see nothing, not even much sky. The jungle was so dense.

My son was looking back behind us when he stuttered in amazement, "thank you God, now I believe!"

Emerging from the jungle behind us, on the path we had taken was a young, tall, blond, blue-eyed, golden goddess.

"Are you real?" we exclaimed.

"Sure I am," she replied with a charming accent.

She was Dutch, was trekking with her boyfriend, had seen us strike out and up and had decided to follow—just like that.

Her boyfriend had decided that he would prefer a pint in a pub and had turned back leaving her to go on her own. We could just imagine the conversation.

Of course we English boys felt smug and superior and showed off a bit, well more than a bit actually and lost our heads a little. Without too much thought we told her that we were not going back down the track we had used to come up but were going to cut our own path through going down.

"Great," she said, "I'll join you."

Oh!!

We set off boldly.

We chose an area less steep and not so dense, but even so it was tough going. I led the way and we saw monkeys, snakes, insects and got a shock when we accidentally caught hold of well camouflaged stick insects and tree snakes on overhanging branches and bushes. No leeches fortunately at that altitude.

The boys were a little worried as to our whereabouts but I pointed out we had come straight up and were going straight down. They were only partially re-assured when we reached a steep gully and I pointed out that this would be a torrent, not a small stream when it rained and would eventually join up with the river and waterfall below. The goddess was unperturbed and remained cool throughout.

The side of the ravine we were on was impassable so we went a little way up to where some trees had crashed down and formed a natural bridge. We crossed and lowered ourselves down into the gully. Here the way was easier and we eventually heard the sound of rushing water and shortly emerged onto the main path.

We were dusty, scratched, bitten, tired and scruffy but elated.

We were full of ourselves.

We got back to our car, said reluctant goodbyes to our goddess and let her go back to her boyfriend.

We saw them later eating outside a restaurant and the two boys went out of their way to go and say hello. They swarmed over the girl, joked about the boyfriend's pint and were telling him of the bravery of his girlfriend. It did not take a Pinkerton detective to realise the boyfriend was not happy and the girl had a fixed smile on her face.

I rescued them from a deteriorating situation and we went on our way. When we saw them again later the boyfriend steered the girl in another direction.

A doomed love affair I thought.

Simply Sarawak

E arly in 1998 we decided to visit Sarawak in North Borneo for the first time

We stayed in the capital city Kuching, which was really only the size of a small town. It was still rural and unspoiled. Amongst the usual small shops, offices and buildings it had a central market, old Colonial offices, a garrison fort guarding the river access to the town and various religious temples. There were taxis and ferries crossing over the river on the other side of which stood the old house of the White Rajah. This was the house of James Brook, the first White Rajah, built for his wife Margaret in 1870. Theirs is a remarkable story and one worth reading.

We rented a 4x4 as we really needed an off road vehicle to tackle the difficult terrain which we were going to have to negotiate.

We left the main road and headed along rutted, bumpy tracks until we found the fishing and hunting village on a river which basically supplied the only way in to the jungle area we wished to explore. The solution was a fast, slim, shallow craft with an outboard motor.

We headed out to sea, crossing shallows in the estuary, frequently needing the outboard to be lifted up and paddles to be used. Once clear of the shallows and sandbanks we picked up speed, hugged the coastline and then turned into the mouth of another river. We coasted upriver until we reached a small village of wooden longhouses perched on the edge of a steep slope. This was the furthest you could get by transport, the rest was on foot. We trekked along a well kept path, passing a family of monkeys playing amongst the trees and foliage. They are natural thieves, daring, cheeky and quite dangerous if challenged.

We eventually reached the Rangers office, the only element of civilisation for miles and obtained our licence to enter the interior.

This was not for the faint hearted as a notice on the left side of the building said, in two languages :-

"The Government of North Borneo takes no responsibility for any persons proceeding beyond this point with respect to injury, mental stress, breakdown, trauma and death."

Besides the path was another notice which said :-

"Danger, beware of falling coconuts!"

No mention of landslips, falling trees, leopards, tigers, snakes and elephants, as well as leeches and poisonous insects to name but a few of the hazards.

We headed for the hills. In my mind I wanted to pick up an old headhunters cannibal trail that rumour had it was marked out by human skulls at various intervals.

We started to climb, easy at first but steadily getting steeper.

We came up to a small rest place with a tree trunk seat facing out over the jungle towards the distant sea. My intrepid partner decided that this was far enough for her, she would sit and meditate while I carried on with the Dr. Livingstone part.

So I did.

Reaching the summit at last, puffing a little, I could see the track running clearly along in front of me.

I followed it for some time, with everything peaceful and quiet. There were none of the usual jungle sounds. This part would never make a good movie as the movie makers love their stereotyped sounds. There were none.

Then I spotted it. Yep, it was a human skull, stuck in a tree. It was naturally very decrepit, having been there for years (well at least I hoped so??!!) with one branch actually growing through the top. I found others at irregular intervals in similar states of disrepair.

I was satisfied, I had been where few had been before, or so I kidded myself until I went a few yards too far. There in front of me was a boardwalk stretching into the distance covering a large area of marshy ground. So I wasn't a lone traveller after all. But it was quiet.

I returned, luckily giving an early warning shout to my partner as I descended. She was in a bit of a nervous state. While sitting peacefully meditating she had decided to read the Rangers pamphlet. It contained many warnings, particularly mentioning care if the jungle was quiet, as stalkers made no noise, only faint rustling noises. That day there was a strong breeze so the whole jungle was full of faint rustling noises. Her imagination had got the better of her, she was very jumpy, and if I had not yelled out before joining her I reckon she would have fainted.

We made our way down, explored out to the shoreline and then went back to check out with the Rangers. Our boat was waiting at the riverside village and shot us back to our starting point. A good day.

Mixed up Myanmar

Going to Myanmar at the turn of the century was a different kettle of fish. I did not want to be seen to support the obnoxious regime in any way shape or form but I must admit I was curious. The opportunity came by way of vacancies on the Orient Express Steamer sailing up and down the Irrawaddy river, a ten day trip, The Road to Mandalay Tour. We took it!

I had a bad start. Just before leaving for KLIA early in the morning I decided to wash up the breakfast dishes. I was distracted with the packing and forgot I had left the water running in the sink.

I remembered a little too late. The sink was full and overflowing. I dived to pull out the plug and switch off the tap and just made it before slipping on the slippery wet floor. I crashed down hitting the side of my face and my nose on the kitchen units. I was bruised and bloody.

A quick repair job left me with a blackening eye and bloodied plasters on my nose and lip. A great way to present myself before airport security and the immigration officers of a military dictatorship.

They didn't turn a hair when they saw me, probably mild damage if you are used to maintaining power by force!

We had flown into Yangon, which used to be called Rangoon before the ruling junta changed it along with the country's name from Burma to Myanmar. Many said that this was illegal and refused to accept the new and maintained the old.

I had promised before arrival to be a good boy and maintain a neutral political position. I would do my best.

In fact it turned out to be easy because the ordinary people were really great.

It so often happens around the world that the lower classes are the salt of the earth and the leaders are crap.

On the principle that ignorance is bliss and knowledge is dangerous the country's leaders kept the people in ignorance of pretty well everything. They had been told that it was the world's fault that tourists stayed away and had no idea of the travel restrictions in place making visits difficult. We in fact were the last party to arrive before a clampdown. The regime was afraid of negative publicity.

We seemed to be allowed to mix and roam freely around the city and chatted to men and women who were eager to speak English. We were often overshadowed by huge posters in two languages warning citizens not to be unpatriotic and critical whether in private or in public. In other words, "keep your mouths shut!"

We of course visited the tourist sights including the Shwedagon Buddhist temple and others.

After a couple of days we flew up country to Mandalay to pick up our cruiser.

We made the obligatory visits to markets pursued by vendors desperate for sales. No one wanted local currency, everyone wanted greenbacks.

In one store we found antique ivory carvings, quite legal, alongside modern bone animals and figures. It's a great pity that irresponsible, criminal poachers and traders have made the ivory trade disreputable. Animals die and if their skins or tusks can be made into articles of beauty then they become in some small way immortal.

It's disgusting that animals are killed because some pathetic Asian man can't get it up any more and believes that a piece of a dead rhino or tiger can help him get a hard on. I reckon that they would be better off eating donkey brains in an attempt to upgrade their intelligence.

Hunting animals illegally and killing purely for profit plays into the hands of those who always go to the other extreme and inevitably take great delight in banning something altogether. Their small mindedness cannot conceive of the fact that rarity increases value and desirability and produces the opposite to whatever it was that they intended. Strict policing and enforcing is much better than banning.

We admired a couple of small pieces.

We told the shop owner that we would purchase them on the way back but he insisted that we take them on credit and pay our tour guide on the cruiser before we left. We thought this unusually trusting but he said that we were English and unlike others the word of an Englishman was his bond.

I liked him!

We got our first sight of the boat and fell in love with it. It was either an original steamer or a clever reproduction. It was long and sleek. Low in the water with three decks. The cabins were on the lower deck with portholes just above the water line. The main deck held the dining room, small theatre, recreation area, cafe and a rear canopied lounge.

The upper deck was really all about rest and observation.

It was broad in the beam and proved to be very stable even in strong cross currents.

We boarded along with a fair amount of fellow travellers but the boat was nowhere near full.

Our guide was a young Burmese, British educated with a scarcely noticeable accent. He was a Buddhist and he was so serene, calm and laid back that at times he seemed to be hardly with us at all. He would speak so softly and act so gently that it made us feel guilty if criticising his slow action.

However his way seemed to work fine as the organisation, if basic, worked very well.

All meals were on board, with most tours being in the afternoon or evening.

The ship tied up every night, getting under way in the early morning.

The first morning I woke up I looked out of the porthole and had to blink my eyes. Swimming strongly up river against the current were dozens of snakes. They were making slow progress with the heavy flow going against them causing ripples and a wake around each one. It took them some time before they passed the length of the boat but they were still going strong as they disappeared out of sight. Goodness knows where they were going or why and none of the locals knew either other than that they did it every day. Perhaps they did it until they were tired and then turned, shouted yippee, and just let themselves rush back down the river with no effort at all. Sort of a snake surf ride to work up an appetite before breakfast.

We went up on deck for our breakfast and saw a sight that had probably remained unchanged for hundreds of years. Long slim wooden craft were criss crossing the river powered by long oars or single sails. Some were carrying vegetables and packages, others carried people dressed in colourful sarongs, while others trawled the water with long nets strung out in a line behind.

On the shore women were washing clothes in the river, first wringing them out then bashing the daylights out of them on nearby rocks before spreading them out to dry. Others were fishing with nets and bamboo rods.

On the opposite bank, set up on top of a hill was a huge golden Pagoda surrounded by a temple.

After our meal, the ship's horn hooted loudly a few times. We then cast off and got underway. All of us lined the sides of the boat, feeling privileged and important, dying to wave and show off to the locals. They took absolutely no notice at all. We were quite disappointed.

Our guide explained that they lived on a few dollars a day and only relaxed after a hard days work. They had earned nothing that early so didn't want to be bothered with trivial diversions.

As far as we knew we had never been trivial diversions before but for sure we had been firmly put in our place.

We were to see similar early morning scenes, minus the snakes, up and down the river every day.

One morning we were dragged up at the crack of dawn and told to get a move on or else we would miss "it."

"It" was a walk to a nearby village. Lined up along the road were a series of stalls manned by local women. On top of lightweight trestle tables were cooking bowls containing rice and vegetables alongside plastic containers full of water.

We became a bit worried as we wondered if this was to be our breakfast but it was not for us. We were the audience.

Shortly a long line of saffron clad buddhist monks appeared holding two bowls, one for food, the other for water.

This was to be their first meal of the day.

The villagers were dirt poor by our standards but provided two meals a day, every day, for the monks from the local monastery. This one at daybreak and the other just before noon. After midday the monks could beg no more and must spend the rest of the day in prayer and meditation.

No true buddhist monk would engage in begging after midday and would certainly not engage in the sale of so called blessed or lucky trinkets. They had renounced earthly desires, including women, so as to be able to concentrate on higher spiritual things and good luck to them. Whatever works for them. It's no good for me though. The more I miss out the more curious I become. Earthly knowledge intrigues me and we know so little I can't waste precious time on dithering about pretending I have discovered some inner mystery that has defied human intelligence for ever. We practice enough self deception every day without adding to it while over exercising a solitary imagination. But then I'm just an ignorant South London brat, so they're probably right.

We returned to the boat all pretending to be terribly impressed and some even tried to discuss it seriously amongst themselves and the guide. For me I couldn't believe the selflessness and devotion of the villagers who gave up so much for others. Working so hard for so little for those who didn't work. Much the same as workers under capitalism I suppose.

The main stop was at the ancient capital of Bagan. Hundreds of years ago this had been a great and vibrant city under the Pagan Kings but wars with Siam, Vietnam, China and India had finally caused the demise of a great empire. The city dwellings were made of wood and burned in a great fire leaving behind hundreds of temples and pagodas within decaying walls.

Most of our travelers were feeling a little jaded and decided that they would relax on the boat. The thought of a ruined city occupied only by pagodas, snakes and rats did not get them going. So they stayed.

There was going to be no organised tour which suited me fine.

The place pecked away at that curiosity of mine. I just had to go.

I walked up the hill away from the river, climbing along an overgrown track with thick jungle on either side. It wound slowly up and around until I came to a gate. Nature reclaims its own from humans so quickly that I almost missed the fact that it was set in a high thick wall.

I thought that the top of the wall would make a good lookout so I looked around to see where and how I could get up it.

Behind me I heard the sound of a horse's hooves and squeaking wheels.

I turned round and there was a smart young horse pulling a very old buggy.

Sitting on the front seat of the buggy, holding a long thin whip was a middle aged Burmese man, smiling at me and saying, "good morning," in very good English.

I said, "hi, how are you?"

He replied perfectly politely that he would be much better if I hired him, his horse and his buggy for a tour.

I declined and said that I preferred to explore on my own.

He said that I wouldn't see much unless someone like him showed the way.

However I shrugged and said that I would prefer to try and manfully climbed the wall. From the top I expected to see it all but couldn't see a thing. When I climbed a small tower I could see even less. Nature and the jungle had won.

I climbed back down to find the man, his horse and his buggy still there waiting patiently.

I thought, "there may be something to this Buddhist approach after all."

I hired him.

He turned the horse and carriage to face back the way he had come, helped me up to sit beside him, and we trotted off along a small road running round the ruins of the city wall which had completely disintegrated in places.

We stopped at a well worn gap in the trees, climbed down and left the horse to munch away happily at the rich vegetation beside the road. There was a brake on the buggy but the driver said that there was no need to secure the cart or the horse. Everyone knew who they belonged to and the horse would be perfectly content where he was.

We set off through the trees.

The walk was short.

We came out on the edge of a flat plain completely covered with pagodas and temples as far as the eye could see. It was totally uninhabited with not a living being in sight. It was staggering and also disturbing because although such an incredible spectacle it was just so desolate.

My guide told me he would show me something that most tourists and others didn't know. Although you could enter pagodas and temples and even climb up some of them the bigger one's had no apparent way up. He would show me a secret passage hidden behind one of the Buddhas in the largest one and I could get right to the top. The view would be fantastic.

Sure enough, in the very darkest, narrowest space behind one of the idols, there was a tiny passage leading to some narrow stairs. I squeezed up the stairs, obviously built for smaller bodies than Europeans and finally emerged into the daylight. I moved along the wide ledge circling the dome taking in the sights.

Laid out before and below me was what would have been a view of the whole city except there wasn't one. As far as the eye could see in any direction the area was covered with temples. Between them were large open spaces covered in undergrowth which on rare occasions allowed a glimpse of ruins underneath.

The site was marvellous but there was little to show of the riches and glory of a past empire bringing to my mind Wordworth's poem "Ozymandias."

All the domes of the pagodas then would have been covered in gold leaf shivering and shining in the sunlight, instead they were crumbling away to dust just like all empires whether famous, physical or financial.

I came back down to meet up with my new found friend who had that 'I told you so' expression on his face.

We went back to the horse and carriage and moved on to the ruins of a monastery close to a small village. He explained that so much of Burma was in decay due to the government doing everything for the army and nothing for the people. He smiled and said that frankly everyone thought that they had been better off under the British. At least the British had not colonised their own people, only others. The so called independent previously colonial nations were being cheated and exploited by their own leaders to a far greater degree than the earlier colonial masters. The biggest issues seemed to be brutality, corruption, cronyism, administration and education.

I had heard so much of this over the years that although I thought at first they were being either polite or sarcastic, I had come to realise that perhaps they were serious. Especially after India's 50 years independence celebration when they officially paid a generous tribute to the UK.

Of course India and Malaysia had been led by men and women of vision who had not been so obsessed with power that they would betray their own country to gain it. They wanted the English out without letting another country in. Unfortunately Burma had Aung San and Ba Maw and China had leaders such as Pu Yi who would change sides so often in their own interest rather than that of their country that they couldn't and shouldn't have been trusted.

Well anyway Pu Yi was jailed, Aung San was shot and Ba Maw, although jailed several times, died of old age.

However History has a strange way of playing funny tricks. Aung San had a most remarkable daughter who married an Englishman and has over the years shown self sacrifice and a love for her country and people while denouncing violence and betrayal. We can only stand, support and admire.

India of course had it's own traitor in Chandra Bose but he apparently died of burns in a plane crash at the end of the war before he could do any more damage and unbelievably managed to salvage his reputation.

Anyone who could so easily be fooled by the false promises of thugs and murderers in the barbaric Japanese Imperial Army was hardly suited to lead a country to freedom and independence.

Fortunately many countries generally found the right leaders at the right time.

While walking amongst the ruins I heard a gentle voice calling.

At the edge of the monastery wall was a young girl gesturing and urging me to go over to her. I ignored her at first but she carried on calling. My guide came over and said it was ok to talk so I went over to her.

She said hello, how are you in presentable English, then asked me to come to her mummy's shop. It was nearby and nothing would cost me more than a dollar.

I tactfully turned down the offer and told her that I wasn't in the mood for buying.

She looked disconsolate so I asked her how she could speak such good English. She told me her mummy had said that if she learnt to speak English she would never again be as poor as they were so she attended classes after school held by an old man in the village who did it free to help the children.

I told her that she was very lucky to have a clever mother and a wise old man.

I asked her anyway why one dollar.

She said because every dollar made a difference.

God the poor ordinary people on this planet tug at your heart strings far more naturally than the selfish so called, successful smart asses who complain at every twist and turn.

I told her that I had to get back, time was running out, but if a dollar made a difference then there were two to take back to her mummy. She took the notes, looked at them in amazement, thanked me very seriously and skipped away.

My friend regarded me quizzically, shook his head, smiled and said, "it's true about the English, you are a good man."

I told him that occasionally I had my moments but they were too few and far between.

He took me back to the path above the river and the boat allowing me to drive most of the way.

I got down, thanked him very much, and asked him how much I owed him.

He hesitated and asked me if I thought five dollars would be too much.

I gave him ten telling him that he deserved it for putting his life in my hands when he let me drive. Was that okay?

He told me that it was as much as he usually earned in a week and the first thing he would do was to go to the temple, make an offering to the Buddha, pray and thank him for bringing him such a fruitful day and kind friend.

For heavens sake, when you look at the puffed up pompous, self important gangster Generals and then look at their people you wonder why there is so little justice in the world.

All over the planet you can see that the ordinary people do not in any way get the leaders they deserve. The leaders of course say they do. Well they would, wouldn't they?

Perhaps they're right.

The next day a shopping tour was organised in the more modern town of Pagan but it was only modern in comparison to the ruins of the old city. The tourist market was the same the world over.

Local products which used to be hand made were being imported cheaply in increasingly large quantities from factories in China smuggled across borders almost impossible to police thoroughly.

Consequently local jobs and skills were being lost as people turned to service industries instead of manufacturing.

One day there would have to be a return to economic fundamentals, and it would not be painless, but it was not going to be soon it seemed.

There was little on show that anyone wanted so the merchants did not have the bonanza day they expected. We were a huge disappointment to them.

We returned to the boat which sailed for a few hours in the early evening before tying up for the night beneath a sheer rock face that led up several hundred feet to a temple built high up precariously overhanging the river.

That was our tour for the next day.

The temple itself was organised for visitors and it was difficult to recognise the same religion as that practised by the humble monks who went down to the village at dawn each day for a bowl of rice, a few vegetables, a piece of cloth or maybe a pair of sandals.

These monks were eager to please, eager to bless and over eager to sell a trinket that had been blessed and was sure to bring good luck.

For a couple of dollars we were allowed to swing back a big log and let it go to sound a big sonorous boom on a giant bell.

The sound echoed and resonated down the river and I could just imagine all the people in the villages hugging the riverside thinking, "oh hell there goes another few wasted dollars that we will never see. Can't those stupid foreigners think of doing anything useful for a change?"

Or perhaps not, perhaps they liked the sound.

From a patio we were able to see far up and down the river and across country. Below us our boat looked no bigger than a matchbox toy and I think we were all relieved to be going down after such a stiff climb up.

Our reward was an on board culture show.

Having seen so many I am no longer a fan.

I am one of those peasants who take the piss out of the English Morris Dancers so I am rarely in the mood to see a band of young girls in strange attire acting out throwing seeds in the fields to an accompaniment of clanging tin cans. They are nearly always followed by a gang of young men trying to impress the young women, who are followed by old women reaping the harvest, and so it goes on.

Our guide was incredible. He would sit on a chair besides the stage, totally serene and immobile, standing up to announce the next act in an expressionless voice. Perhaps he had also seen too many.

However we had to endure—it was obligatory tourist fare.

Some of our crowd seemed to enjoy it. I bet they liked Morris Dancers!

Give me the fantastic exuberant Russian Cossacks anytime. They certainly keep you awake.

We were nearing the end of our tour and more difficult jobs had to be undertaken such as paying the bar bill and deciding on who to tip and how much.

As we were packing there was a knock on our cabin door. It was the guide who asked if we would like to settle up the bill for the Ivory figures. No need to find our way into town. He would go, no problem. So that's what we did. We had paid and he would get his commission.

As we disembarked and picked up coaches to go our different ways we all swore in deadly earnest to keep in touch with the friends for life we had met on board.

Of course it never happened.

One hell of a tour though.

A few days later the government clamped down on visitors as someone in the foreign press had slipped in as a tourist and written a critical report.

Murderous gangster Generals in charge of vast armies were terrified of one slim, determined woman with a lot of guts leaving her home and talking to anyone and everyone. She had left her understanding and supportive English husband and children to pursue the cause of freedom in her native country.

Who will history remember I wonder?

My money is on the great Lady.

Let's hope she lives up to it.

Myanmar was off the list and would remain so for quite some time.

Mounting Mount Kinabalu

I had often had it in the back of my mind that I needed to climb Mount Kinabalu in the state of Sabah for the age old non-reason— that it was there!!

Kinabalu was the highest mountain in South East Asia attaining a height of 4,095 metres or 13, 342 feet.

I thought that as I had "done" Snowdon and Ben Nevis in the UK and Gunung Macinggang in Langkawi plus a bit of rock climbing in Cheddar Gorge and the Lake District then why not Kinabalu? I conveniently ignored the fact that it just happened to be four times higher.

Being a failed family man I decided to attempt to redeem myself a little. I put out feelers to my sons and grandsons in the UK to see if they fancied joining me on a possible bonding "Jolly Boys Outing" climbing Mount Kinabalu.

Within hours what had been just a feeler and a possibility had become a firm yes and I had a contingent of two sons and two grandsons ready, willing and able. It was no good telling them it was just an idea I had—they were on their way, flights, itineraries and back packs already organised.

I stimulated their enthusiasm by promising that I would provide and carry cans of Lager in my pack to drink and celebrate with on reaching the summit. Not for one second did we doubt we could do it.

While awaiting their arrival I studied up a lot on Kinabalu and what was needed so as to be prepared. This was just as well because once the lads arrived it was all get up and go. It was, "don't bother us with details, let's just get on with it." Oh boy, the joys of youth.

We flew by MAS to Kota Kinabalu and hired two taxis to take us and our luggage to the base mountain lodge where we would check in and the next day start our climb complete with guide.

The taxi drivers were confident that we would get there in good time even though the vehicles seemed to labour while still on the flat.

Soon after we reached the foothills and we began to climb it was chug chug for a while, then it was chuck it in for a while to let the engine cool. Then it was panic as we had lost the other taxi which should have been right behind us. We stopped and waited.

After some time it came up wheezing more than a sixty year old smoker and stopped beside us. We were worried as after a short chat amongst themselves the drivers told us that the cabs were not going to make it and suggested that we should pay them and they would leave us with our luggage and they would go back and send a van out for us.

We countered with a few suggestions of our own which convinced the drivers that if they wished to continue to live long and happy lives then we should all rest awhile, we should all cool down, including the taxis, and that we should then go slowly on and complete the journey.

Well we made it eventually even though we could have picked daisies on the way.

We paid up, checked in, registered, and met our guide. After a few wisecracks, which the poor guy must have heard a million times before about him not looking much like Sherpa Tensing, we allowed him to check our kit, and make sure we were well and properly prepared with the necessary equipment to proceed the next day.

We had dinner and then turned in for an early night. We shared inter-connecting rooms so it took a while for every one to settle down and tire of the inevitable jokes and pranks.

The grandsons ran about and wrestled, played silly buggers in the shower, then arm wrestled, then ran about until one of them decided to run, leap in the air and crash down backwards onto the mattress on his bed. These were lads used to soft home comforts not mountain lodges. The mattress was wafer thin and the bed rock hard. He crashed down all right. For a while there was silence as he tried to get some air back into his lungs. Still not speaking he investigated slowly to see if he was still intact, quietly pulled the blankets over himself and didn't say another word. We all managed to get some sleep.

Our party consisted of myself, my eldest son David in his early forties—a chain smoker and practised trencherman, Tarik my son in his twenties—a non smoker and social drinker and my two teenage grandsons Lee and James, who, if you believed their stories, were already alcoholics, drug addicts and pimps who feared nothing and no man. Oh yeah!

We breakfasted early and reported to our own Sherpa Tensing.

Everything was checked, we had our passes and certification, backpacks with necessities and lots of enthusiasm so off we set— DOWNHILL. Yes, actually downhill which worried me as it meant we were going backwards before going forwards. Any downhill walk meant a longer climb back up and to climb over 4,000 metres was way back up enough anyway.

All climbers are recommended to leave the greater part of their luggage at the lodge so as to reduce the load to be carried up the mountain. In accordance with conservationist requirements and the laws of gravity everything that goes up must come down and the only way up or down is on foot. No cable cars, mountain railways, helicopters or pack horses are available.

The aim is to reach the summit in two stages. Stage one gets you to the base camp just above the tree line. The number of hours or days this takes depends on your fitness and determination. There you rest, eat and sleep until waking at 2am then you charge straight off for the summit in order to be there just in time to catch the sunrise at around 6.30 am.

First however you have to reach the base camp.

Once we passed through the gate which marks the official entry to the mountain reserve park we soon began to climb in earnest.

At first the route wound its way up a not too difficult track but the higher we climbed the steeper it became. It varied from being dirt steps, to staggered footholds, to just a solid climb up a very steep, seemingly never ending bank where we stuck our feet and hands into slots worn well into the mountainside by hundreds of climbers who had gone before. Just when we felt we really had had enough of it we stumbled onto steps again which led up to a small clearing containing a bench and a first aid hut. These emergency stops were placed at intervals on the route, which we disdainfully disregarded at first, but were grateful to reach in the later stages of the climb.

The view was restricted due to the fact that the vegetation was thick all around due to being in the tropics, even at 9,000 feet. Such lush growth would not be found at that height in Europe.

Hardy porters carried everything in very heavy packs on their backs secured by a cap or band around their foreheads. They handled everything that was needed by official occupants and visitors to the base camp and check points. They carried consumables and equipment up and waste products down. They were as tough as nails. Men as well as women undertook these journeys nearly every day, all at their own steady pace. It was a bit off putting to be resting, gasping for air, rubbing aching legs, and seeing these guys coming resolutely past, relentlessly tackling the toughest slopes in a routine manner—for them just an every day affair.

At the beginning I had impressed on the younger ones to stay close and work as a team, not as individuals. Youthful egos however got the better of them and they changed the rules into a race for the top. They disappeared using other guides as and when they caught up to other parties and left myself and eldest son David with our guide to plod steadily on.

All the family had expressed concern over David attempting anything as strenuous as mountain climbing due to him apparently being a bit of a couch potato as well as a heavy drinker and smoker.

Well at every rest stop he was glad of a break, not because of exhaustion, but because he needed a ciggie. At every possible opportunity he lit up a cigarette, took a sip from the hip flask lodged in the back of his old jeans, puffed away for a while then stubbed out the remains with his dilapidated trainers.

Much to the guide's concern and relief he picked up the dog end and put it in his pocket and being well fortified, after a few minutes, he was ready to go on.

Other climbers, all dressed up, some dressed for Everest, trying desperately to look as professional as possible, looked in amazement at a casual David, as they staggered, puffing badly, up to the resting place.

That's my boy!!

I took a great delight in pointing out that perhaps we all took things far too seriously and should take a leaf out of my son's book—exercise less, smoke more, drink a lot and break out occasionally. Such comments did not go down too well. Some climbers got a bit abusive and personal. Obviously people who had problems of their own whether on or off the mountain—no sense of humour or the ridiculous.

So ever onwards and upwards we went with our guide offering encouragement along the way. He told us, when we were close to despair, that the hardest part was behind us, only for us to find out that it was still in front of us. We soon gave up asking, "how much further?" and saved our breathe for the struggle.

Those going up frequently had to pass those coming down and the news was mixed. Some, on the way back down said, "marvelous, keep going, it's worth it," while others suffering badly exclaimed, "we just want to get this torture over with now."

One woman was crying and telling us to turn round and go back, shouting, "just get off this damned mountain!" She hadn't reached the top.

Our three young men, who had been well in advance of David and I, were at last suffering.

Although still well ahead of us, they had finally come to a standstill, and were asking those passing that if they found they were close to the base camp up above would they please shout back down to tell them. They would then revive and keep going but if they heard nothing then they would have to take a break and rest awhile.

No more than 30 seconds later came a voice from immediately above them telling them that the base camp was in sight no more than 200 metres away. The lads weren't sure whether this was a leg pull or not but decided to go with it and after a 100 metres easier climb they saw the base camp. Utter relief for them but David and I were nearly two hours away.

By the time we made it they had rested and eaten and were full of themselves.

The scenery had changed dramatically over the last 1,000 metres. Rain forest, trees and plants, including the famous insect eating plant, The Monkey Pot, had been largely left behind and we were now on solid rock, which looked and was very volcanic. The black rock extended unevenly all around and went up in overlapping layers towards the summit.

We sometimes spotted the highest peak way up through breaks in the cloud before darkness fell but it still looked a long way off. We also caught glimpses of the towns outlined like toy towns thousands of feet below, but they were more often obscured by the clouds which clung to the mountain in dense layers beneath us.

We were over 10,000 feet high and a number of people were suffering from altitude sickness. This varied from little more than normal tiredness to sickness and fainting. Some just couldn't face going on and looked forward to a good night's sleep and a measured descent in the morning. Two Japanese girls fainted face down into their plates of food and, not surprisingly, couldn't be encouraged to go to the summit. Many others found that the base camp was their limit and turned back immediately after a light meal and short rest. They refused to spend a night on the mountain. We wished them luck as some of the way down would have to be made in the dark.

For those of us who wanted to go all the way the aim was to reach the summit in two stages. We were to rest at the base camp, eat and sleep until rising at 2 am. Then we would charge straight off for the summit just in time to see the sunrise at around 6 am.

The first stage was to climb up to a check point through which every one had to pass, stop and be recorded whether going up or down. Any one failing to report was considered lost or dead and search parties were sent out. The mountain, as with all mountains, had claimed its fair share of fatalities over the years.

After being checked you were free to carry on up or down.

The conditions in the base camp were adequate but primitive. Males and females slept separately in shared dormitories and had to use communal toilets. Centrally heated radiators gave out some warmth but were smothered in wet clothes that we were all trying to dry. Between rain, mist and humidity every one was soaking wet. We had left the rainforest behind but not the rain.

In spite of the noise of people arriving and departing we managed to snatch a few hours of sleep and were up in time to collect our torches which fitted on our heads like miner's lamps. We set off on schedule in the pitch dark at 2 am. We were told emphatically to follow the rope and use it to climb where necessary. If you lost sight of the rope then you had to stop and blow a whistle to attract a guide. On no account were you to try to find your way back on your own as doing so could well put you in the wrong place. The wrong place could mean plunging down thousands of feet in the dark—it had happened before and was a bad idea.

So we found the rope and dutifully followed it to aid our upward progress and to climb where needed. At one particular difficult spot my grandsons decided to be helpful. After a 25 metre climb on the rope they looked back down to encourage me, telling me to hang on and where to put my hands and feet. Of course they were looking straight down and I was looking straight up so I couldn't see a damned thing as their torches were shining directly into my eyes completely negating any help they were giving. A short heated discussion ensued whereby we decided that we were all capable of sorting things out for ourselves.

We reached the checkpoint and were speedily tagged and listed after which the three younger ones raced ahead again—this time non stop for the top.

By then the darkness was less intense and the sky was just beginning to lighten with the false dawn which spurred us on passing between lesser mountain peaks slowly coming into view on our way up.

It had become a question of a hard sloping slog upwards, just making sure we put one foot in front of the other before having to hitch a hefty climb straight up. Then a slog again—always up.

Eventually silhouetted against the skyline we could see the main peak not too far away and we could hear my noisy grandsons yodelling their triumph at reaching their goal, their voices echoing through the mountains.

We clambered and scrambled up the remaining rocks and stood on the summit just as dawn was breaking—and it was incredible—truly spectacular.

Before us traces of mist and cloud floated between the sharp black shapes of the surrounding peaks against a background of a flaming red, orange and golden dawn.

Behind us we could see the way back, looking down through a high valley, past the dull volcanic strata to the tree line far below still in shadow.

As the blazing sun lifted higher in the sky so the shadows started to give way to daylight.

We watched a new day emerge.

Then we amazed the other climbers by breaking out the cans of lager and celebrating. Their faces were a picture—they couldn't believe we had the dedication to carry an extra load so far up and down (no waste could be left behind). The beer was deliciously cool because of the altitude and seemed extra bubbly. We spread a few cans of joy around which was greatly appreciated.

Also it was pointed out that every one else was dressed for Everest whereas we were dressed for a mere chilly spring day in England.

The climate to us was mild and with the climb making us warm we had even stripped off a little. We were feeling hot, they were feeling cold and they couldn't believe it.

We captured what we needed on video and still camera, enjoyed a bit more of our moment of glory and started on our return.

At one stage I was ahead. Having come through an awkward stage on the rope I turned to video Lee emerging from around the side of a rock face following me on his way down. I called out to him that he was on video and should make it look difficult whereupon he told me in no uncertain terms to shut up as it was already difficult enough.

On reaching the check point we were "detagged" and eventually arrived at the base camp where we had breakfast before setting off back down in earnest towards the ground lodge.

We set a cracking pace and were moving at some speed, allowing gravity to do the work. However it was a little too fast for me as I slipped and fell, rolling down some metres before coming up hard against a rock. I suffered no real damage other than to my self-esteem. Then my legs went all wobbly, waving about all over the place. Apparently this was due to the altitude and lack of oxygen in the muscles. Going up had challenged me but not beaten me—going down had reduced me to looking like a drunkard. The loss of control was hilarious but dangerous so the guide obtained a pair of ski poles from a first aid hut which did the job and allowed me to regain some control.

We were dropping sharply down, making progress.

Then it rained—in buckets.

This was hard enough on those going down but sheer murder for those going up. We encouraged them best we could which made me feel good until one woman remarked that if I could do it, being disabled, then she should be able to do it being fully fit.

I nearly threw the ski poles away but our guide sensibly talked me out of it.

The three musketeers had pressed on ahead leaving David and the guide to look out for poor old grandad whose progress was painfully slow and not at all good for their image.

Slowly, as we descended to lower levels, I started to regain control again, and on arriving on relatively flat ground I jettisoned the ski poles, walking more or less normally back to the lodge.

On returning to our rooms we showered, changed clothing, collapsed on the beds and slept soundly until the evening. We were done in.

When we woke up and stood up I had my revenge. None of us could move—we were all so stiff and sore. The short journey from the rooms down a steep slope to the dining hall for dinner more closely resembled the progress of casualties in a disaster movie rather than the triumphal return of successful climbers of the highest mountain in South East Asia.

We returned the next day to KL. We still all had a bit of trouble getting up and down and in and out but the youngest ones inevitably were the first to recover.

We washed and dried our smelly wet clothes, throwing some away that were past redemption, rested a while and then set off for some R&R on the island of Langkawi.

We were highly pleased with ourselves.

Indonesia—What a Riot!

We were approached by a major concessionaire in Jakarta Airport. The contact was a well connected government official who wanted a company who could plan, design and effect extensions at the airport in an original way but which would also fit in with the existing structure.

Original was a word we understood, fitting in however was always a problem.

I flew by the Indonesian airline Garuda which was a test in itself. At the time Garuda had the worst safety and maintenance record of any airline. This was quite an achievement considering the state of many airlines at the time. In the not too distant future they would be grounded for a while.

Jakarta airport's main terminal was in the form of an incomplete circle so, in my estimation, it would be fairly easy to sort out, improve and understand.

When you are in business you have to take note of worldwide situations and developments but still have to carry on regardless. I had been accidentally landed in the middle of revolutions, takeovers and fundamental changes in many countries and sailed through them as though they were nothing to do with me.

Maybe the luck of the Irish, inherited from my father.

We left the airport in an official car with darkened windows and an escort. It was the middle of the afternoon on a fine hot day. The driver and my companion's bodyguard were constantly talking on radio and handphones and looking increasingly anxious.

After a while they apologised but said they thought it necessary to put up the darkened screen between passengers and driver.

I was talking away, oblivious to everything as usual, when a big crash stopped me, and I saw a rock bouncing away down the roadside.

This caught my attention and looking out I saw crowds on both sides of the road yelling, screaming, waving fists and throwing sticks and stones. At us!

I was assured by my colleagues that the car was armoured with non-puncture tyres and we wouldn't be stopping no matter what. That was fine by me. The crowd did not seem to be in an amiable, reasonable mood.

We did slow down and just edged forward through the crowd who banged on the sides, jumped on the bonnet and tried to lift the car up on one side. It was futile as the car was built like a tank but they still kept banging away with increasing frustration.

We came up to a road block consisting of what appeared to be iron sprung bedsteads standing upright on small wheels.

The crowds were thickest around them and even more threatening.

The driver sounded the horn several times in what sounded like a pre-arranged pattern. From somewhere behind the barricade a loud roar erupted.

We could just glimpse two large heavily screened riot police buses parked in a lay by. Riot police were pouring out, helmeted, in padded suits smashing batons on plastic shields.

To my amazement they just rushed into the crowd with no advanced warning, smashing and beating everyone in all directions. Those falling to the ground were stamped on and kicked, others beaten unconscious and left.

A senior police officer saluted and waved us through a cleared space, we shot through and sped away down the highway.

I looked back and saw the police filing back into the buses, people picking themselves up and helping others and replacing the barrier.

Apparently just another day at the office.

The protests were over the government's decision to follow the demands of the IMF and World Bank. The conditions for the loans needed to bail out the country, it's financial institutions and the banks were seen as too severe. Consequently thousands of Indonesians had gone on strike, blocked the main roads into Jakarta and attacked any official or prestige car that was passing in order to show their displeasure.

The main square in the city centre, with the Hotel Indonesia Roundabout and Monument in the middle was full of protestors but pushed well back to the sides by police and military so that the roads were clear.

The arranged meeting went well, well enough anyway to agree to meet again.

I was taken back to my hotel, situated just off the main Airport Jakarta highway. We negotiated the barriers easier this time as the crowds were more interested in those coming in than those going out from the city.

My colleagues asked me where I would like to go for dinner. Would I prefer to stay in the hotel for safety or would I like to go into town to a nice restaurant? They told me that due to the troubles people were not socialising much, so business was slow and that if we went to a good class restaurant, although running the risk of attack, we would get fantastic personal service. "Let's go for the service," I said.

Strangely enough the streets were deserted, even the centre roundabout. No protesters.

Where had they all gone?

They were all at home eating with their families watching themselves on CNN. They viewed the foreign media as naive and superficial. "You can play CNN like an old worn out violin," I was told. "They want action and drama above anything else so that's what the demonstrators give them. They go into overdrive when the cameras are around and the media just lap it up."

"We just love it when they bring on those rather ridiculous, so called pathetic experts, discussing things we never thought off, nor would in a million years! Our favourite is when the anchor man asks the reporter, 'give us some idea of the mood there,' when that's just what he's been reporting."

"The West will never understand us."

I was to hear a lot about this place called "The West" and the people who live there called "Westerners" during my years in Asia. A suitably convenient, meaningless phrase, as to me, everywhere is west of everywhere else.

If you keep going north you go over the pole and then you are going south. If you keep going south you go under the pole and then you are going north. If you go west however, no matter how far you go, you are still going west.

So "western" is an archaic comment based on Mercator's projection and not on the globe.

The world is round you ignoramuses, not flat.

The problem was, irrespective of the media, they attacked the Chinese, burnt their homes and businesses and used them as the usual scapegoats on which to take out their frustrations. Once such riots got out of hand they frequently harmed themselves also. The very situation that Dr. Mahatir of Malaysia was determined to avoid.

Our second meeting yielded more detail. The good news was that everything was planned and in place, the bad news was that it hadn't been approved.

Our input was needed but of course not readily available as we had no prior knowledge of what was required. I would have to go away and work on it. No problem, so my host suggested a last night celebration at a club.

The club was bigger than an aircraft hanger. It was divided into sections with bands, DJ's, dancing, cabaret and live sex shows all running alongside one another quite comfortably irrespective of the noise levels. We were shown into a VIP section with sofas and armchairs and scantily clad waitresses all over the place.

As soon as we sat down we were besieged.

Our host was obviously well known and had to be well looked after. We were accompanied by two young Chinese businessmen from Singapore.

A young mama san approached, knelt down graciously in front of us, and after passing on our drinks order to one of the waitresses, signalled to a row of very pretty but very scantily dressed young girls of all shapes, sizes and races.

One of these delicious, subservient dreamboats wriggled into my lap, sweetly caressed me, and told me I was handsome, sexy and so, so interesting.

I was enjoying this, sipping my drink, when mama san clapped her hands. The girl jumped up, scooted away and another took her place. The routine was the same.

This happened three or four times—well who wouldn't enjoy it— when mama san came over.

"Ah, Mr. Denis," she said knowingly, "Sometimes I get the experienced, sophisticated gentleman like you here. You know that I would always keep my precious ones back for just a moment like this. You bad man you knew I only allow my pearls to come out on special occasions."

She spoke tersely into a communicator.

Almost immediately a vision wriggled sexily into view, working her way suggestively over towards one of the handsome young Chinese. Mama San fervently redirected her in my direction. She covered any disappointment very well. Boy this time I really felt the heat. This girl was not only lovely but extremely skillful and hard to resist. Hard being the operative word.

I lay back and was enjoying it so much I ordered another drink. Suddenly the girl was gone.

"What is wrong sir?" cried Mama San. "I have sent you my best. Mr. Denis, haven't you really felt the urge, haven't you ever looked at a woman and thought you must have her, no matter what?"

"Yes, of course," I replied.

"Then who is she Mr. Denis, where is she?"

"I married her."

No more girls came which was a great pity.

"You're supposed to fuck them," one of the Chinese said helpfully.

"Yeah but I don't, used to, but not anymore." I said, a bit defensively.

"Well I will, lay one on, let's go" And he went.

He was soon back. Obviously the girl was very good or he was a five minute max type.

"That was awful, the room stank, the mattress was bare and stained and the girl was impatient," he groaned.

Our host was not happy. Two wouldn't go for it and the one who did was moaning.

When we left soon after we reassured him that we had really enjoyed ourselves but he remained unimpressed.

We obtained a few contracts but the main project never took place.

The Phillipines—More
Pleasure than Business

We were approached by the airport authorities in the Philippines regarding the opening up of Subic Bay. This was being evacuated by the Americans, who were removing most of their naval base, consequently creating a large vacant lot.

The plan was to turn it into a huge duty free area with port facilities and retailing.

Were we interested in investment and development?

We were.

We had initial meetings in the Makhati area of Manila where provisional projects were outlined to us. Many of them were so ambitious that they were well beyond our financial scope. This seemed to disappoint our interviewers as they were expecting high flyers. We were, but we were not that high financiers. We requested a more consultative role. It soon became evident that it was not our expertise they wanted but our money. The same old story, over and over again.

What they wanted was a milk cow so that they could drive around in Mercedes, buy expensive condos and go overseas all at some one else's expense. Don't we all? But most of us have to earn it first.

Discussions ground to a premature halt. We left it that we should stay in touch and if they needed us they would give us a call. They never did and the project achieved nowhere near what was originally planned.

We however had a few days before our flight. Bookings were firm and penalties heavy if changed. We were told that they couldn't be changed so we decided to look around. We booked a mini van with driver. There were three other tourists to split the cost and the driver brought along a friend who he talked to most of the time.

The Philippines is a colourful country with great people, great potential and a basically corrupt government. A decent government with the needs of the people as their objective would have long ago removed so much of the dire poverty seen everywhere.

Instead of getting decent government they got the "Marcos" and what followed was not much better. We got the whole story on our way out and more detail on the way back.

We were shown items not on the approved tourist route. We visited the "Imelda Marcos" township she created for the poor. This was enclosed with a rusting corrugated iron fence, collapsing in places. Inside were the homes.

They were portacabins and shipping containers piled on top of each other, "multi-story" apartments with no running water, sanitation or power.

She obviously had a big heart as well as a closet full of shoes!!??

We went into a restricted area that used to be the International Convention Centre for Film and Music festivals.

A multi-million dollar project for the Marcos' egos that no one supported for longer than two years. It was in a dilapidated state.

From a different location we looked up at a palace in the skies that could only be reached by helicopter. This had been built for exclusive use by family and cronies of Marcos. The authorities were attempting to build a road up to it so as to open it up for tourists. All this when the ordinary people were struggling to make a bare basic living. As always the political excuse is that it is an investment that will eventually benefit the people. Strange that it usually only benefits a relatively small amount of cronies.

Of course visiting politicians and dignitaries never get to see the dark side because they always look from the top down, never from the bottom up. They are force fed a diet of propaganda amid a self congratulatory environment. They all seem to think they are very fine fellows and can't wait for the photographic shoot.

I loved the Jeepnys. These were old American jeeps, saved, restored, stretched and decorated. They were canopied with wooden seats along the sides and used as jump on, jump off buses.

The decorations were incredible with highly painted metal symbols and patterns welded in place along sides and tops, supplemented with floral and abstract designs interwoven into the canopy supports. All had sound systems blaring out local and western pop music and strident motor horns blasting away every minute or so. Bright, multi coloured lights covered any available space while some musical horns completed the package. Safety regulations did not apply—to implement such things cost money that was not available—transportation was risky but so was starving.

We stopped off to view the bamboo organ in a very ancient church, Las Pinas, and also one or two shrines.

We stood reverently on the spot where the Spanish executed Philippine independence fighters, especially admiring the hero, Jose Rizal, who the Spanish insisted should be shot in the back as a criminal. At the last minute he was turning, in an act of defiance, to face his executioners.

The prison where he spent his last days is now a museum to his memory and the walk of over a mile he was forced to make in chains has been marked with metal footprints.

History is inclined to show the Spanish to have been very cruel destructive conquerors, a bit along the lines of the Huns and Mongols, more interested in pillage rather than trade.

No wonder the Dutch and English turned to piracy??!!

They spread the Spanish language though, which is musical and pleasant and where would we be without the gypsies and the Flamenco?

The cost of freedom really came home to us when we visited the Allied War Graves, at a cemetery outside Manila.

Here there were 38,000 graves plus memorials to thousands more missing in action. The endless rows of white crosses disappeared into the distance. The dead there were from Bataan, Corregidor, the Coral Sea and other areas. I was later to see similar sites on Guam, Hawaii and other islands, all those young men and women. If you ever really want to know the real reason why the bomb was dropped just pay a visit and think awhile. Anyone in their right mind, who possessed a means of ending it all quickly, would have done so. Contrary to some minority modern opinions there were no signs at all of Japanese surrender prior to the bomb, their actions were completely opposite.

Easy for later generations to speculate, conjecture, and condemn, from a safe distance, but if you actually lived it, and I did, there was just a great sense of relief that it was over and the tyrannical bastards who had started the horror had got their just deserts.

Fort Santiago, was an old Spanish fort built to protect Manila from the sea. It used to be much closer to the waterfront but was now sited well back due to later landfill. It had been used by the Japanese secret police, the Kempitai, during the second world war to interrogate and torture prisoners.

The lower dungeons were used to murder people because they were flooded every high tide.

Please drop the bomb Mr. Truman!!

We eventually ended up at our main destination, high up on a ridge above a small town on the edge of the vast Lake Taal. Across the lake, in the middle, stood a large smoking volcano. Below the volcano we could see a small fishing village.

Our guides explained that this was as far as they could take us. The whole area was an exclusion zone as the volcano was deemed unstable and close to eruption. They would lose their tourist guide permit if they took us any further. We could go on only at our own risk and could not involve them if we were challenged. We asked how we could go on, go down and go across.

When our guides realised we were serious, one spoke on his handphone, told us to stay where we were and walked away.

Shortly after another van laboriously climbed up from the town, urged us quickly to jump in and we went off down the hill to the town below. We left our other colleagues behind as they felt they already had a good view and were safe and close enough.

We went straight to the waterfront where there were fast fishing boats lined up. The boats were canopied, long and slim, with huge powerful car engines at the rear. The driver would start the engine and lower a propeller at the end of a long drive shaft, into the water.

Our new guide asked if this was far enough or did we want to go across. "If we can, then we go," we replied.

We did a deal, boarded, and shot off, bouncing precariously over waves caused by the wake of other boats going ahead.

When we landed we were greeted by a host of villagers all offering horse rides to the top of the volcano. We selected the mounts we needed and set off for the top. My legs nearly touched the ground on either side but this was one tough pony who knew the way and knew his job.

We looked apprehensively at the columns of grey smoke erupting from the mountainside as we passed. We were told that they had been instructed to evacuate but wouldn't do so as long as the smoke was grey and not black.

When it turned black they would go—very fast. I hoped that grey turning to black would be warning enough.

My pony struggled the last 50 metres or so and I had to dismount and haul him up. Fair enough, he had brought me most of the way.

I peered over the edge of the crater, standing on the rim and looked down on a bubbling lake full of floating sediment. A guide explained that the weight of water would increase the pressure and add greatly to the explosion—very dangerous.

I believed him but said I thought that I had seen more smoke coming from our Marketing Director April than from the volcano.

Two years later it blew with catastrophic results.

After taking photos we journeyed down, with the pony much happier and trying to trot, stumbling on the rough surface. I pulled him in as he threatened to fall head over heels a few times taking me with him.

We arrived safely at the bottom, paid up and took a boat back to the mainland. We walked up the hill and rejoined our fellow travellers and van.

We dropped off the two Indonesian guys at their hotel first. As soon as we drew up, they slid open the door, shouted bye bye and ran for it. We had all prepaid but they ran to avoid the tip.

Our guides depended on tips to make up their salaries as our tour ticket prices went to the tour company not to them. They were not amused. The Japanese guy heard their muttered complaints and argued to me that they shouldn't just expect tips as being a right. I pointed out that we should be ashamed to run like that. We could afford to come to their country, enjoy a tour, and eat and drink at the best restaurants whereas we knew that they could not even afford to go back to visit their families on a nearby island.

A tip in US dollars was nothing to us, but everything to them.

When we got to his hotel, he jumped out, asked the driver to wait and came back a few minutes later with a good tip. He said he had needed to change his currency to US.

When we got out we gave a good US dollar tip also. I told the two guys that this was to make up for the Indonesian runners.

They were delighted of course and I felt better for it—well you always do, don't you?

Our hotel was not quite in Makahti itself but was along the water front. I was still in training most days for the Marathon, running my last two in the future Millenium 2000. So I had traced a route along the water front, round several corners, turning to run along a road behind the hotel until eventually turning back to the start. This was just over two miles. The first time around raised smirks and a few ribald comments from workers taking the mickey along the way. The second time around they looked surprised and after the third or fourth time they had formed my new fan club. The fifth and last time raised cheers instead of jeers and I graciously acknowledged the applause.

The next morning we journeyed to the Pansanjan Falls in Laguna. The only way up to the falls was by canoe. There are a number of rapids which have to be negotiated on the way up before the exciting ride down. It was a fitness test. First came what we found was the easier part—paddling upstream against the current. This was child's play compared to shoving the canoe up over rocks in the teeth of cascading water. In some places bamboo poles had been laid over jagged sections to avoid the canoe being ripped apart.

The canoe was long and slim, not particularly stable, but was fortunately comparatively light.

At the top of the rapids was a small lake and across the other side of the lake were the falls.

The next stage was to run the falls by means of a bamboo raft propelled and steered by one guy with a bamboo pole.

Behind the falls was a deep cave and you went on the raft, through the falls, into the cave.

This was where most opted out.

On our way over the man with the pole explained that the force of the water made it difficult to stay on board. If you were swept off then you should swim into the cave, not out.

Of course we all intended to stay on and waited with some trepidation as we approached the roaring base of the falls.

As soon as we entered the foaming, heaving waves the raft pitched about crazily. Then came the tough bit. We pushed on into the falls to reach the sanctuary of the cave.

Naturally most of us were knocked off. We struck out strongly but found to our surprise we didn't need to. The backlash from the tumbling water just picked us up and swept us in. No problem. The guide of course had known this all the time and was ready with his pole to haul us out.

A body count ascertained that we hadn't lost anyone and we explored the interior of the cave. Thousands of years before it had been an underground river but the terrain had changed.

It had also been much deeper but the falls above had steadily eroded the surrounding rock and probably in thousands of years time the cave would have disappeared altogether.

It had been inhabited from time to time and remains had been discovered but never categorised. After the noise and turmoil of the falls this really seemed a haven of peace but of course we had to get out. We had to make a run at it in order to crash through the inward driving current. Once this was done the outward current swept us through and into the strong daylight.

As we knew what to expect this time we all stayed on.

So we soggy gladiators returned to the canoes and the hectic run down the rapids. Great and over all too quickly. We used the changing rooms to dry off and dress up and make our way back to the hotel taking in Intramuros, the quaint old town of Manila, and its ancient cathedral.

We returned to Malaysia, without any contracts but lots of memories.

A Little Taste of Real India

I needed to go to India so I had to get a visa. An Englishman needing an entry visa for India—how dare they. Admittedly the country was no longer a colony but hadn't they heard of the Commonwealth? Apparently they had but it made no difference—get in line and get a visa.

For me the actual paperwork was the easy bit—the queues and bureaucracy at the consulate were not. For most of the others the opposite was true—most of the applicants seemed to love the queue but hated the paperwork. That is if they bothered to turn up with any.

When they reached the counter they looked mystified by the questions asked by the consular staff. Being asked, "where are you going, why are you going, when are you going and how are you going," caused great concern and needed consultation with the small army of relatives accompanying them. The queue had been a joyful family reunion, the application was an unwelcome interruption.

The staff coped wonderfully under the circumstances but for anyone in the queue behind who wanted to get in and out quickly it was enough to drive you mad.

I had travelled so far and so often in my life that I had long forgotten what an adventure it still was for many people.

The crowds in Asia deemed necessary to send off one person fascinated me. That is until they got in the way.

Even with everything in order and submitted I had to wait several days before I was cleared and my passport returned complete with visa. My destination was Chenai, previously called Madras. Why the name change—what was wrong with Madras? Surely they hadn't struggled for independence just to change names!

God I loved Indian food. One of my favourite dishes was Chicken Curry Madras mopped up with Keema Nan. What did I do now—order Chicken Curry Chenai with Keema Nan? No sorry, didn't have the same ring about it.

The flight across the Andaman Sea and the Indian Ocean by Air India was comfortable. Not much to look at out of the windows except water, so I watched a movie.

Thank heavens the flight was quiet and restful because India was not.

I had visited a number of times in the past, Bombay mainly, (now called Mumbai) and Calcutta, (now called Kollkata), (aiyee—what is it with these people??!!) and each time I was staggered by the sight and sounds coming from every possible direction.

Absolute colourful chaos from the moment of touch down.

Nobody seems to know where to go but they're all going somewhere and no one seems to know what to do but they are all earnestly doing something.

This, to me, is typical of all poor under-developed countries, so many people doing their own unco-ordinated thing trying to survive, but actually achieving very little.

Immigration was there waiting, how you got to them was something else. Customs too were there waiting, how you got to them, let alone past them, was a miracle. Asia is not great on queueing and very low on patience. In spite of uniformed security and police trying to enforce order, sometimes violently, every one just barges forward shoving through, with men the worst offenders, knocking women and children aside.

Brought up in the old fashioned culture of women and children first I always found this most distasteful. Bloody hell I was starting to sound like a Hooray Henry.

Of course the British are too good at queueing but it does have it's advantages.

I finally erupted onto a concourse trying hard to keep a grip on my two bags which porters were attempting to rip out of my hands. I was a prime target. Why help poor Indians when there is a rich white man to milk of a few dollars? All westerners are rich in the opinion of Asians, especially the young women who see a means of escape not just from poverty but from prejudice. Who can blame them?

One guy was particularly persistent and I was about to give him a load of abuse when I cottoned on to the fact that he had been sent to meet me.

You don't just see India, you feel it and taste it. Poverty and distress are inextricably mixed with wealth and majesty. You walk out of your plush hotel, where you have been surrounded by luxury, spoilt and pampered by superb service, into the street full of noise, dust, cars, bicycles, carts, people, animals, and a cacophony of sound.

You step around a bundle of rags on the pavement only to realise the rags clothe a beggar who had died in the night. I was told whatever you do, do not throw coins to the little boys running beside you begging for money, and especially don't favour the smallest. As soon as the small ones have the money, bigger ones suddenly appear and beat the daylights out of them while stealing the cash.

Nobody bothers to interfere, it's normal.

Old men, with withered, gnarled muscles, push overloaded two wheel carts, straps cutting their shoulders, agonisingly slowly along the uneven road. They are steadily losing a contest they were never destined to win.

I visited a number of sites with my contacts who were would be investors and developers. They had cash and influence but no expertise. They desperately needed us as we did not bullshit but actually performed. They liked what we had done. They had tried several other local options but had been let down each time.

The sites were typical of the city. Modern office, shop and apartment blocks next to old settlements. These settlements were a mixture of mud huts, corrugated iron, wood and foliage. Inside were animals, children and elders all mixed up among the dirt and smells of sweat, urine and faeces. What a way to live. Back to nature with a vengeance.

Although obviously a problem to me I had to come to terms with all this. How to put brands such as Gucci and Dior and others into a suitable environment separated only by a tumbledown wall from destitution.

I wasn't to be confronted with the issue of this sort for long. My contacts took me out to dinner each night and at first were reasonably behaved. Slowly as the alcohol flowed their standards slipped. By the third night I was in despair. Two of them were roaring with laughter at dirty, racist jokes, another was crying over missed opportunities and yet another was slowly sliding under the table completely out of his head.

When I finally got the three still left upright to pay attention they became over serious and repeatedly asked me what I thought and what I could do for them, unfortunately over and over again without taking any notice of my replies.

After an hour of this I gave up—I ordered a fine cognac as consolation followed by two Irish Coffees made just the way I liked.

Outside I got hold of my Malaysian Indian contact who had made the introductions and told him that no way could we be involved with this lot of clowns. He became really worried and excited, promising good behaviour in the future. I told him that it had become apparent listening to all the talk that these guys were onto a vague promise that was not going to materialise—there was no point in wasting any more time, let's just go.

And that's what we did.

Opportunities were opening up around the region, some ideal, some not so, but they would probably turn out better than this episode.

Well, that's what I thought anyway.

Vietnam Revisited

Although we had made little money from our Liquor company adventure we had made some useful contacts and picked up a lot of handy information.

James Bonaparte from Singapore was one such contact and yes his name really was Bonaparte, and not being young he was often called "Old Boney." He didn't find this amusing.

He was the regional agent for a number of liquor brands, was well established and operated mainly across the east of South East Asia. You could almost call him a leftover from Colonial times. He didn't like that much either but he was a good enough bloke. Vietnam was one of his hunting grounds.

He and his Chinese partner David approached Louis, our International Chairman, to see if we were interested in a possible venture in Vietnam.

"OK, what is it, when do we go and who do we see?"

Our contact was to be Madame Mai. She was a middle aged lady, and although it was ungallant to say so, she had seen better days and better men. Before we left for Saigon (so few called it Ho Chi Minh City) I was told my knowledge of French would be a big help. But it was not. Most of the Vietnamese we met either spoke English or wanted to.

Madame was full of wonderful opportunities or so she said.

She was certainly well connected but most of the opportunities seemed to involve a million US dollars of our money up front. This aroused my suspicions which unfortunately adversely affected my attitude towards the whole deal.

I was constantly looking for the catch which, being the nature of the beast, was always there. We toured the airport. Plenty of retail concessionaires, just a few vacancies that were poorly situated. "No problem" said Madame.

She told us that she had promises from her senior government and airport contacts that if she came up with the finances then she would be given the best sites.

I asked if she had anything in writing, even memo's of understanding. These frankly were mostly exercises in futility, but at least would give us some indication of intent and influence. She hadn't but assured us it would all be all right.

Yeah, right. OK, next.

We flew to Da Nang. I was interested to see that the protective bunkers built by the Americans years before were still in place. Getting off the aircraft I asked the crew if they still towed the planes into the bunkers to limit damage. They all laughed and said not any more but that they were left there for illicit liaisons after dark. I told them that times hadn't changed that much then. This greatly amused them but horrified my companions.

We did the tour, had meetings, with everything very similar to Saigon. It could have been that Madame was right in her belief, but there was too little to catch hold of and she just seemed far too desperate.

While we were in a bar discussing what had transpired we were approached by two tall, very attractive Vietnamese girls. They spoke good English with American accents. Without any invitation, they sat down full of confidence between David and I. James was somewhat pushed to one side. Well we were the younger bones, not by much, but enough. They ordered drinks for us and themselves then asked if that was okay.

Not really but what the hell. The usual sparkling conversation took place—"where do you come from, what do you do, you are so handsome?" Everything we said to them appeared to be witty and funny as they laughed after every sentence. A bit like those corny American Sitcoms with the implanted canned laughter.

We soon got bored, stood up to leave, paid the bill and started to move out. This shook the laughter out of them, suddenly they were serious and all action.

"How much you pay us?"

"What for? Nothing of course."

"You pay fifty dollars US each?"

"No way, Jesus, that's real inflation. Fifty dollars for 15 minutes chat. Hell, you used to get boom boom all night long here for ten bucks. Bye girls."

I gave one girl ten dollars, told her it was nice talking to her and that's that. Enough.

"What about my friend,"

"What about her, tell her to ask my friends, that's what friends are for."

By now we were on the street so David said, "disappear, or I call the police."

They went, really put out, not looking nearly as glamorous as they had when they came in.

My colleagues were aware of my disappointment at the way business things were going and tried to build up the positives but there were too few of them.

On the road just north of Da Nang we had to wait for a freight train to pass, very slowly, with a guard sitting on the front of the engine. He was there to stop anyone jumping on for a free ride and there were others like him along the train doing the same thing. I drew attention to what I thought was a similarity with 1930's America but it didn't go down too well.

We moved onto Hanoi. Hanoi was a different kettle of fish. Madame Mai seemed to tread more carefully. Although still very friendly, people approached things more seriously and thoughtfully. There was much less of the "give us your money now" attitude and more of the "what have you got to spend, why, and what do you expect for it?" Madame Mai, who had seemed so at home in Saigon, appeared out of her depth here in Hanoi.

She didn't have automatic access to everywhere and everyone as before and became uneasy and displeased with my skepticism.

I had done enough looking and now wanted detail. Without detail there would be no joint ventures and without a clear and transparent joint venture with attainable objectives there would be no money.

Madame didn't like the sound of this very much so she decided to talk to me through a third party only, as though I was not there. She pointedly snubbed me.

My two companions could see that this was going downhill and so decided that it was time to reveal the grand finale.

We were going north to the Chinese border. We hired a small van and a driver as no one in their right mind wanted to drive in Vietnam. Pure anarchy. Of course there were rules—they were made up as they went along. Any side of the road was okay as long as there was just enough space to get through, which there often wasn't. So they played chicken in which frequently there were no winners. The casualties stayed by the roadside for ever.

Cyclists and the little motor bikes, with engines the size of hairdryers, came from all angles without the least intention of slowing down or giving way. Madame was not involved with this project so she stayed behind in Hanoi. James and David arranged for us to meet on our return.

This would prove to be a mistake but she had insisted against my objections. James and David were in a difficult position, caught in between, as Madame was a customer of theirs with some influence and I had come on their say so at my own and my company's expense.

Vietnam, undeveloped, was a charming country. This seemed to be true of so many places in Asia. In an effort to gain so much they seemed unaware of what they were losing.

French colonial architectural influence was still very much in evidence and mixed well with local styles. The wonderful relaxed French style of living could still be seen in cafes, bistros and shops along the streets and tree lined boulevards, which even indiscriminate American bombing had not managed to totally destroy. It all mingled well with traditional, basic Vietnamese lifestyles. I was intrigued that there seemed to be more residual resentment of the French and suspicions of the Chinese than there was of Americans.

Perhaps because the French and Chinese had wanted to conquer and rule Vietnam where the Americans didn't, they just wanted their side to win. Unfortunately the wrong side!!

Vietnam had moved on, well aware of its history but much more looking to the future while having to deal with the present.

There was a lot to do. We headed north through the suburbs of the city, still on presentable roads that just happened to be overcrowded.

Every one on the road defended their territory as though they owned it. Progress was slow.

Eventually we cleared the city limits and as the view improved so the roads deteriorated. This was not predominantly padi country, the climate being different to that of the south. Animal husbandry was much more in evidence as was subsistence farming.

The small towns along the way were more of the traditional shophouse type with seemingly hastily erected shanties spread around.

The dress was changing also. At first I thought that maybe it was festival time but our driver told us that this was normal in these areas and it would be much more noticeable the further north we went.

I was intrigued by the country buses with their suspensions raised well above the ground. I was told this was because they had to ford rivers and travel rocky roads in outlying districts. Usually the city people wore a mixture of western styles and what we regarded as Vietnamese, having seen it all in newsreels. It was rare to see men dressed other than in western clothes, jeans being common everywhere but the women varied greatly. The silk and cotton trousers covered by a long loose flowing top in pale colours looked so elegant that I enjoyed seeing it around—well any excuse to look at the girls would do?

As the terrain grew steadily harsher so the colours of the dress became more strident, texture more coarse, and the material much thicker. Beaded head ware, intermingled with fabric, was common. According to our driver the styles were very tribal and regionalised and had changed very little over many, many years. Then we came over and around a small mountain range and there in front of us was Ha Long Bay—truly breathtaking.

The road ran along the edge of the bay, sometimes cutting through crevices that had been widened to accommodate vehicles until the full splendour was revealed on our right hand side. There were the dozens of top heavy islands with trees and foliage clinging to the sheer sides in plain view.

The town itself had been built by the French in imitation of the Riviera and was still picturesque.

Flowing serenely between everything were sailing boats in a mixture of styles, mainly resembling the Chinese Junk but much more colourful.

Different coloured woods and paint made up the hulls while the sails, supported by bamboo spars, varied in texture and hue. It was all so natural and tranquil that we heard with some distaste that there were plans to develop it into a resort area in an effort to attract hundreds of tourists with foreign currency.

Well who were we to deny people their chance for a better life but we wondered if it would in fact turn out to be that way. As so often happens, change makes thing different but not always better.

We stayed a while but reluctantly moved on as our driver said he did not want to drive up into the mountains at night.

Very wise, as it turned out. Not many people wanted to tackle it by day either. A journey to be made only if you had to.

Sometime later we came to what appeared to be a wide river estuary but was in fact an inlet cut in from the sea.

We had to cross by ferry. There was no ferry boat, just a very large flat barge tied to a tug. There were two in operation, passing each other from opposite sides round about the halfway mark.

There were no safety procedures, no life rafts, no safety jackets, no guide rails or lines, only very low sides on the barge. The jetty, sloping gradually down into the water, was yellowed concrete and battered with age, usage and weather.

Waiting close to us was an old woman water carrier with four buckets at either end of two long bouncing bamboo poles supported on her narrow, skinny shoulders.

She carried these all day and every day and if she sold every drop she could earn the equivalent of two US dollars a day!!

As the ferry gently collided with the pier, workers, their heads covered in conical straw hats, literally hurled a metal ramp from the barge onto the jetty. Before it could be secured dozens of people on board began to leap, push, pull and shove their way ashore. In between the crowds were legions of cyclists driving forward followed by motor cyclists, three trucks and one car. No one seemed concerned about their own or any one else's safety.

As if this total chaos wasn't enough, waiting passengers on shore charged forward elbowing and jostling through those disembarking forcing their way onto the barge.

No one took charge, everyone was left to sort it out for themselves.

At first we stood back, laughing our heads off, waiting for people to drown, crash, fight or collapse. No one did.

They'd all done this many times before and were old hands.

We were not.

While we had been hanging about feeling superior, our driver had got the van on the ferry. His shouts jerked us into action and we got on board just as workmen on the jetty were chucking the ramp back onto the barge.

We took stock of our fellow travellers. A totally mixed bunch of housewives, young and old, many traditionally dressed. Manual workers, smartly dressed office workers, and ruddy country peasants all mingling together without any signs of racial or monetary discrimination. I occasionally took photos on trips, not many as I travelled often, but I had taken pictures in Ha Long Bay and I took a few of the ferry. Also I had taken a picture, just before boarding, that intrigued and revolted me.

An older man had a motor bike with two wire panniers on the back. Crushed inside these panniers were adult dogs, still alive, whimpering and trying to move, but movement only created more pain.

A world war and army life had removed a lot of squeamishness from me years ago but not compassion.

I drew the attention of our driver to this and he laughed and said their suffering wouldn't be for long as they were going to market and would be slaughtered that evening. They would be sold as fresh dog meat. Not to worry—it was normal.

Not for me it wasn't—I didn't like it and said so but no one cared or took any notice.

We reached the other side, alighted amid the usual chaos, and resumed our journey.

It wasn't long before we started to climb, slowly at first on a road that was reasonable but did tend to lose it's outline and surface occasionally. This made it a little act of faith for vehicles trying to pass in opposite directions.

As for overtaking—well forget it, or so we thought.

The higher we climbed the poorer and narrower the road became. All of a sudden we rounded a bend where the road came out upon the side of a mountain, opening up a fabulous view of valleys, rivers, gorges and bare mountain peaks.

The road snaked up ahead for miles, in full view, clinging to the mountainside thousands of feet up with a sheer rock wall on one side and a sheer drop on the other. We could see clearly for the first time that we were not the only ones on the road, and more disconcertingly, that not all were traveling in the same direction.

Our nerves were tested many times as we were forced to edge painstakingly past cars and trucks coming towards us as though they were on an expressway. We, being on the right hand side of the road,(where there was a side!) and going up, had to move as close to the edge as possible and sometimes further to allow those going down to move through.

We frequently alighted, one of us on each side at the front, walking backwards, guiding the driver, with the tires sometimes partly over the edge. When we had scraped through we jumped back in, very relieved.

Along the route, some valleys and crevices below were littered with debris of cars, trucks and buses, which didn't do much to steady already shaky nerves.

Thank goodness we only had a small van. Large trucks often had to back up, which they didn't really want to do and so played chicken with each other until one gave way. No one seemed to worry too much about the delay, just sat and waited patiently.

Two or three times we saw the ultimate challenge—a car overtaking a truck facing a truck coming the other way, usually on a blind bend.

The more usual situation of two trucks trying to pass in a too narrow part of the road, and one having to back up, rarely resulted in the drivers having to get down to sort it out. Three vehicles in a deadlock did. The drivers alighted and consulted, poring over the same details again and again, often assisted by other drivers caught in the tailback.

With arms waving, heads nodding, hands pointing to the trucks, and standing on the edge of the precipice they stated the obvious. They seemed oblivious to the fact that even more traffic was building up behind them.

Now we knew why our driver had wanted to push on. Eventually the build up behind was backed up, allowing the guilty parties to manoeuvre enough to pass by and we all went on our merry way once again.

For us this was probably a one time up and down. For the locals this was an every day event.

We had taken the A class road out of Hanoi and then turned onto the QL18. This was an A, B or C class road, or no road at all depending on which bit you were on, but it did take us all the way to Mong Cai on the Chinese border.

It was late afternoon when we arrived. Remarkably the road opened out onto a flat plain high in the mountains right on the Chinese Vietnamese border. The border line was a river, deep in a gorge with a bridge connecting it to Djongxing Park on the Chinese side leading down to Fangcheng Harbour.

And there was Mong Cai, a small town, parts of it comparatively modern, developed and totally unexpected after the difficult climb and lack of human habitation on the way up.

It had a few hotels, no stars but clean. A few restaurants, also no stars but clean, and a few bars, as well as shops, offices and houses, all surrounded by high cliffs and mountain sides. It even boasted a neon Karaoke sign. On either side of the bridge were situated the customs and immigration posts of the relative countries. The bridge itself appeared to be suspended in no man's land.

We met up with our contacts for dinner at the hotel after we had checked in.

They ran the duty free concessions in town which were performing well but needed to expand, particularly with respect to renovation, product and world brands. Without considering location and accessibility we seemed a natural shoe in. We fixed up to meet for a tour of the stores next day after breakfast.

David discovered a Chinese tractor close by belonging to a local farmer. These tractors were multi-purpose workhorses during the day and acted as generators at night by hooking up the power supply to the flywheels on the side of the engine. We all took a drive, not recommended on a full stomach.

The relevant buildings were located on what passed for the main street. The stores were on opposite corners of an intersection.

They catered for every one and sold everything under the sun.

The most intriguing department for me was the largest—a selection of electrical goods that was not only comprehensive but was in duplicate. One of each of them. One made in the West and the other made in Asia.

"Why? Who the hell bought them?"

There had to be a good reason for importing them and transporting them miles up a dangerous mountain road to a remote border crossing.

There was. The Chinese Immigration, Customs Officials and Border Guards did three month tours of duty at this border post.

The journey down to relative civilisation was just as hazardous on their side as it was on ours.

They came up and down in large military trucks. During the course of their tour they came over to the Vietnamese side and placed their duty free orders for themselves, their families and friends. The list was formidable.

Anything not in stock was ordered and shipped up.

On their changeover day several trucks were backed up over the bridge against the Vietnamese border and loaded to the brim with their purchases, all paid for in US dollars! They drove off when full.

This was a real eye opener for me. TV's, Hi Fi's, fridges, washing machines, vacuum cleaners, kitchen utensils all went over including of course the more usual duty free stuff such as liquor, tobacco, perfume and jewellery etc.

Articles made in the west were greatly preferred over Asian made and fetched a premium price. Branded goods were essential.

On top of this "official" business came the more normal trade from the drivers and visitors cross border traffic.

The owners were desperate for more of the high profile brands and so were their customers.

We were sure we could help and we hammered out a basic supply, upgrade and management agreement that we planned to put into a more detailed and finished state in Hanoi. We celebrated at the Karaoke.

Next day, after more due diligence and surveys, we made the trek back down to Hanoi. A journey down equally as adventurous as on the way up. We had a puncture and the driver just sat by the roadside looking at it all forlornly doing nothing. David took charge and we all got stuck in. We changed the wheel ourselves. If David hadn't taken over we would probably have been there for hours.

I had completely forgotten about Madame Mai who pounced on us almost as soon as we arrived.

James and David told her the story before I could brief them. I had wanted to keep it away from her but failed.

When we were joined by our mountain colleagues she straight away cut herself in and we were back on the old merry go round of come up with a million dollars first.

Our prospective partners lost sight of us and the original proposition, and were put off by Madame Mai. She made it clear that if she couldn't have it, nobody else could either. They didn't understand why she was in and neither did I, but there she was and James and David couldn't see a way to leave her out—so the talks broke down.

We tried different tacks but our new colleagues were put off by our apparent associations with Madame and all came to an end, unfortunately completely.

We tried a number of ways to resolve our differences, issued a few MOU's, and conceded quite a bit of ground as we came to understand the problems of doing business the Vietnamese way.

We could not take any money out of the country earned through services and management—that was a basic problem as that was how we earned our living. We decided that we would form a joint venture company with James. We would supply James with product at a price covering our fees which he would onward sell to Madame Mai's company. We would manage and develop the stores.

We were all set up to go but Madame could not be satisfied, she wanted this and that to such an extent that we all became more than a little peed off with her. She wanted her million dollars.

She wouldn't commit to paper, nor could she produce anything resembling a contract at any of the airports or downtowns that were of interest and essential to make it all financially viable.

If we were to proceed then we would have to make a giant, very expensive leap of faith.

We were people of fact, with little faith, so it all faded out to nothing.

A pity really as with a better Vietnamese partner it could have worked out.

James was right however, although Madame's star was definitely on the wain she still possessed enough clout to be a spoiler if she was shut out or we went with someone else.

So we came away from Vietnam with nothing.

We had joined the French and Americans but with far less casualties!

The Great Wall of China Business

Mark had several contacts in Hong Kong that knew of opportunities in China.

One looked very promising.

The Diplomats had their own downtown duty free stores, principally in Beijing, Shanghai and Guangchou. They needed upgrading to be more in tune with China's ongoing emergence into the modern business world as well as a large scale brand revision.

Just the job for us.

Kevin Ng, Mark's contact fixed up the appointment with the managers in Beijing.

This being an official visit, visas and airport clearance was soon arranged.

We did the usual tour, saw clearly what needed to be done and what we could do.

We repeated the dose in Shanghai.

Based on information given to me we drew up business, range and renovation plans.

At the meetings we seemed to understand each other and appeared to agree on what had to be done and by whom so we drew up a memorandum of understanding.

This seemed clear enough so we proceeded on the basis as laid out in the memo.

April and I alerted suppliers, had meetings and came to certain hard fought, tough deals with prominent brand names who had a million and one reservations about dealing with China at that time. Most only agreed as long as we were the customer, we were the stockists and we were the sellers.

As this was in accord with our proposed management, supply and renovation contract we happily committed ourselves.

We confirmed everything at the Cannes Duty Free Exhibition and relayed the good news to our future partners.

Luckily for me, as it turned out, I just happened to have temporarily mislaid my copy of the MOU and asked for one to be sent from Kevin and one to be sent from my office. Better two than none I thought.

When they turned up they were not the same. Kevin's did not agree with our office copy nor with my original which I had eventually found amongst a pile of my traveling paperwork.

His version was a few sections shorter and had a few vital sentences missing.

When I queried this with Kevin he insisted that his was just a copy of mine, so therefore it had to be my agreement.

I smelt a big rat. The revised copy took away the more profitable parts of the business from us and kept it with our partners to be. His copy was not only in a smaller print but also in a different font style so could not have been the same as my original.

It made a hash and joke of our business plan.

I tried to explain at first calmly, then less calmly, then impatiently, then irritably and finally angrily as I met total intransigence.

I queried again, and again, and got the same answer. No revision, no discussion, no change. Kevin claimed it was certainly my agreement so that was that. But it wasn't.

I did a revised business plan and it didn't add up. We would be the unprofitable busy fools.

If there were no changes then there could be no deal.

I could see Mark was concerned and Kevin was not only upset, he turned nasty.

He committed a fatal error. He went above my head, not in a business like manner, but whining and complaining about me a bit like a silly kid.

I had never worked in a vacuum so regular reports went to Louis and Hans in Amsterdam. They were well updated anyway but they had also seen me in Cannes and had a firm grip on the background.

The command came through to me, basically saying, "Stop the silly nonsense on both sides, drop the deal and get rid of the nuisance."

I did.

This could have just been a case of genuine misunderstanding or lack of accurate translation. Maybe it could have been solved by re-negotiation but once Asians feel face is lost then all is lost.

Far too often after we had put our all cards on the table and had circulated copies of our final detailed plans we had been faced with an about turn or modification of an agreement. Entirely to our disadvantage of course. When confronted out would come the old hoary chestnut, "no, you're mistaken," or, "no we had already thought of it." Always after we had handed everything over of course, not before.

Just a coincidence? Perhaps! But there were just too many coincidences.

During the course of our research we visited Beijing and Shanghai several times.

Of course when in Shanghai it is necessary to visit the Bund and also the park which still keeps the sign, placed there by the British many years ago, on prominent display.

It says, "Dogs and Chinese not admitted."

The world should move on but its not difficult to understand any residual resentment that may be hovering around.

Nanking road still seemed romantic and it was easy to be nostalgic about the clubs, jazz bands, dance halls and high life that had existed all around it.

The old Bund financial buildings were still there but separated from the river by highways, underpasses, overpasses and riverside walks. The view across the river was entirely new. The Puchong development of high rises out to the new airport dominated the landscape.

While posing for a picture on the promenade I was approached by a tall, gaunt, elderly man. He spoke excellent English.

He was interested in my nationality and background, and enquired most particularly about my University qualifications.

I was interested first off in his very good command of English.

He told me he had been a young student after the second world war and had studied in an English religious school. He had gone on to University and qualified as a teacher.

He had survived the Communist takeover and done well, becoming a professor of literature, until the Red Guards came. He had been beaten, tortured, humiliated and dismissed to a labour farm.

He had been rehabilitated years later but had never recovered his earlier status.

He viewed that generation of Chinese as a completely lost generation that would hold China back for years.

We had talked for a while about the world and it's problems and potentials when he asked me a favour.

With no trace of irony he said he appreciated what Britain had done for China so he wanted me to send him copies of The Economist, Time, Forbes Magazine and National Geographic on a monthly basis.

I nearly choked. This was only ten years after Tianamen Square. China was changing but not that much. Countries run by dictators had redefined the words transparency and sensitivity. They used them as a trap.

He could have been secret police. Friends of mine had been detained before for less, or he could just have been a genuine straightforward guy with a thirst for knowledge but with a death wish!!

Regrettably I had to turn him down.

We amicably arranged to meet for coffee later but he didn't turn up.

Maybe I over reacted, maybe not. Better to be safe than sorry.

We moved on to Beijing.

We took a rickshaw ride around Tianamen, negotiating the price in Remnimbi, only to find the guys trying to pull a fast one. They wanted the agreed amount but in US dollars, just four or five times as much.

The situation became threatening so I told them I was going for the police hanging around the square. This calmed it down and we agreed to meet halfway on the price.

Tourists beware!

We went into the Forbidden Palace and had some luck.

Many of the luxurious throne and residential rooms had been closed for restoration for some time and were only opened for certain occasions. Our visit co-incided with with one of these occasions so we had a wonderful sneak preview of what was to come.

We walked in and on areas that had been for the Emperor only, forbidden on pain of death to all people, no matter what their status. Here we were with thousands of others treading all over without fear.

All the Emperors were long dead, we, the ordinary people were very much alive. The pompousness and stupidity of heredity monarchies is beyond belief to me. Oh boy how they love to dress up and parade around particularly in uniform. They can't stop awarding decorations especially to other monarchies. That people suffered and died because of their greed and selfishness seems ridiculous. I suppose I'm a republican at heart, not a monarchist. I would definitely have served with the Parliamentarians and tried my best to stuff the Cavaliers during the civil war in the UK.

Never destroy the history though, no matter how unpalatable. It is a part of every one's heritage. It is how the unchangeable past becomes a visible part of the ever changing present and the unknown future.

We visited the Ming Dynasty "Valley of the Kings," Chinese style. This is a cut down version of the Egyptian, with impressive Pyramids and Tombs but nowhere near as magnificent as those of the Pharoahs.

After this we had to tackle the great wall.

We went to Badaling, north of Beijing where huge sections of the wall had been preserved.

This was stunning. It was in a mountainous area and from only just a fairly low position it was possible to see a great deal.

We started off up the wall's main path accompanied by a substantial crowd with two high towers in sight far above.

"Not too far to the top," we thought.

Colourful flags and banners fluttered in the breeze and everyone started forwards walking the determined strides of Shaolin monks.

By the time we reached the first tower the crowd had thinned substantially and so had the size of the wall!

By the time we reached the second tower the flags had disappeared and so had the crowd. Those of us left were not striding like Kung Fu Fighters any more, it was more of an Ali Shuffle.

We looked up expectantly only to see three more towers in view rising up the wall further into the mountains.

It was only then we remembered the comments of our taxi driver guide.

"If you want to reach the top it is a long, long way up. Leave plenty of time to get up and down."

Well we had the time, let's see the top.

By the fifth tower we were alone. The trickle of stiff and soar people coming down had fizzled out entirely. Most looking disabled on the way down had been fit enough on the way up apparently.

We were not deterred.

We carried on climbing, and climbing and climbing, putting tower after bloody tower behind us.

Finally we could see the end. Beyond the next tower up there was blissfully nothing except magnificent scenery.

We entered the tower to be confronted and congratulated by two young men.

Unbelievably they did this climb every day. They welcomed those who had managed the climb. Then for the sum of ten US dollars they would hand over a signed certificate with your name on it declaring you to be, "A Plucky Hero of the Great Wall". Well worth every penny—I cherish my certificate to this day.

After a rest and a chat, we started back down.

This should have been the easy part and at first it was. Then it became a never ending two steps forwards, one step down, for ever. What had seemed a tough climb became a tougher descent.

April's legs gave way. The muscles would not send her legs in the direction she wanted. They went every way but the right way.

There was this tough boardroom cookie rendered almost helpless by a lot of steps.

We managed slowly, but not surely, with April hanging onto the wall on one side and me on the other.

Reaching the bottom was hardly sanctuary because instead of going down April now had to go forwards. Not easy when two legs were going in ten different directions at the same time.

She got to the cab near to collapse so the cab driver drove us to a Chinese Traditional Medicine Centre.

Getting in to the taxi had been difficult, getting out was hard labour. I was stiffening up also after the climb and the ride so my expert help was deteriorating fast.

We made it to the reception rooms where we were entertained by three martial arts practitioners controlling electric currents passing through their bodies and various other antics supposed to impress us.

Fine but we were just too done in—get on with the cure.

For around five hundred dollars US we were given dozens of different herb pills which would clean us and cure us of everything over a period of three months.

What! No way did they do that! I will never go near the stuff again. For me, if you haven't got it then Chinese medicine will give it to you.

We did eventually recover back in good old KL but it took time.

Spa-Ring Partners

Our partners decided we were looking a bit jaded and suggested taking us to a spa.

"What sort?" we asked.

"The Asian sort, relaxing massage, Thai style."

"Wait a minute, Thai style, no way, they crack your bones, jump up and down on your spine, grind their knuckles into your flesh and smile while they torture you. That's not a massage, it's their revenge and you pay."

Grinning at one another Don and Zuhl said, "no they don't crack your bones," they hesitated a while, then followed up with, "they will crack your balls though," and burst out laughing.

Oh oh!

We jockey parked in a swank hotel and were ushered through to the elevator and went down two floors.

This was the VIP Spa area. Lights were dim, decor a bit jaded, carpets somewhat worn but plenty of indoor plants to add ambiance.

Pretty girls, with skirts around their necks and tank tops around their ankles, checked us in and showed us to our cubicles, handing us towels and perfume. The cubicles were spacious with an adjustable bed in the middle and a shower unit in the corner. Otherwise it was rather bare.

I was invited to shower. I was disappointed that the girl disappeared and left me to it saying I would be attended to soon.

I showered, dried, perfumed, wrapped a towel around my waist and sat on the bed.

A few minutes later my masseuse came dressed in a white, knee length robe. She indicated for me to lay face down, oiled my back and legs and slowly massaged all over confidently but gently.

No rough stuff so it really was relaxing and enjoyable.

She turned me over and started on the front. Great.

My eyes were closed and I was dreaming away when I sensed a change. I opened my eyes and the masseuse had dropped her gown on the floor and was totally naked.

Although the light was dim I could see well enough as she climbed on the table, straddled me and started bouncing up and down on my stomach while frantically massaging her breasts.

I think this was supposed to turn me on but it didn't.

She looked a bit boney to me and her breasts although small pointed down instead of up. She threw her head back and started panting just like the videos.

Well perhaps she was enjoying it, good for her, but it was leaving me cold.

"Hey, hey, hey," I said, "can we get back to the massage, I liked that?"

Without stopping for a second she lent back and started massaging my penis just as frantically as her breasts.

This was just not on.

She leaped off, licking her lips and unrolled a condom.

This was one enthusiastic, impatient young woman, who couldn't see that I was not rising to the occasion.

Enough was enough, I called a halt.

She started to cry, "If you don't do, if you no happy, me get fired, no work, have baby, bad master."

"Hold on, hold on a minute, carry on with the brilliant massage, you're better at that than the sex. Then we shower together, I say I'm happy, tell my friends you were great. They will pay, you'll get paid, we'll all be happy, OK?"

She smiled, "OK."

When I got to the lounge I was the last to arrive, which to my companions meant the last to finish.

"Wow, Denis what a man, I bet you gave her a real going over, she says you were great, she's exhausted you old dog, we're all jealous, ha, ha, ha."

No matter how I tried to tell them the truth they thought I was just being modest.

All except Johann. He was in the doghouse because he didn't "go." So he complained to me, "I thought you said you didn't do this sort of thing."

"Johann, old mate, I don't and I didn't, you have to fake it and lie to make the boys happy. Then everyone's happy."

And everyone was.

For a while anyway.

Phoning Home

My father was getting progressively harder of hearing, so much so that conversation was impossible when he had the TV on and he avoided answering the phone if he could.

One day I called the UK to tell them I would be visiting later in the year.

Dad picked up the phone.

"'ello, 'oose that?"

"Hello, is that dad?"

"Is anyone there, speak up, I'm a bit deaf you know?"

"HELLO, IT'S ME, DEN."

"Rene, it's the phone, I can't hear anyone," Dad talking to my mum.

"HELLO DAD, CAN YOU HEAR ME NOW, I'M SHOUTING LOUD ENOUGH TO RAISE THE DEAD? I JUST WANT TO TELL YOU THAT I'M COMING BACK TO THE UK FOR A WEEK, PROBABLY CHRISTMAS IF I CAN."

"Rene, it's the damn phone gone wrong again, there's no one there."

"It's Den, he's coming back for Christmas."

"'ow do you know?"

"Cos he said."

"When? Why didn't you tell me?"

Mum, giggling away, "well I didn't know before did I?"

"Oh Gawd woman, 'ow do you know now?"

"Cos he's on the phone, shouting his head off, I can hear him from here. He said he's trying to raise the dead."

"Blimey, sorry Den, 'ow are you, here comes mum."

"Hello Den, mum here, how are you?"

Absolutely fabulous.

James

We had a friend, James, who was a giant Scot, with a strong accent. He was a top class chef at a first class hotel in KL.

He was gay. Being gay may seem not too unnatural in some countries but is totally incongruous in a huge, hairy Scot. There was this incredible hulk with a gay, fey intonation and an effeminate walk and mannerisms wondering why everyone kept bursting out laughing when he went into detailed descriptions of his experiences.

This particular time he was after sympathy and understanding. He had decided that he was no longer in touch with nature. Where he lived had previously been in the country but had latterly been swallowed up by big city expansion. He had moved further out and loved the raw feel of the surrounding jungle.

Until two days before.

He had come out of the house, and gone down the drive to get into his car to go to work.

The path, drive and car were covered in monkeys who were using the whole area as a playground. As always their play could be destructive and James explained how he threw up his hands in horror at seeing one of his windscreen wipers being used as a cane by one big fellow on a smaller guy.

He said, "I thought, James you are a such a big boy, not a silly billy, so go and sort out your car but don't, positively don't, bully those precious little pets. You big monster, be gentle with them."

He tried.

The monkeys all stopped doing what they were doing and closed ranks.

James said, "I thought, come on now big boy, these are only small monkeys, take control, don't be a soppy girl. Shoo now monkeys, come on shoo, shoo please."

The monkeys advanced, windscreen wiper user to the front, and started jumping up and down snarling, baring their teeth and hissing. They moved forward—James moved back.

The monkeys were fast, James was faster.

The monkeys kept James a prisoner all day and it was James who gave up first and retired for the night.

James moved back to the city soon afterwards.

Marathons

I had found the climate suitable for marathon running. Friends thought this strange but having trained in the UK through countless winters of freezing hail, sleet, ice and snow the heat was paradise.

Here even before I started I was warmed up.

I could just slip into shorts, shirt and shoes and be ready to go. This was very different from the times I had experienced piercing headaches from the bitter cold rain beating on my forehead. The icy wind pushed against soaking wet track suit bottoms spread flat, and chills crept through the women's tights underneath and the newspapers on my chest. These were all vain attempts to keep warm.

No need in Malaysia—just drink a bit more.

I had run a number of international marathons including London and New York so I decided to enter for the Penang Bridge Run here. This was a race of various lengths involving the Penang Bridge and included a full marathon.

I was in.

It was a beautiful run but due to Southern Asian temperatures it was decided to start the race at 5 o'clock in the morning. This was not my favourite time of day.

It involved actually getting up at 3 o'clock in the morning to get to registration at the start by 4 o'clock.

I was sound asleep on the start line only being wakened by the sound of the starting pistol.

I jerked into action and was off. Sort of.

At that time in the morning it took me a while to get into my long distance running rhythm.

Not so two women Indian runners. They were running barefoot and were running fast.

I was going one way over the bridge with a little way still to go when they passed me on the way back.

Beautiful. One was Indian from India and the other was Malaysian Indian. There were only a couple of Chinese women runners and three or four chubby, track suited Malays in Tudongs who were staggering around even before reaching the bridge. I passed them on my way back. I was told they had no idea what a marathon was and had only entered for fun. When I saw them they obviously no longer felt it was fun.

The race started between two schools, just outside Georgetown, which were used as registration stations, and headed towards the bridge. Just before reaching it the course doubled back towards Georgetown before passing the schools again and then crossing the bridge both ways.

The run headed south nearly to Bayan Lepas by the airport before backtracking once more all the way almost into Georgetown itself. It then swung round doing a u-turn almost back to the bridge where it looped over into a recreation park for the finish.

More than forty two kilometres.

The race organisers had judged it well. Runners started in the dark and were crossing the bridge at sunrise—incredibly spectacular—and were passing the finish line well before the midday heat.

I had learnt a lot of the tricks from previous marathons. I put vaseline in my socks, wore two pairs, spread vaseline on all the movable joints and also crevasses and nipples. I avoided getting wet if possible, didn't stop for toilet and kept walking about after I finished. I always trained hard so that I only hit the wall well after halfway and after running I could still go out shopping or visiting, but not before relaxing in a good hot bath.

Even so the next day I still knew I had run a marathon.

By the time I retired I had run ten full official international marathons and a dozen others. I had run about eighty half marathons, finished more than sixty triathlons and competed in one iron man. I had run hundreds of miles in training and worn out dozens of pairs of shoes. I had raised thousands of pounds for charity.

I was inspired by a commentator on the London Marathon one year who after covering the race with the champion runners said, "and now we'll look at the other runners, the real champions, who don't run for their own glorification, but run for the benefit of others."

I thought," OK, yeah, that'll be me!" And two years later it was.

I happened at the Millennium to be the first and probably only runner to run the London Marathon for Malaysia. I ran for charity and presented a cheque for the Veteran Police and Military retirement fund to the Malaysian Prime Minister along with the t-shirt I ran in for his museum. It was covered by the press.

During the run people cheered on the various runners picking out their various nationalities from their shirts or emblems. As I ran I heard "come on Uganda," "go go Jamaica," and "yeah go for it Malaysia," followed by "Malaysia ???"

They didn't think an Anglo-Irishman looked very Malaysian. This happened again in the embankment tunnel around Holborn in the final stages passing a group of Malaysian student observers. They were startled, recovered and called out the slogan on my shirt. Malaysia Boleh! (Malaysia can do it). This echoed away down the tunnel and was a great moment.

Running the Penang Marathon was a plus for me. Usually I started towards the back with the slower runners, all say thirty six thousand of us, and by the time we crossed the start line and began running we were already fifteen or twenty minutes down. My finishing position was generally around seventeen or eighteen thousand in a time of say four hours plus.

Ha ha, not in Penang. My time was similar but my finishing place was below two hundred.

People were impressed until I told them that there were not that many runners and although the drop out rate was much lower than in the more famous marathons there were not so many starters either.

Many people cannot conceive of running so far and don't understand the effort needed.

Consequently some enter unprepared or with little understanding or experience. St John's Ambulance, those wonderful people, are kept busy and unfortunately para medics are often needed. The marathon is unforgiving but as with many challenges the feeling of achievement is worth it.

The idea one year in Penang was that my partner would drop me off for the Marathon, go for breakfast, and then pick me up at the park afterwards.

During the run I noticed that many roads were closed for the race and wondered how she was going to get to the finish. Thinking that she was a resourceful sort of person I pushed it to the back of my mind. I expected she could sort it.

Passing the bridge running on my way back up from Bayan Lepas I noticed two police motor cycles, going in the other direction on the Marathon course, towards the park. They were escorting a 5 series BMW flying Malaysian Pennants.

"Oh, Jesus," I said to myself, "Another bloody self important, self indulgent official."

"Just a minute," I thought, "that's my bloody car!"

My partner had sorted it. She had told the police that I was a runner, she needed to pick me up at the finish but couldn't get there. "Could they be a couple of absolute sweeties and help?" They could and did. She had a VIP escort to the finish line! Some people have style.

Bob and Janice

B ob and Janice were two typical Australians. Bob couldn't stop laughing and his wife Janice couldn't stop talking.

Bob had done well enough in Malaysia working for a large corporation but decided that with the contacts he had made it was worth going it alone.

He succeeded.

Of course immigration and the tax man eventually caught up.

The solution was for Bob to form a company. As a foreigner he couldn't just have a registered company he had to form a Sendirian Berhad. (a limited company).

In order to register this he had to have a partner—a Bumiputra partner.

"Why?" said Bob, not unreasonably.

"Because that's the law."

"Whose law?"

"Our law."

"Funny bloody law, ain't it?"

"You have to award 51% of the shares to your partner."

"Whaaaaat! Does he pay?"

"Not necessarily."

"Well I think it's necessary. Any partner of mine has to pay and earn it, I tell ya."

"Well you may not find a partner."

"So what?"

"No partner, no company."

"I'll tell you what"

"What?"

"You go and fuck yourselves, because you're not fucking me. This country's a joke."

Bob was given forty eight hours to leave the country.

He was missed.

He had a lot of humour in him and a typical Aussie down to earth view of the world.

A popular series at the time was the "Crocodile Hunter" with a clown called Stevie Irwin performing theatrical stunts in a manic manner with a variety of snakes and animals. All under the pretence of survival.

Bob's comment on it was, "oh you mean that stupid bugger from Oz who goes chucking himself around everywhere frightening half the species on the planet? One day one of them's going to bite him back. Anyone who puts his kids up front just to make a TV show is a right berk. He's an accident about to happen."

Tragically he was.

All Sorts of Climate Change

A round this time global warming was beginning to become fashionable. The millennium bug had proved to be a big expensive profitable con for some so it was obvious that the smart money wanted to invent another one. Especially as it could be attributed to human misbehaviour which was also becoming fashionable.

The fact that we lived on a restless, constantly changing earth, hurtling pell mell through space, over which we had no control whatsoever seemed to have completely escaped the eternal doomsayers and bandwagon jumpers. Climate change, natural convulsions, energy conservation and preservation all got lumped into one parcel. The humans were decimating the planet.

Which was true, but only because of the uncontrollable birth rate.

Populations were growing at an unsustainable level and China, the one country prepared to face the fact, was condemned.

Populations needed to reduce, not increase. The Catholic church especially needed to get it's brain in gear, but how could you expect so much from male eunuchs living a life of secluded security accompanied by luxurious pomp and circumstance.

It led the world in pious statements of little use to the very people it purported to care so much about.

It seemed that most religions quietly encouraged population increases so that they could claim greater membership of their flocks. Captive membership from birth!

From the industrial point of view huge labour resources were no longer needed so workforces and work practices would have to be fundamentally revised as robotic machinery could do the job more effectively.

The antiquated political and economic ideologies previously so useful in promoting growth now had no long term answers. Accumulating so much capital at the top hoping for the much vaunted trickle down effect benefiting the majority of the population hoping and working hard for a break was no longer feasible. There were just too many humans justifiably wanting so much, when too much was held by too few. What was needed was a torrent not a trickle.

Mankind was accused of lowering the number of species on this planet at a faster rate than ever before.

No one could know that.

Millions upon millions of species had come and gone before mammals were invented by evolution, many leaving little or no trace, but still various so called experts dished out the same old crap trying to gain their fifteen minutes of fame.

One came to KL.

He was American of course, possessed of all the fervour of a marketing maniac from the good old USA. He came to promote awareness of global warming, human excesses, and of course his book.

He was so typical of his kind, pacing up and down, waving his arms, creating an impression of energy and know how, in fact so energetic that he was probably warming up the planet all on his own. He dished out, what he thought, were smart witty statements but were in fact quite shallow comments.

He showed with a huge number of statistics that throughout the history of the planet there had been a great number of periods of global warming. During these periods the evidence suggested that there were excessive levels of carbon di-oxide in the atmosphere.

Human beings were producing high levels of carbon di-oxide emissions hence humans were the cause of global warming. Game set and match as far as he was concerned.

He also mixed in rather haphazardly, as most global warming protagonists were inclined to do, climate change, conservation and destruction of forests.

I rose up and he eagerly invited my question.

I had a number.

Firstly he never mentioned the ice ages and their causes—humans were around then. What froze the ice? Cold is a reasonable guess—neat trick for humans fifty thousand years ago. Also the planet had warmed, formed and reformed many times before human beings were invented either by evolution or God.

The earth was restless, great changes had and were taking place that had nothing to do with humans.

Continents shifted, the earth moved and erupted, one volcanic eruption emitted more pollution than hundreds of cities, had more power than the greatest bombs ever invented, grounded airplanes and displaced thousands, while earthquakes, hurricanes, typhoons and tornados ripped apart towns and villages as though they were toy models.

Remove us and nature reclaimed what was hers in no time. Look at how much earth or jungle had to be removed to explore ancient civilisations from not that too long ago.

Secondly according to Julius Caesar, two thousand years ago, England was covered in forests, the climate was wet and windy, warm and chilly often on the same day, and the people were primitive.

Since then, over time all the great forests had long since disappeared but the climate and the people were still the same.

Explanation please.

He started to waffle so I interrupted.

I had noticed that another period of heating up had occurred during the time that the dinosaurs ruled the earth.

Could he please tell me what car the Tyrannosaurus Rex drove, maybe a "gas guzzler" (didn't they just love that meaningless expression?). What jet engines did the Pterodactyl use and what jet skis did the Velociraptor favour?

I suggested facetiously that as modern cows passed methane gas due to them being vegetarian, then perhaps all dinosaurs had been vegetarian, and we had been mistaken that many were carnivores. Their farts heated up the planet. I said that surely nobody would be stupid enough to suggest that—would they?

Also vehicles emitted carbon monoxide, not carbon di-oxide. So realising that after sometime the experts conveniently started to omit the di-oxide bit and fixed on carbon. But isn't carbon one of the most common elements in the universe?

Also the billions of trees, plants and algae converted many gases into oxygen so weren't we really in danger of over oxidisation. We could all go rusty.

Did he really think that silly posing on green instead of red carpets was going to conserve our oil and gas reserves?

Did he really think that abandoning plastics, which were mainly made from milk and oil derivatives, would really reduce global warming?

Didn't he think that there was too much confused and ignorant posing in an attempt to appear with it and concerned rather than offering sensible actions?

I finished with the remark that when I did post graduate studies incorporating statistics we were clearly taught to differentiate between causal, contemporary and co-incidental facts.

For instance for decades it was a fact that in March and April millions of bananas were imported into the UK. This co-incided with an increase in the number of road accidents.

No one was bold or foolish enough to suggest that one caused the other.

Also had he not thought that maybe the increase in carbon was caused by climate change as in the remote past before the time of mankind rather than being a cause of it? Just a thought!

What about mentioning the new glaciers being formed and growing as well as those diminishing.

There had always been climate change, the world and it's weather never standing still, so as we have only been scientifically studying the weather for such a short period of time how can we come to such broad based conclusions.

When some of the most freezing conditions in history occurred all the global warmers went quiet only popping out again on hot days.

We could be at the peak of the earth's warm up after the last ice age and be heading towards another. That could be the reason for the weather becoming possibly more unpredictable. Total "Global Warming" is one hell of a step up from localised climate change.

I told him he had got himself into a fashionable box and I wouldn't be buying his book.

He fluffed and faffed about great lakes forming in the arctic, the antartic disappearing, half the world's land mass submerged, doomsday was coming if we didn't use more public transport etc.

The managing director of HSBC stood up and said that he had just flown in from Sabah and all he had seen was green, jungle and sea all the way from Borneo. Not all of it may have been virgin jungle but weren't rubber, palm and tea plants green and natural? These replants then formed ecosystems again. Anyway the tigers loved them!!

The speaker got himself into an incoherent muddle, all his former bombast and confidence gone, just like the waiters in the USA who recited all of the day's specials in one joyous monologue until interrupted with a question. This always threw them and they had to go back and begin again. Good fun, try it when next there.

The chairman broke in with, "well then we'll just have to agree to differ and leave it there!"

That confused him even more.

His book didn't sell very well.

Closure of Sorts

I was past retirement age. I was a great grandfather but not of the typical great grandfather material. Not for me. I was never going to sit peacefully in front of the tele watching soaps, going to bingo and waiting for the kids to visit.

No pipes, cloth caps, furry slippers and pullovers as Christmas presents please and the first young member of the family who spoke to me as though I was a senile village idiot would have a short career.

Throughout my life as fast as one door closed I was searching for another to take me on a new adventure. I rarely looked back, I just got on with what I had whether up or down. Down could be hard.

I realized, and had often been told, that I had a too casual attitude to women and relationships and that I shouldn't be so full of myself and conceited. Possibly true, but not really. The truth was that I had never been a handsome hulk who brought a roomful of women to their knees when I entered so I was casual in that I didn't think they could care for me that much.

I had been married three times and was now wedded for the fourth. I don't know whether that made me an optimist or a fool. Probably a bit of both.

It seemed that I could never please any of my wonderful ex-wives who constantly accused me of doing everything wrong and my very existence appeared to displease them.

I could do nothing right so when I decided that it was best to go and see if I could please someone else, somewhere else, then that turned out to be wrong also!

I wished them well and really did hope they would find happiness but such a charitable attitude was rarely reciprocated. It only succeeded in upsetting them more.

To me it was a shame that when one person in a relationship wanted to talk through the problems they were accused of being unreasonable and out of order. Then when that person gave up and left the other person decided it was time to talk. Bad timing.

Anyway there was now still time for me to seek a new adventure but to show a little more stability. Maturity was never in it. The day I really grew up would be the day I really gave up.

It was not going to happen. I needed to make mischief.

However much of my "Hard Travellin' Man Blues" days were over. I was retired and no longer on salary and subsidised company expenses.

Perhaps it was time for a new outlook.

Maybe time for all the music and books that had been in me for so long to make an appearance.

A time for a bit of "Ole Man Blues."

The Hayes Family wish you all a beautiful life.